The European Court of Human Rights

The European Court of Human Rights

Implementing Strasbourg's Judgments on Domestic Policy

Edited by Dia Anagnostou

EDINBURGH
University Press

© in this edition, Edinburgh University Press, 2013, 2014
© in the individual contributions is retained by the authors

First published in hardback in 2013

This paperback edition 2014

Edinburgh University Press Ltd
The Tun – Holyrood Road
12(2f) Jackson's Entry
Edinburgh EH8 8PJ
www.euppublishing.com

Typeset in 10/12pt Goudy Old Style by
Servis Filmsetting Ltd, Stockport, Cheshire,
and printed and bound in Great Britain by
Printondemand-worldwide, Peterborough

A CIP record for this book is available from the British Library

ISBN 978 0 7486 7057 4 (hardback)
ISBN 978 0 7486 7060 4 (paperback)
ISBN 978 0 7486 7058 1 (webready PDF)
ISBN 978 0 7486 7059 8 (epub)

Contents

The contributors

Dia Anagnostou (PhD Comparative Politics) is an assistant professor in the Department of Public Administration, Panteion University of Social and Political Sciences and a senior research fellow at the Hellenic Foundation for European and Foreign Policy (ELIAMEP) in Athens.

Dragoş Bogdan is a practising lawyer who has worked in the Romanian delegation at the European Court of Human Rights in Strasbourg.

Kimberley Brayson is a postgraduate research student at Queen Mary, University of London. She is working on a doctoral thesis on human rights and Muslim women in Europe.

Kerstin Buchinger (PhD Legal Studies) is a law clerk at the Austrian Constitutional Court. Before that, she was a legal researcher at the Ludwig Boltzmann Institute of Human Rights in Vienna with a research focus on asylum law and anti-discrimination issues.

Yonko Grozev is a legal expert on human rights and programme director of the Centre for Liberal Strategies in Sofia.

Haldun Gülalp is Professor of Political Science and director of the Center for Global Studies at Yıldız Technical University in Istanbul.

Christoph Gusy is Professor of Public Law, Constitutional Law and Constitutional History at Bielefeld University.

Dilek Kurban (MA, JD Columbia Law School) is a researcher and programme officer at the Democratization Program of the Turkish Economic and Social Studies Foundation (TESEV) in Istanbul.

Barbara Liegl (MA Political Science) is Resident Twinning Adviser for the project 'Establishing a Comprehensive System of Anti-discrimination Protection' in Zagreb, Croatia, on behalf of the Ludwig Boltzmann Institute of Human Rights (Vienna).

Sebastian Müller (PhD Human Rights Law) is a member of the Faculty of Law at Bielefeld University.

Alina Mungiu-Pippidi is Professor of Democracy Studies at the Hertie School of Governance in Berlin.

Evangelia Psychogiopoulou (PhD European Law) is a research fellow at the Hellenic Foundation for European and Foreign Policy (ELIAMEP) in Athens.

Serena Sileoni (PhD Public Comparative Law) is a lecturer in public law at the Faculty of Political Science and a research fellow in constitutional law at the Faculty of Economics, University of Florence.

Astrid Steinkellner (MA Legal Studies) is a legal researcher at the Ludwig Boltzmann Institute of Human Rights in Vienna on the topics of human rights in development cooperation and business and European human rights protection.

Gabriel Swain has worked as a researcher and consultant for the Council of State Governments, an American think tank.

Acknowledgements

I would like to acknowledge the generous financial support provided by the European Commission's 6th Framework Programme, which funded the research for this volume as part of the JURISTRAS project ('The Strasbourg Court, Democracy and Human Rights: Patterns of Litigation, State Implementation and Domestic Reform', contract no. FP6-028398, 2006–9). Further information on the project's findings can be found at http://www.juristras.eliamep.gr. I would like to especially thank Angela Liberatore, the European Commission's project officer, whose enthusiastic support for the subject of this research was from the start and throughout the project extremely encouraging and motivating.

This book was originally conceived at a project meeting in Strasbourg in June 2009 where its basic structure was also defined. As so commonly happens with collective volumes, it has taken much longer to complete it than was originally planned, partly due to some unpredictable setbacks along the way. Since then, the rapidly increasing case law of the European Court of Human Rights and changes in the state of execution of the judgments under study necessitated substantial and constant updating of the country-based chapters. I would like first of all to thank the contributors to this volume, who have sustained an unmitigated interest in and commitment to this book project during its lengthy process of preparation. They were extremely responsive throughout our collaboration, being willing to revise their chapters a number of times without losing their patience or temper.

I would also like to thank John Watson, commissioning editor at Edinburgh University Press, who believed in the value of this book project from the beginning, and his excellent support team, among them Rebecca Mackenzie, project manager, and Eddie Clark, managing desk editor. Special thanks go to the artist Holly van Hart from the San Francisco Bay area, who once again has kindly given her permission to use one of her paintings, *All Distances*, for the book cover. Even though we have never met in person, her paintings formed the bridge that brought us into contact, reifying their underlying concept about how we are all connected across nations, distances, time and cultures.

The bulk of the editorial and writing work on my part was completed during a Marie Curie fellowship at the Law Department of the European University Institute in Florence in 2010–12. It provided a highly stimulating and conducive environment for thinking about human rights in Strasbourg and Europe, as well as an ideal place for research and writing, for which I can only be grateful.

Finally, on a personal note, I would like to acknowledge the contribution of my husband Yorgos Kaminis, which, although indirect, is significant. Without realising it, he transmitted to me his passion about human rights both as a constitutional lawyer and as a practitioner. Our heated discussions about the proper place and scope of rights in a democratic society helped me open up a new and exciting intellectual horizon at the crossroads of law and politics that continues to animate my academic research.

Athens, August 2012

Introduction

Untangling the domestic implementation of the European Court of Human Rights' judgments

Dia Anagnostou

Over the past couple of years, the European Convention of Human Rights (hereafter ECHR or Convention) and its judicial arm in Strasbourg have attracted renewed scholarly interest. The European Court of Human Rights (hereafter ECtHR or Court) is a paradigmatic instance of a transnational tribunal that fundamentally differs from an international court based on inter-state processes:[1] it allows individuals, but also other civil society actors, to raise claims against states, once they exhaust domestic remedies. Over time, poised between judicial restraint and activism, the Court has expansively interpreted the basic civil and political rights contained in the Convention, as well as scrutinising states' restrictions of those rights. Through individual petitions, a large array of state laws and practices, including areas that are sensitive for national interests and security, such as those pertaining to minorities and immigrants, have come under its purview. Through both dynamic interpretation and enforcement, the ECtHR has over time substantially upgraded and expanded human rights standards across established European democracies, and also vis-à-vis the democratising states of the ex-communist world. Having come a long way from its obscure origins in the 1950s, it is now increasingly constitutionalised and it is characterised as the single most important rights-protecting tribunal in the world.[2]

Among the Convention's most remarkable characteristics is the obligation of national authorities to implement adverse judgments issued by the ECtHR. This involves a decentralised system of institutions and actors assigned responsibility for implementation at the national level, along with robust supervisory and enforcement mechanisms at the European level. Implementation is thoroughly rooted in the principle of subsidiarity: national authorities must define the nature and scope of measures that are necessary to remedy a violation detected by the ECtHR, in cooperation with the supervisory bodies of the Convention system, and the Committee of Ministers (CoM) in particular. While some judgments mainly require just satisfaction and an individual remedy, most rulings necessitate domestic legislative and administrative reforms to prevent recurrence of infringements of the Convention in the future, as well as shifts in national judicial approach and interpretation. Far from being overlooked, state compliance with Strasbourg Court rulings that find a state to have infringed Convention provisions is actually remarkably high, and it has been described as 'as effective as those of any domestic court.'[3]

Despite such widely held appraisal, the issue of domestic implementation of judgments has emerged as particularly salient and problematic in connection with the current caseload crisis that is confronting the ECtHR.[4] Owing to an excessive backlog of cases threatening its stability and viability, the Convention system and the Strasbourg Court are currently at the centre of an ongoing reform process, in regard to which the ability of the Court to continue to provide individual justice is profoundly strained and challenged.[5] Available data from the CoM indicates that the overwhelming backlog of cases pending for judicial review and execution is largely due to clone or repetitive cases: these reflect persisting structural problems, which domestic execution measures and remedies have failed to effectively redress.[6] While most states sooner or later execute the ECtHR's judgments, a substantial implementation gap persists, at least in part due to the fact that the adopted measures do not remedy the root causes of rights violations.

This volume explores the processes of domestic implementation of the ECtHR's judgments and seeks to identify and understand the factors that account for variable patterns of implementation within and across states. It inquires into the reasons that national authorities and the various institutional actors involved in implementation sometimes respond positively and promptly to adverse judgments but at other times are recalcitrant or strongly resistant towards them. While the country cases mainly focus on the actions and measures of national authorities in response to judgments in specific issue areas, some of the contributions also probe the potential of these judgments to influence national policies and broader social-political change within states.[7] Domestic implementation may be a response to strings of similar adverse judgments necessitating fundamental reform of an entire issue area or area of state action. What is the impact of the ECtHR's case law on the legal norms, institutional structures and policies of national states that participate in it? Do national authorities implement the adverse ECtHR's rulings, and what factors facilitate, or conversely restrict, implementation? Do these judgments influence rights-expansive policy change at the national level? These are some of the questions that have guided the empirical research on which the individual contributions are based.

While domestic implementation of the ECtHR's judgments has received increasing scholarly attention over the past couple of years, important gaps both in the empirical focus and in analytical perspective remain. For a long time now, legal scholarship has analysed the legal and institutional characteristics of the Convention system and the Strasbourg Court, the modes of execution of its judgments, as well as the supervisory role of the CoM. The domestic effects of the Convention and the Court's case law are largely understood in reference to the legal structures and hierarchies within each state, the extent and forms of national constitutional review, and the formal relations between the legislature and the judiciary, among others.[8] These studies are mainly confined to descriptive accounts of the processes and modes of execution of judgments, without systematically inquiring into the conditions and factors that influence their domestic implementation.[9] This, however, is a crucial aspect for understanding the domestic dynamics that state acceptance of the jurisdiction of a transnational tribunal elicits, as well as the domestic effects that it has. More recently, scholars have taken a more interdisciplinary approach to domestic implementation, exploring how, through what mechanisms and to what extent the national legal orders of the respondent states are coordinated with, adapted to or adjusted by the ECHR and ECtHR case law. While this interdisciplinary approach is more systematic and comprehensive than earlier studies, it mainly provides a broad and descriptive overview,[10] and it only begins to inquire into the factors that account for variable patterns of domestic implementation within and across states.[11]

In sum, attempts to explore the national and non-legal factors that influence domestic implementation of the ECtHR's judgments are still at an embryonic stage. Making progress in this direction, though, is essential in order to move beyond a descriptive and still mainly legally centred institutional analysis. A multi-faceted set of processes has over time led the Strasbourg Court to assume an authoritative role in the European institutional landscape and the region's integration processes. Understanding variable patterns of domestic implementation is also important in order to relate the Convention and the Court as a case of a transnational and judicialised human rights regime to the broader international legalisation processes that we encounter in other parts of the world, as well as to existing scholarly approaches to state compliance with human rights.[12] An overview of the Convention-specific literature cannot fail to notice that it has abstained from engaging with a sizeable international relations and comparative politics scholarship on enforcement of and state compliance with international law, including human rights law.[13] While the analyses in this volume do not link the domestic impact of Strasbourg Court judgments to these international and comparative politics approaches, their findings can contribute to scholarly analyses in this direction.

As a regional human rights regime, the Convention system is defined by the institutionalised participation of its contracting states in transnational legal processes. The processes of litigation in the Strasbourg Court and the domestic implementation of its rulings involve sustained interaction among individuals, civil society actors, governments and legal-judicial actors, as well as between European officials and national diplomats. Notwithstanding a vast legal and non-legal scholarship on the Convention and the Court, we have an insufficient understanding of the domestic institutional and societal dynamics that this highly successful and in many ways uniquely European regime elicits. By focusing on domestic implementation processes, this volume provides an interdisciplinary perspective of the multi-faceted ways in which the Strasbourg Court's judgments come to scrutinise and influence human rights standards, laws and policies at the national level.

Eight country-based case studies focus on particular areas of law and policy to examine how national authorities implement the ECtHR's judgments, as well as whether state compliance with these actually influences legal and policy change in the direction of expanding rights. This is also the first book to explore the dynamics that develop as civil society and minority actors mobilise Convention provisions and seek to challenge state laws, policies and practices in Strasbourg. It sheds light on the ways in which individuals, civil society and political actors have been implicated in the processes of litigation and domestic implementation of the Strasbourg Court rulings. This bottom-up dimension, which is the focus of the second part of our volume, is an aspect of domestic implementation of international human rights law that is highly underexplored in comparative politics and international relations, and also in the Convention-specific literature.

The next part of this introductory chapter depicts the basic contours of the Convention's institutional evolution and its enforcement machinery. The third part expounds the methodological and analytical considerations guiding the present set of studies, while the last two parts elaborate on and provide an overview of the two main sections of the book.

THE ECHR'S INSTITUTIONAL EVOLUTION AND ITS ENFORCEMENT AT THE NATIONAL AND EUROPEAN LEVEL

The genesis of the ECHR system is to be found in the post-World War II geopolitical context shaped by the Cold War and driven by the aim of deterring the future rise of fascism and authoritarianism. Originally lacking institutional autonomy, the foundations of its initially obscure structure were put in place by national governments of western European states amidst conflicting national interests over the direction of European integration and at a high level of diplomacy.[14] Yet, over time, the system evolved away from its political origin towards a more legalistic and dynamic approach. Such an approach sought to harmonise European human rights standards and extended the initial catalogue of rights way beyond those contained in the original text,[15] leading to increasing intervention in the legal and political systems of the contracting states. This transformation occurred particularly during the 1970s, when the Strasbourg-based court began to enforce its doctrine of the Convention as a 'living instrument'. Allowing for a dynamic interpretation of the rights contained within it in accordance with shifting social values, this change prompted an increase in the Court's caseload.[16]

The 1990s provided another turning point when nineteen new states from central and eastern Europe and the former Soviet Union acceded to the Convention. This placed enormous strain on the system not only by greatly expanding the pool of potential petitioners, but also by confronting it with structural and large-scale rights violations from countries with deficient democratic standards such as Russia and Turkey. Partly in response to the new situation facing it, a major institutional overhaul of the system abolished the European Commission on Human Rights and created a single court, while it also rendered mandatory the individual right to petition the Court. By 1998 when the new monitoring system was in place, the Court's jurisdiction and the right to individual petition had been accepted by all states party to the Convention, making it possible for more than 800 million people to petition the Court.[17] Today, all forty-seven member states of the Council of Europe have ratified the ECHR.

By applying and interpreting the fundamental rights contained in the Convention in the context of individual complaints, the Court reviews national laws and practices, thereby exposing domestic legal and political systems to European supervision and scrutiny in human rights matters. Since the 1990s, the extraordinary increase of its caseload appears to have been accompanied by a qualitative transformation in the status of Strasbourg jurisprudence vis-à-vis national legal orders, as well as in the nature of the Convention as an originally international treaty adopted by states. Legal scholars have for long now spoken of the Convention as 'a constitutional instrument of European public order'.[18] In examining individual petitions after all domestic remedies are exhausted, a domain customarily reserved to constitutional law, the ECtHR resembles less an international tribunal and more a court of final appeal. Over the past couple of years, the Court's initiative in ordering states to undertake structural measures in order to redress the systemic causes of human rights infringements (the so-called 'pilot' judgments) has been seen to strengthen its law-making and constitutional propensities.[19] Further reinforcing its European quasi-constitutional qualities is the fact that the Convention system has in practice become slowly incorporated into and intricately fused with the legal and governance structures of the EU.[20] Even though it remains formally separate from the EU, this is expected to change in the near future with the accession of the EU to the ECHR, which is provided for by the Lisbon Treaty.

The institutional architecture and the rules of the Convention system impose explicit and fairly demanding obligations upon national authorities to comply with the ECtHR's adverse judgments. When a state is found to have breached Convention provisions, national authorities are required to comply with the Court's judgment by undertaking both individual and general measures to rectify the injustice (Article 46 ECHR). Besides just satisfaction in the form of pecuniary compensation, individual measures may involve the reopening of judicial proceedings domestically, the cancellation of a person's criminal record as a consequence of a conviction, or changing/

overturning the administrative act in an individual case which was found to be in violation of the Convention. Individual measures aim at restoring the individual's condition to what it was before his/her conviction along the principle of *restitutio in integrum*, even if this may not always be possible in practice.

More important and harder to determine are the general measures that a respondent state, found to have violated Convention norms, is required to take. These are broader measures that extend beyond the specific individual case and are aimed at preventing the recurrence of similar infringements in the future. It is in the obligation to institute general measures that the potential for the ECtHR's rulings to exert broader influence in legal, judicial and policy reform at the national level lies, in areas that come under the Court's purview in the context of individual claims that it reviews. General measures may involve legislative (and in rare instances even constitutional) amendments, the adoption of administrative or executive measures (that is, ministerial circulars or regulations), or a shift in domestic judicial approach and interpretation in conformity with the ECtHR's jurisprudence, and also educational activities and other practical measures.[21] Legislative changes correspond to somewhat more than 50 per cent of the general measures taken by states.[22] These general measures are of cardinal importance to the Convention system. The extent to which states undertake reforms and measures to improve human rights protection at the national level beyond an individual case is decisive for the longer-term effectiveness, legitimacy and the credibility of the system.

While national authorities are obliged to implement Court judgments, responsibility for overseeing whether states actually do so lies with the CoM (Article 54 ECHR), to which a final judgment is first transmitted. Comprising the ministers of foreign affairs of all contracting states and their permanent representatives, the CoM is the political arm of the Convention system. It reflects its intergovernmental underpinnings, which were aimed at ensuring that the Convention would not pose any challenge to the sovereignty of the contracting states. In performing its supervisory role over the execution of judgments, the CoM enters into contact with the competent national authorities and reviews the adequacy of both individual and general measures that they undertake in response to adverse judgments. When the CoM considers that such measures are sufficient to provide an individual remedy and/or to pre-empt future violations, i.e. through a shift in national jurisprudence or through reform of national laws or practices in line with the Convention and the Court's rulings, it closes the case by adopting a final resolution.

Despite the fact that Convention rules prescribe extensive obligations and European supervision over member states, a number of factors can compromise the implementation of Court judgments and their ability to influence national human rights standards. For most part, Strasbourg Court judgments enunciate interpretations only to the extent strictly necessary for the decision of a particular case.[23] They refrain from considering the broader laws and institutional structures to which the issues raised by the individual case at hand may be linked. With the exception of the recent 'pilot' judgments mentioned earlier,[24] the Court has for the most part refrained from ordering the respondent state to undertake specific measures, taking the position that it is not empowered by the Convention to do so. Confining a judgment to the specific conditions of a case, however, creates uncertainty as to how the legal principles enunciated in the latter can be generalised, and obfuscates its implications for broader legal and policy change. The Court has been reluctant to explicitly pronounce a national law to be in violation of the Convention. It instead confines itself to finding fault with the application or interpretation of the law by national courts, and allows national authorities a wide margin of discretion to determine the appropriate general measures. Court judgments are not directly enforceable by national authorities, that is, they do not have *erga omnes* effects. They do not in and of themselves have the effect of overruling national courts or of quashing a decision of state authorities which was found to infringe upon Convention principles.[25]

Furthermore, significant political constraints regarding the effective national implementation of the ECtHR's judgments are built into the Convention's monitoring mechanisms. In particular, the supervision exercised by the CoM has generally been viewed to be lax and deferential to national authorities, exercising a rather 'soft' kind of control in enforcing the execution of judgments against states.[26] It arguably fails to substantively examine the conformity, the appropriateness or the adequacy of the measures instituted in response to an adverse Court judgment. Whether or not the measures instituted are actually implemented, or are effective in preventing the recurrence of violations, is also arguably overlooked by the CoM.[27] As a political body representing states, the CoM relies on information provided by national representatives and has tended to refrain from putting pressure on the latter. It may accept minimal government action, such as distributing the content of a judgment, as sufficient to acknowledge compliance and terminate its proceedings on a case.[28] Critical of this approach, a former judge has noted that 'what is at stake is . . . not only whether remedial legislation is passed at all, but also whether, if passed, it is adequate and meets the requirements implied in the relevant judgment'.[29]

Since the late 1990s, however, the CoM's originally lax and timorous approach has evidently shifted to a more rigorous kind of supervision. The Committee requires national authorities to provide evidence for legal reform or change in judicial practice, before ending its supervision of a judgment.[30] The new rules adopted in 2006 have further empowered the CoM to assume initiative and exercise greater pressure towards national authorities in executing Court judgments.[31] Its supervisory role has also been increasingly assisted by the Directorate General of Human Rights and further bolstered by the activities and initiatives undertaken by the Parliamentary Assembly of the Council of Europe.[32] Important as they may be, these changes do not undercut the substantial influence that competing and mutually accommodating state interests may have upon the CoM's work, especially with regard to judgments that involve nationally sensitive issues.[33]

Notwithstanding the institutional, political and jurisprudential limits of the Convention regime, its norms and the ECtHR's case law have gradually acquired a persuasive and authoritative character which national judges, legislators and other domestic actors are for most part disinclined, at least openly, to contradict. The influence and authority that the ECHR norms and case law have acquired in national legal orders is striking if we consider that the ECHR involves a largely self-restrained court, a lax intergovernmental system of European-level supervision, and extensive national discretion in implementing the orders. The authoritative position that the ECtHR has acquired along with the extraordinary rise of its caseload shows that it interacts dynamically with national legal and political systems and exerts substantial influences over them. Ample evidence shows that the Court's jurisprudence influences substantial legal, judicial and institutional changes, as well as human rights practices at the national level.[34] Why else would large numbers of individuals embark on the 'long and arduous road' to Strasbourg seeking a judgment against their own states, if in the end such a judgment had little result in providing redress and – even if only occasionally – a better kind of justice?

DOMESTIC IMPLEMENTATION OF THE ECtHR'S JUDGMENTS: ANALYTICAL AND METHODOLOGICAL CONSIDERATIONS

Domestic implementation of the ECtHR's rulings varies not only across but also within states, across different kinds of rights claims, and even across issues or policy areas. In some cases national authorities may provide an individual remedy but shy away from adopting any broader measures that may be called for by a judgment. They may confine general measures to minimal forms of action such as translating and distributing the Court's judgments among the judicial and other competent authorities with the goal of diffusing knowledge of Strasbourg case law. Not infrequently, national authorities respond in a formalistic manner, failing to engage in the substantive changes called for by a judgment. In other cases, though, they initiate legislative and/or institutional reform to bring national law, practice and policies in line with the human rights norms pronounced in the ECtHR's judgments. In some areas and issues, the execution of the ECtHR's judgments may inspire little interest or controversy. In others, it may involve mobilisation by interested individuals and actors to pressure governments for reform, or conversely, strong opposition among competing social and political actors to stall change.[35]

If national-level implementation and the broader legal and policy impact of the ECtHR's judgments are significantly constrained, and yet cannot be dismissed, then what are the domestic legal and institutional factors that promote or undermine implementation? What are the responses of the domestic actors and institutions to the implementation of the ECtHR's judgments, as well as the relevant dynamics that develop among them? And how do they vary across issue and policy areas? There is ample room for comparative research into the variable and multi-faceted ways in which European human rights judgments are implemented and the extent to which they influence domestic laws, judicial norms, policies and politics. The contributions in this volume examine such differences and identify and analyse the conditions and factors that promote or conversely restrict implementation and the potential of judgments to trigger rights-expansive policy change. Analytically, they employ a dual approach that explores the national-level institutional structures and dynamics (Part I), as well as the political and societal conditions (Part II), that shape the domestic implementation of the ECtHR's judgments.

The first part of the volume explores the implementation responses of, and interactions among, different institutional and governmental actors. The chapters on Germany, Italy and Romania examine the responses of national judges, as well as of the administrative, executive and parliamentary actors, in instituting individual and general measures following adverse judgments issued by the Strasbourg Court. These three countries are selected because they capture the diversity of domestic implementation institutions, processes and performance records in Europe. Germany has a decentralised structure of implementation, strong judicial review of rights and one of the best implementation records. Italy has a highly centralised implementation process, moderate judicial rights review and one of the worst implementation records. Romania lacks a tradition of and structures for judicial rights review, it has a rather dismal implementation record and it has undergone post-communist democratisation and EU accession, both of which have distinctly shaped the context of domestic human rights implementation. The volume and nature of rights violations across these three countries also differ markedly. They touch upon a broad spectrum of law and policy, ranging from the structure and functioning of the national judicial system, to respect for privacy for groups and individuals who find themselves in a status of reduced rights, nationalisation of property, state expropriation of land, journalists' freedom of expression, and the powers of the secret services, among other things. They involve isolated infringements but also so-called 'clone' cases manifesting repeat violations symptomatic of deeper systemic problems.

The enforcement of Convention rights and the Court's case law, however, is not only the task of formally designated national institutions. It is also diffused among individuals and other social actors who claim their rights in

litigation before the ECtHR and may subsequently mobilise for implementation of its judgments. Focusing on the cases of Greece, Bulgaria, Austria,
Turkey and the UK, the contributions in the second part of this volume
examine the national authorities' responses and interactions linked to the
implementation of the Court's case law, but they also go beyond this to examine
the political and societal context. Interested in processes of legal mobilisation
as a prerequisite for the ECtHR to exercise its judicial review, they explore
how marginalised individuals and social actors from various kinds of minorities mobilise and claim Convention rights. They take recourse in Strasbourg
in order to address a variety of issues and demands vis-à-vis their governments. How, in what ways and to what extend does social, legal and political
mobilisation affect the domestic implementation of the ECtHR's judgments,
as well as their potential to exert broader influence over policy reform?
This can only be meaningfully explored in countries which have generated
a substantial number of adverse ECtHR's judgments in minority-related
cases.

We have selected the five countries listed above (Austria, Greece, Bulgaria,
Turkey and the UK) as they are longstanding parties to the Convention and
have over the years generated the most voluminous minority-related case
law from the ECtHR. The country-based contributions explore the ECtHR's
judgments pertaining to immigrants, ethnic and religious minorities and
homosexuals. While human rights litigation does not necessarily lead to
progressive legal and policy reform that expands the rights of individuals
and social groups, the Strasbourg-based regime does provide opportuni-
ties for legal recourse beyond the national level. In this way, while it does
not enhance the representative aspects of democracy – indeed, it is seen to
undermine them – it can (and does) contribute to its accountability through
individuals enforcing human rights law and claiming their rights under the
Convention in respect of states. From this perspective, the contributions in
the second part of this volume shed light on the decentralised and participa-
tory processes that this transnational regime of the ECHR involves, with
implications for democratic governance.[36]

The eight country-based case studies focus on the precedent-like norms
pronounced in the ECtHR's judgments rather than on the domestic reception of the Convention in general.[37] The reason for such a focus is that the
ECtHR's case law interprets and therefore renders concrete the abstract
Convention norms (which are to a large extent contained or replicated in the
constitutional texts of most contracting states) by applying them to a variety
of practical contexts and areas of law and policy.

The final resolutions issued by the CoM, when it considers that national
authorities have adequately remedied a violation, contain substantive information about the measures and reforms that have been adopted in response
to judgments, but these measures must be contextualised. Merely affirming
state compliance when the CoM issues a final resolution in fact obscures a

great deal of variation in the nature, let alone the efficacy, of the legislative and other measures that national authorities institute in response to judgments. Such variation is in part linked to the ambiguity but also flexibility of the appropriate measures that may be called for by a judgment, as well as to the fact that the CoM may close its proceedings on a case on the basis of minimal measures undertaken by state authorities. Both the CoM delegates and the national officials involved in the execution of the ECtHR's judgments operate through 'shared expectations of flexibility': while they ostensibly observe normative principles in some cases, they may abide more substantively in others.[38]

In sum, the country case studies examine the reports and resolutions issued by the CoM in each judgment in order to identify the measures that national authorities undertake in response. At the same time, the analyses place the reported measures and reforms in the broader institutional, political and societal context in order to appraise critically their scope, quality and effectiveness. The authors analyse the information reported in the resolutions in the light of a variety of national- and European-level documentation obtained through several interviews with relevant actors, from reports issued by governmental and non-governmental organisations, as well as from the press. They trace the actions and interactions of state officials, judges, and non-governmental actors to uphold, improve or correct domestic rights protection in response to the ECtHR's judgments in particular areas of law and policy.

Country-based case studies are not the appropriate methodological tool to test a set of pre-existing hypotheses, and this volume does not purport to do this. Yet, drawing from existing studies on the implementation of international and European legal norms, a number of factors and conditions can be identified as instrumental. By engaging in intra-country comparisons, the case studies in this volume consider the plausibility of factors influencing the nature and scope of implementation (or the lack of it) on the basis of the empirical data they review without, however, claiming to test specific propositions. The goal is to identify in which direction further research could be pursued to build more general propositions. In this sense, this volume moves beyond a descriptive overview without, however, advancing a consistent causal argument or a theory about the factors promoting and obstructing the domestic impact of and compliance with ECtHR case law.

INSTITUTIONAL DYNAMICS OF DOMESTIC IMPLEMENTATION

Legal scholarship has emphasised the incorporation of the Convention and its rank in the domestic legal order as an important factor in determining state compliance with its human rights provisions.[39] Yet there is now a broad consensus that the influence of this factor is at best mixed and decisively mediated by other factors such as the presence or absence of an indigenous bill of rights and judicial review, and the relationship between the judiciary and the government, among others. It is also linked to the extent to which contracting states, like Switzerland for example, routinely verify the compatibility of draft laws with the Convention, by also taking into account Court judgments that pertain to other states.[40] Even as early as the 1980s, Andrew Drzemczewski noted that irrespective of the domestic status of the ECHR, a general presumption existed that national courts should interpret domestic law in compliance with the Convention.[41] Today all contracting states have incorporated the Convention in their domestic legal order. Differences in its domestic status (that is, whether it has a constitutional rank, a supra-legislative status or another status) do not bear any notable impact on the implementation of Strasbourg Court judgments domestically.

States that are parties to the Convention have set up domestic structures and designated national bodies that are responsible for the implementation of the ECtHR's judgments, which the CoM monitors. Such structures reflect a largely top-down implementation process. While they vary considerably across states, they overwhelmingly share a common feature: their institutional arrangements predominantly rely on the executive and in most countries they are characterised by a strong degree of centralisation in the latter. In six out of the eight countries covered in this volume, the dominant government institution assigned with responsibility for execution is either the ministry of foreign affairs and the officials, departments or bodies that belong to it, or the head of government (for example the Prime Minister in Italy and the Federal Chancellor in Austria). On the other hand, the involvement of parliamentary actors in the implementation process is limited, even if in certain countries it is significant (UK) or not entirely absent (Germany). Overall, the domestic implementation of ECtHR judgments is closely linked to the ability of particular institutional settings and decision-making processes to amass and transform political will to effective policy action.

Domestic implementation of the ECtHR's judgments involves a variety of national institutions and actors that must align national laws, policies and practices to the Convention. Their responses do not necessarily conform and indeed may conflict with one another. In the first place, national courts, especially higher and constitutional ones, play a fundamental role by being able to align their judicial approach to the Convention and the ECtHR's case law. Even though the ECtHR does not have direct links to national courts, akin to the Court of Justice of the EU and its preliminary ruling mechanism, and even though the Convention lacks supremacy and direct effect, the Strasbourg Court today is the centre of a system that has moved far beyond its origins in traditional precepts of international law.[42] In this transformation, national courts have been instrumental in progressively attributing a higher status to the Convention domestically than what had been assigned to it through its formal incorporation in a country (for example, in Germany, Italy and France, among others).[43] In general, familiarity with and adherence to the ECtHR's jurisprudence have over time substantially grown among national judges in many countries.

The attitude of judges in national higher and constitutional courts towards the Convention and their (shifting) willingness to modify their interpretations in line with the ECtHR's rulings is a complex issue shaped by a variety of factors. Scholars have debated the extent to which the evolving relationship between national courts and the ECtHR resembles one of hierarchy akin to a constitutional order,[44] or conversely an open-ended and pluralist one.[45] Irrespective of which paradigm most accurately depicts reality, the extent to which national judiciaries accept and comply with the ECtHR's case law is clearly influenced by the degree to which domestic legal norms of human rights and the relevant jurisprudence are congruent with the Convention.[46] The existence and effectiveness of domestic rights review, in which individuals can pursue a remedy, as well as a national judiciary well acquainted with and responsive to Convention standards, are arguably important factors. They contribute both to low violation rates in countries such as Germany, Belgium, the Netherlands and Sweden, and to the implementation of the ECtHR's case law.[47]

National judges of higher and constitutional courts may align with the ECtHR's interpretations as a means of enhancing their domestic position and power, but they may also be defensive of indigenous constitutional norms and judicial approaches vis-à-vis those advanced by the Strasbourg Court.[48] Aligning with Strasbourg jurisprudence may be perceived to strengthen their judicial authority domestically, but it may also be seen to threaten it. National courts seeking to maintain their autonomy may attempt to retain their role as the ultimate authority over a European tribunal. In addition, competition among different courts within a jurisdiction may also play itself out in relation to the ECtHR's jurisprudence. For instance, one can observe a notable evolution in the attitude of French tribunals and of the Council of State in particular. Their approach to aliens' rights has shifted and become more consonant with Strasbourg case law, resembling the attitudes of their Dutch counterparts.[49] Such a shift is attributed to changing judicial interests arising from competition with other domestic courts and the need to prevent being short-circuited by these.[50]

The attitude of national judges towards the Convention and the ECtHR's case law is determined not only by the legal culture and established jurisprudential practice, but also by the interests of national judiciaries in maintaining or enhancing their authority with respect to other actors and branches of power domestically. Evolving perceptions and interests of national judges in relation to the ECtHR may be constrained by established institutional balances between the judiciary, parliament and the government, but they may also challenge such balances. In post-communist countries, upholding European norms of human rights has arguably enabled the relatively young constitutional courts to bolster their authority and gain leverage with their governments.[51] Generally, scholars have not considered or explored the possibility that implementing the ECtHR's judgments may trigger changing dynamics among state institutions and different branches of power, as well as between societal actors on the one hand and the state on the other.

Besides the role of national courts, scholars of international relations and public law have highlighted the existence of sufficient domestic political will as a necessary precondition for compliance with international and human rights law and its potential to influence social reform. Because courts lack implementation powers, they can promote significant political and social change only when there is ample support from legislative and executive officials, as well as significant elite and public support for their rulings.[52] The willingness of political elites and officials in key executive institutions to promote rights-conscious policies has also been identified as crucial in complying with the Convention and the Court's judgments.[53] Political will varies depending on the magnitude of domestic public opposition or expected resistance, as well as on the anticipated political costs that the implementation of human rights norms may have. Parliamentary representatives, whose support for legislative changes is indispensable, often have agendas beyond protecting rights in accordance with the Convention.[54] For elected officials in general, considerations of political cost for pursuing unpopular policies (especially with a view to their chances of being re-elected) weigh heavily upon their willingness to promote rights protection in particular areas of state policy. The dynamics of party politics can also bear an important influence. The presence and the relative strength of strongly conservative, populist and nationalist political parties in Parliament, which tend to be opposed to international human rights, may be inhibiting factors that restrict the implementation of Court judgments, especially with regard to immigration and asylum policies or historical minorities.

The first part of this volume explores the domestic structures and processes involved in the implementation of the ECtHR's judgments, and the efforts of and interactions among the competent national authorities in instituting individual and primarily general measures. Focusing on Germany, Italy and Romania, the three country-based chapters in this part show considerable cross-national but also intra-country variation in the responses of national authorities to Strasbourg Court judgments. Why do national authorities implement adverse judgments in some cases but do so highly restrictively, or even fail to do so, in other sets of cases and policy areas? How do courts, especially higher and constitutional ones, but also ordinary courts, respond to Strasbourg judgments? Do the influences and pressures exerted by the need to implement and comply with rights interpretations advanced by the ECtHR's judgments embolden and/or enhance judicial authority vis-à-vis the legislative and executive branches?[55]

The chapter on Germany explores the national system of rights review and the constellation of the domestic structures and actors involved in the implementation of the ECtHR's judgments. These encompass government, administrative, judicial and legislative actors at both the state and the federal level, along with the involvement of a variety of non-governmental actors without a designated role in implementation. The small number of adverse judgments issued by the ECtHR against Germany cannot be understood independently from the highly developed and effective system of rights review domestically, dominated by the Basic Law and the Federal Constitutional Court. It is also linked to an apparently preventive approach often adopted by state authorities: the review of draft legislation for compatibility with the Convention and the consideration of the ECtHR's case law issued also against other countries. Nonetheless, the domestic implementation of the ECtHR's judgments is a sometimes controversial and conflict-ridden process, for reasons that are explored in the German chapter.

The chapter on Italy examines the domestic consequences of the ECtHR's judgments in the most problematic areas that have generated a large volume of case law, such as fair trial and length of proceedings, property rights and the right to family and private life. The chapter argues that the ineffective and delayed implementation of the ECtHR's judgments in Italy has been due to factors concerning the legal system as well as the cultural attitude of Italian politicians and the civil society. In spite of the Italian authorities' persistent failure to undertake effective legal and judicial reform in response to major violations of the ECHR (such as those regarding Article 6), the past couple of years have seen renewed and more determined efforts in this regard. These have gone hand in hand with greater receptivity towards the Convention and its binding quality. Especially important has been the role of the national higher courts, which have sought to partly counterbalance political inertia to enforce Strasbourg Court judgments, even if they do so by exercising substantial self-restraint.

The Romanian chapter explores the profound influence that the ECtHR's judgments have had in the post-communist period, in spite of significant opposition to it. Besides the infrastructural weaknesses of the main institutions assigned the task of execution of judgments, political elites accord an overall low priority to the implementation of the Court's judgments. In spite of such deficiencies, these judgments have proved to be a major source of policy change in areas such as freedom of expression in the media, the criminal justice system, judicial reform and property laws. In these areas, laws, structures and practices inherited from the communist regime were sharply incompatible with the Convention's provisions and ECtHR case law. The large volume of petitions taken to the Court and the resulting condemnations on the one hand, in tandem with the country's EU accession process on the other, turned out to be the major sources of pressure and policy change in these areas.

LEGAL MOBILISATION AND THE POLITICAL CONTEXT OF IMPLEMENTATION

While state implementation of the ECtHR's judgments is a top-down process shaped by designated national institutions and actors, it may also involve decentralised enforcement by interested individual and social actors that begins with litigation. Scholars of EU integration and international relations have over the past couple of years highlighted litigation in domestic and European courts as a central mechanism of enforcement of EU and human rights law.[56] They have also probed into the factors that determine variable patterns of judicial rights claiming at the European level.[57] Even though the Convention establishes a decentralised system of enforcement through the right of individuals to lodge their complaints in the ECtHR, aspects of litigation and legal mobilisation until recently went unnoticed by researchers. The second part of this volume focuses on specific areas of rights that are raised in claims advanced by various kinds of minorities, ethnic, religious, sexual and racial, immigrants and asylum seekers. It explores the social and political conditions and dynamics that characterise the processes of implementing Strasbourg Court judgments, while also paying attention to the politics of human rights on behalf of less privileged social actors.

Less privileged and marginalised social actors such as minorities have engaged with legal processes to claim their fundamental rights. Their resort to courts and the legal system to claim and protect their rights is a longstanding phenomenon. In general, litigation through courts has been a means of pursuing rights and empowering individuals and groups who are less likely to be influential through electoral politics and the legislative political process. While it was originally prevalent in countries like Canada and the US, it has also been increasingly evidenced in continental Europe both at the national and the European level.[58] Not infrequently, legal action by individuals from less privileged and marginalised social groups in Strasbourg originates from 'strategic litigation', namely, the 'use [of] the court system to attempt to create broad social change'.[59] It is premised on a widespread but also highly disputed expectation that judicial rulings can vindicate minorities and exert pressure upon governments to change their relevant laws and practices. The purpose of such litigation is to clarify or reform national laws, promote human rights practices, pressure governments, document injustices or change public attitudes. A good number of minority-related cases are defended by public interest law firms and NGOs from various countries across Europe.

Mobilisation through the legal process and the courts is necessary for the Strasbourg Court to exercise its review powers over specific national laws and policies, yet it is far from sufficient for achieving implementation and influencing policy reform.[60] Even when the claims of individuals from marginalised groups are vindicated in court, judicial decisions are seldom enough to create policy change on their own. In fact, litigation in courts is often part of a multi-pronged strategy with the goal of gaining leverage in political contestation and generally in extra-judicial negotiations. By 'following through' on a legal victory, successful litigants, activists and their supporters continue to campaign on behalf of their goals and to underscore the political and financial costs of persisting non-compliance.[61]

Less privileged groups like ethnic minorities are more likely to take recourse to courts, and to the ECtHR in particular, in some of the countries covered in this volume. At the same time, they may also be less capable of combining litigation with lobbying efforts in legislatures and administrative agencies. It is argued that those more likely to pursue their interests effectively in legal and political arenas are actors with intense and concentrated interests (such as employers' associations) rather than weak and dispersed ones (such as consumers' or immigrants' groups).[62] Unlike the latter, the former can overcome the problems endemic in collective action and coordinate legal and political efforts. Specifically in reference to rights claims, other scholars attribute less importance to the specific characteristics of interest groups as such and more to the development of a strong rights culture, as well as comprehensive and vital structures of legal support to engage in sustained judicial battles. Such structures of legal support comprise rights advocacy organisations, willing and able lawyers, and the availability of financial aid, as well as state agencies such as equality bodies and national human rights institutions.[63]

Pressure from societal and other interest groups may influence the willingness of government and legislative elites to implement human rights judgments and reform policies accordingly. The ability of different groups, political, professional, issue based or otherwise, to forge dominant coalitions and pressure the government may be decisive in bending opposition against legal and other reforms that are called for by the ECtHR's judgments. Their ability as such is in turn determined by the domestic structure of state–society relations, and in particular by the degree to which state structures and policy-making processes in different countries are open to pressure from societal interests.[64]

In sum, the ability to exert government pressure is also shaped by the nature and organisation of different kinds of societal interests, as well as the extent to which they can enlist sufficient support from public institutions or influential political actors. Those who do dispose of material and organisational resources and structural power are more capable of combining litigation with other political tactics (that is, lobbying) towards gaining a legal victory and using it in the political arena to press for certain reforms and policies. In the end 'the will of governments to align policies with innovative legal interpretation depends on the likelihood of institutional support for legal claims and government responsiveness to the preferences of actors with structural power'.[65,66]

The second part of the volume examines domestic implementation of the ECtHR's judgments related to various kinds of minorities by focusing on their legal and political mobilisation to pursue different rights claims against states, and the responses of legislative, judicial and governmental actors. By comparing the ECtHR's judgments concerning the rights of homosexuals with those related to claims raised by foreigners and immigrants, the chapter on Austria seeks to identify the factors that account for divergent patterns of state compliance in these two issue areas. Why has the implementation of the ECtHR's judgments played a central role as a trigger of domestic legal reform and policy change in the former, but has only exerted at best a limited influence on the latter? While civil society mobilisation emerges as an important precondition for the implementation of the ECtHR's judgments and their ability to exert domestic legal and policy change, whether sufficient or effective (general) implementation measures are taken seems to be only marginally dependent on the resources and structures of legal support for the individuals concerned. What seems to be more important is the existence of the political will to initiate changes, as well as the personal commitment and influence of individuals in high-level positions within the administrative machinery.

The chapter on the UK compares four sets of cases that have produced markedly different implementation outcomes: those concerning rights claims by homosexual and transgender applicants on the one hand, and cases brought by Gypsies as well as victims of police violence and wrongful imprisonment in Northern Ireland on the other. While in the former set of cases the ECtHR's judgments led to the adoption of legal and policy reforms that enhanced the protection of their individual and group-specific rights, the judgments in the latter have been characterised by sluggish and restrictive implementation in the few cases in which applicants were vindicated by the Strasbourg Court. The analysis of the UK chapter shows that such variation in domestic implementation between the two sets of cases has been determined in large part by social and political factors, such as support from civil society, the extent to which an issue area is linked to national security and public order issues, political will on the part of government and legislators, and the degree of public support.

The chapter on Greece compares the effective implementation of the ECtHR's judgments originating in petitions by members of non-Orthodox communities (mainly Jehovah's Witnesses) with the refusal by national authorities to give effect to the judgments concerning the rights of individuals that assert an ethnic minority identity. What accounts for such different national responses to the implementation of the ECtHR's judgments concerning two distinct kinds of minority groups, towards which public attitudes have been equally prejudicial, if not hostile? The analysis of the Greek case shows that Strasbourg Court judgments do not prompt in themselves legal and policy reforms but they can still act as important catalysts in a process of change. The variable domestic implementation of the ECtHR's judgments in the two sets of cases can be understood in reference to the level of existing political support to promote reforms, in tandem with low or diffuse public opposition against legal and policy changes pertaining to minorities. These political and societal preconditions have direct repercussions for the approach and position of national judges.

Since the late 1990s in Bulgaria, a significant number of the ECtHR's judgments have raised procedural and substantive legal issues pertaining to the rights of political participation and/or protection of ethnic, racial and religious minorities. While the authorities eventually implemented domestic measures in judgments involving procedural issues, they have implemented minimally or not at all adverse judgments concerning the rights claims affecting religious and ethnic minorities, with the majority of cases seeing only partial general measures and limited individual measures. The chapter on Bulgaria argues that such variation is significantly determined by factors such as political party interests and public attitudes. Where the issue raised by a judgment does not affect negatively any political or institutional interest, or where there is significant public support for it, there is a greater likelihood of effective implementation, as well as legal and policy change. As in other countries, the position taken by national judges can be a pivotal parameter, which, however, in the Bulgarian case has been highly reluctant and restrained in upholding the rights claims raised by members of minorities.

In Turkey, most of the thousands of cases taken to the ECtHR in the 1990s were in response to the violations originating from the actions of security forces, committed in the name of 'combating terrorism'. The chapter on Turkey shows that the ECtHR's case law has played a significant role in bringing these violations to light. The consequent pressure from the international community has forced the Turkish government to revise its mode of dealing with the insurgency and with the Kurdish political and cultural demands more generally. Additionally, the EU's accession criteria, which require candidate countries to protect minority rights, have pressured Turkey not only to execute the ECtHR's judgments related to the Kurdish question, but also to go beyond it and grant Kurds limited linguistic rights. At the same time, though, the authors argue that the improvements have not resulted in the eradication of the problem or even in any substantive change in governmental policy. In a struggle with the two institutional pillars of the nationalist position, the military and the judiciary, the AKP government of Tayyip Erdoğan has held an ambivalent position and followed a policy of negotiating for power rather than displaying a principled commitment to human rights.

Notes

1. Robert O. Keohane, Andrew Moravscik and Anne-Marie Slaughter, 'Legalized Dispute Resolution: Interstate and Transnational', *International Organization*, vol. 54, no. 3 (2000), pp. 457–88.

2. Alec Stone Sweet, 'A Cosmopolitan Legal Order: Constitutional Pluralism and Rights Adjudication in Europe,' *Global Constitutionalism*, vol. 1, no. 1 (2012), pp. 53–90.

3. Laurence R. Helfer and Anne-Marie Slaughter, 'Toward a Theory of Effective Supranational Adjudication', *Yale Law Journal*, vol. 107, no. 2 (1997), p. 296.

4. While in 1999, 12,600 applications were pending before a judicial formation in Strasbourg, by 2011 this number had risen to 151,600 applications. See *European Court of Human Rights Analysis of Statistics 2011* (Strasbourg: Council of Europe, 2012), p. 7.

5. See Steven Greer, 'What's Wrong with the European Convention on Human Rights?' *Human Rights Quarterly*, vol. 30, no. 3 (2008), pp. 680–702.

6. In December 2010, only 11 per cent of all cases pending before the CoM were leading cases (that is, important cases that reveal a new structural/general problem in a respondent state), while 89 per cent were clone/repetitive or isolated cases. In the same period, 14 per cent of all judgments that became final in 2010 were leading cases, while 86 per cent were clone/repetitive or isolated cases. The high ratio of clone and repetitive cases has not declined since 2004 and remains around 80–85 per cent. See Council of Europe Committee of Ministers, *Supervision of the Execution of Judgments and Decisions of the European Court of Human Rights: Annual Report 2010* (Strasbourg: Council of Europe, 2011), pp. 42–6.

7. On this latter issue, see Lawrence Helfer and Erik Voeten, 'International Courts as Agents of Legal Change: Evidence from LGBT Rights in Europe', available at http://ssrn.com/abstract=1850526 (accessed 8 October 2012).

8. See for instance Benedetto Conforti and Francesco Francioni (eds), *Enforcing Human Rights in Domestic Courts* (The Hague: Martinus Nijhoff, 1997); Jorg Polakiewicz, 'The Application of the ECHR in Domestic Law', *Human Rights Law Journal*, vol. 17, no. 11–12 (1996), pp. 405–11; Jorg Polakiewicz and Valerie Jacob-Foltzer, 'The ECHR in Domestic Law: The Impact of Strasbourg Case-Law in States Where Direct Effect Is Given to the Convention', *Human Rights Law Journal*, vol. 12, no. 4 (1991), pp. 125–42.

9. See for instance Theodora A. Christou and Juan Pablo Raymond (eds), *European Court of Human Rights: Remedies and Execution of Judgments* (London: British Institute of International and Comparative Law, 2005). See also Fredrik G. E. Sundberg, 'Control of Execution of Decisions under the European Convention on Human Rights: A Perspective on Democratic Security, Inter-governmental Cooperation, Unification and Individual Justice in Europe', in Guðmundur Alfreðsson et al. (eds), *International Human Rights Monitoring Mechanisms: Essays in Honour of Jakob Th. Möller* (The Hague Martinus Nijhoff, 2001), pp. 561–85; Georg Ress, 'The Effect of Decisions and Judgments of the European Court of Human Rights in the Domestic Legal Order', *Texas International Law Journal*, vol.

40, no. 3 (2005), pp. 359–82; Elisabeth Lambert-Abdelgawad, *The Execution of Judgments of the European Court of Human Rights* (Strasbourg: Council of Europe, 2002); R. Ryssdal, 'The Enforcement System Set Up under the ECHR', in M. K. Bulterman and M. Kuijer (eds), *Compliance with Judgments of International Courts* (The Hague: Martinus Nijhoff, 1996), pp. 49–69.

10. Helen Keller and Alec Stone Sweet (eds), *A Europe of Rights: The Impact of the ECHR on National Legal Systems* (Oxford: Oxford University Press, 2008); Leonard Hammer and Frank Emmert (eds), *The European Convention on Human Rights and Fundamental Freedoms in Central and Eastern Europe* (The Hague: Eleven International, 2011).

11. Steven Greer, *The European Convention on Human Rights: Achievements, Problems and Prospects* (Cambridge: Cambridge University Press, 2006).

12. See for example, Harold Hongju Koh, 'The 1998 Frankel Lecture: Bringing International Law Home', *Houston Law Review*, vol. 35 (1999), pp. 623–82; Xinyuan Dai, *International Institutions and National Policies* (Cambridge: Cambridge University Press, 2007); Thomas Risse, Stephen C. Ropp and Kathryn Sikkink (eds), *The Power of Human Rights: International Norms and Domestic Change* (Cambridge: Cambridge University Press, 1999).

13. Beth A. Simmons, *Mobilizing for Human Rights: International Law in Domestic Politics* (New York: Cambridge University Press, 2009), which, however, does not examine the implementation of the Convention and the ECtHR's case law.

14. Andrew Moravscik, 'The Origins of Human Rights Regimes: Democratic Delegation in Postwar Europe', *International Organization*, vol. 54, no. 2 (2000), pp. 217–52; Mikael Madsen Rask, 'From Cold War Instrument to Supreme European Court: The European Court of Human Rights at the Crossroads of International and National Law and Politics', *Law and Social Inquiry*, vol. 32, no. 1 (2007), pp. 137–59.

15. Since it was adopted in the early 1950s, the Convention has been supplemented by fourteen additional protocols, most of which have expanded the set of rights contained in the treaty.

16. Rask, 'From Cold War Instrument to Supreme European Court', p. 153.

17. J. G. Merrills and A. H. Robertson, *Human Rights in Europe: A Study of the European Convention on Human Rights*, 4th ed. (Manchester: Manchester University Press, 2001), p. 274.

18. Andrew Drzemczewski, *European Human Rights Convention in Domestic Law: A Comparative Study* (Oxford: Clarendon Press, 1983), p. 19.

19. Wojciech Sadurski, 'Partnering with Strasbourg: Constitutionalisation of the European Court of Human Rights, the Accession of Central and East European States to the Council of Europe, and the Idea of Pilot Judgments', *Human Rights Law Review*, vol. 9, no. 3 (2009), pp. 397–453.

20. Laurent Scheeck, 'Solving Europe's Binary Human Rights Puzzle: The Interaction between Supranational Courts as a Parameter of European Governance', *Questions de recherche*, no. 15 (2005).

21. Lambert-Abdelgawad, *The Execution of Judgments of the European Court of Human Rights*, pp. 20–1.

22. Sundberg, 'Control of Execution of Decisions under the European Convention on Human Rights', pp. 573–4.
23. Paul Mahoney, 'Judicial Activism and Judicial Self-Restraint in the European Court of Human Rights: Two Sides of the Same Coin', *Human Rights Law Journal*, vol. 11 (1990), p. 87.
24. On pilot judgments, see Philip Leach, 'Beyond the Bug River: A New Dawn for Redress Before the European Court of Human Rights?', *European Human Rights Law Review*, no. 2 (2005), pp. 161–2; J. A. Frowein, 'The Binding Force of ECHR Judgments and Its Limits', in Stephan Breitenmoser et al. (eds), *Human Rights, Democracy and the Rule of Law* (Zurich: Dike / Baden-Baden: Nomos, 2007), p. 266.
25. Ress, 'The Effect of Decisions and Judgments of the European Court of Human Rights in the Domestic Legal Order', p. 373.
26. Sundberg, 'Control of Execution of Decisions under the European Convention on Human Rights', p. 575.
27. Greer, *The European Convention on Human Rights*, p. 71.
28. Occasionally, however, the CoM may adopt an interim resolution when it considers that the information provided by the government of the state found to have violated the Convention does not show satisfactory execution of an ECtHR judgment. See Lambert-Abdelgawad, *The Execution of Judgments of the European Court of Human Rights*, pp. 36–7.
29. S. K. Martens, 'Commentary', in M. K. Bulterman and M. Kuijer (eds), *Compliance with Judgments of International Courts* (The Hague: Martinus Nijhoff, 1996), p. 73.
30. Elisabeth Lambert-Abdelgawad, *The Execution of Judgments of the European Court of Human Rights*, 2nd edn (Strasbourg: Council of Europe, 2008), p. 37; Sundberg, 'Control of Execution of Decisions under the European Convention on Human Rights', pp. 574–9.
31. Nicholas Sitaropoulos, 'Supervising Execution of ECtHR Judgments Concerning Minorities: The Committee of Ministers Potentials and Constraints', *Annuaire international des droits de l' homme*, vol. 3 (2008), p. 532.
32. Philip Leach, 'The effectiveness of the Committee of Ministers in Supervising the Enforcement of the Judgments of the European Court of Human Rights', *Public Law*, no. 3 (2006), pp. 449–51.
33. Sitaropoulos, 'Supervising Execution of ECtHR Judgments Concerning Minorities', p. 539.
34. See the contributions in Keller and Sweet (eds), *A Europe of Rights*.
35. D. J. Harris, Michael O'Boyle and Chris Warbrick, *Law of the European Convention on Human Rights* (London: Butterworths, 1995), p. 30.
36. At an analytical level, these kinds of question are raised in Rachel A. Cichowski, 'Introduction: Courts, Democracy and Governance', *Comparative Political Studies*, vol. 39, no. 1 (2006), pp. 3–5.
37. Helen Keller and Alec Stone Sweet, 'Introduction: The Reception of the ECHR in National Legal Orders', in Helen Keller and Alec Stone Sweet (eds), *A Europe of Rights: The Impact of the ECHR on National Legal Systems* (Oxford: Oxford University Press, 2008), pp. 11–36.

38. Richard Bilder, 'Beyond Compliance: Helping Nations Cooperate', in Dinah Shelton (ed.), *Commitment and Compliance: The Role of Non-binding Norms in the International Legal System* (Oxford: Oxford University Press, 2000), p. 69.
39. Polakiewiz, 'The Application of the ECHR in Domestic Law'.
40. Helfer and Slaughter, 'Toward a Theory of Effective Supranational Adjudication', pp. 306–7. See also Helen Keller, 'Reception of the European Convention for the Protection of Human Rights and Fundamental Freedoms (ECHR) in Poland and Switzerland', *Zeitschrift für ausländisches öffentliches Recht und Völkerrecht*, vol. 65 (2005), p. 307. Greer argues that none of these factors are decisive in promoting lower versus higher rates of compliance with the ECHR. See Greer, *The European Convention on Human Rights*, pp. 85–6.
41. Drzemczewski, *European Human Rights Convention in Domestic Law*, p. 260.
42. Ibid., p. 18.
43. Leslie Friedman Goldstein and Cornel Ban, 'The European Human-rights Regime as a Case Study in the Emergence of Global Governance', in Alice D. Ba and Matthew J. Hoffmann (eds), *Contending Perspectives on Global Governance: Coherence, Contestation and World Order* (Abingdon: Routledge, 2005), pp. 154–77; see also the chapter on Italy in this volume.
44. Sadurski, 'Partnering with Strasbourg'.
45. Nico Krisch, 'The Open Architecture of European Human Rights Law', LSE Law, Society and Economy Working Papers 11/2007, available at http://papers.ssrn.com/sol3/papers.cfm?abstract_id=1018991 (accessed 19 September 2012).
46. Ibid., p. 30.
47. Greer, *The European Convention on Human Rights*, p. 87.
48. Keller and Stone Sweet, 'Introduction', p. 27.
49. Virginie Guiraudon, 'European Courts and Foreigners' Rights: A Comparative Study of Norms Diffusion', *International Migration Review*, vol. 34, no. 4 (2000), p. 1095.
50. Ibid., p. 1104.
51. Nancy Maveety and Anke Grosskopf, '"Constrained" Constitutional Courts as Conduits for Democratic Consolidation', *Law and Society Review*, vol. 38, no. 3 (2004), p. 468.
52. Gerald Rosenberg, *The Hollow Hope: Can Courts Bring About Social Change?* (Chicago: University of Chicago Press, 1991).
53. Greer, *The European Convention on Human Rights*, p. 132.
54. Keller and Stone Sweet, 'Introduction', p. 31.
55. Ibid., p. 29; Goldstein and Ban, 'The European Human-rights Regime as a Case Study in the Emergence of Global Governance'.
56. See Simmons, *Mobilizing for Human Rights*; Tanja Börzel, 'Participation through Law Enforcement: The Case of the European Union', *Comparative Political Studies*, vol. 39, no. 1 (2006), pp. 128–52; Rachel A. Cichowski, *The European Court and Civil Society: Litigation, Mobilization and Governance* (Cambridge: Cambridge University Press, 2007).

57. Elizabeth Heger Boyle and Melissa Thompson, 'National Politics and Resort to the European Commission on Human Rights', *Law and Society Review*, vol. 35, no. 2 (2001), pp. 321–44.

58. See Carlo Guarnieri, 'Courts and Marginalized Groups: Perspectives from Continental Europe', *International Journal of Constitutional Law*, vol. 5, no. 2 (2007), pp. 187–210; Michael D. Goldhaber, *A People's History of the European Court of Human Rights* (New Brunswick, NJ: Rutgers University Press, 2007); Dia Anagnostou and Evangelia Psychogiopoulou (eds), *The European Court of Human Rights and the Rights of Marginalised Individuals and Minorities in National Context* (Leiden: Martinus Nijhoff, 2010).

59. *Strategic Litigation of Race Discrimination in Europe: From Principles to Practice*, published by European Roma Rights Centre, INTERIGHTS and Minority Policy Group (Nottingham: Russell Press, 2004), p. 35.

60. Carol Harlow and Richard Rawlings, *Pressure through Law* (London: Routledge, 1992).

61. Karen J. Alter and Jeannette Vargas, 'Explaining Variation in the Use of European Litigation Strategies: European Community Law and British Gender Equality Policy', *Comparative Political Studies*, vol. 33, no. 4 (2000), pp. 462–4.

62. Ibid., p. 473.

63. Charles Epp, *The Rights Revolution: Lawyers, Activists, and Supreme Courts in Comparative Perspective* (Chicago: University of Chicago Press, 1998).

64. Jeffrey T. Checkel, 'The Europeanization of Citizenship?' in Maria Green Cowles, James Caporaso and Thomas Risse (eds), *Transforming Europe: Europeanization and Domestic Change* (Ithaca, NY: Cornell University Press, 2001), pp. 180–197, at 189–190.

65. Lisa Conant, *Justice Contained: Law and Politics in the European Union* (Ithaca, NY: Cornell University Press, 2002), p. 31.

66. Ibid., p. 25.

Part I

INSTITUTIONAL DYNAMICS OF DOMESTIC IMPLEMENTATION

Chapter 1

The interrelationship between domestic judicial mechanisms and the Strasbourg Court rulings in Germany

Sebastian Müller and Christoph Gusy

The European Convention on Human Rights (hereafter ECHR, or Convention) has gained more importance within the multi-level system of judicial protection of human rights in Germany in recent years. The number of adverse judgments against Germany delivered by the European Court of Human Rights (hereafter ECtHR, or Strasbourg Court) has been relatively low compared with other member states of the Council of Europe.[1] In 2007 and 2008, the ECtHR found a violation of the Convention in seven and six judgments respectively.[2] The number is even lower when one looks into the records before the Strasbourg Court became a permanent institution in 1998.[3] However, since 2009 an increase of adverse judgments against Germany can be observed, with the ECtHR delivering twenty-nine adverse judgments in 2010 and thirty-one in 2011.[4] Even though several of the judgments concerned repetitive cases, the Strasbourg Court has for the first time decided on significant topics like preventive detention in Germany. It also issued its first pilot judgment against Germany regarding excessive length of court proceedings, as well as judgments on freedom of expression and the protection of whistleblowers. The increase in adverse judgments, as well as the importance of the issues they involve, raise significant questions concerning the role of the ECtHR's judgments in the domestic system of human rights protection.

First of all one must bear in mind that the ECtHR complaints mechanism is just one component of a broader set of mechanisms that exist in Germany to protect human rights. They comprise a complex system consisting of judicial and non-judicial channels, as well as systematic monitoring structures. The vast majority of human rights claims brought before a court are redressed within the domestic judicial system. At the same time, some human rights claims will never become a subject of court proceedings due to the legal status of the person concerned, for instance when s/he is a migrant without a residence permit.

The domestic court system is very efficient, and with the mandate of the Federal Constitutional Court (FCC) to quash any state act, it has considerable power. Exploring the interrelationship between European and national judicial protection of human rights therefore has to start with the domestic court system (in the next section), before probing into the system of domestic implementation of adverse ECtHR judgments and the complementary mechanisms (in the following two sections). Some human rights issues do reach the European stage and they sometimes present difficulties for state authorities in implementing the judgments issued by the ECtHR. This chapter explores these difficulties, and seeks to identify and understand patterns of restrictive or evasive implementation. An example of problematic implementation can be evidenced in the issue of and conflict over adopting a domestic remedy for lengthy court proceedings, which is discussed in the final section.

THE DOMESTIC SYSTEM OF JUDICIAL REVIEW OF HUMAN RIGHTS: COURT PROCEEDINGS AND CONSTITUTIONAL COMPLAINTS

Any description of the German court system regarding the protection of human rights should start with the German Basic Law (*Grundgesetz*). In Article 1, paragraph 3, the Basic Law stipulates the legally entrenched understanding of who is addressed by fundamental norms: 'The following basic rights shall bind the legislature, the executive and the judiciary as directly applicable law.' This norm has very practical implications for the work of all three branches of state power, as it obliges them to abide by all basic rights and any comparable rights in the Basic Law. The role of the judiciary is especially important in this regard.

Judicial review has a decisive role in the protection of human rights in Germany.[5] This is because German legal culture is still very much based on the predominant role of court proceedings in pursuing individual interests. This applies not only to human rights issues, but to all kinds of claims that are often brought before the courts. The very broad scope of the Basic Law leaves almost no area untouched by the basic rights, although they will not necessarily be decisive in all areas of litigation. Furthermore, the domestic court system is highly developed in terms of its expertise, accessibility and acceptance within society. The expertise of each court is displayed in the structure of the system itself, which is subdivided into five branches (civil and criminal in one branch, administrative, social, tax and labour). It must be emphasised that all judges in the different branches are compelled to abide by the Basic Law, irrespective of the legal issue which they are competent to decide. The basic rights precede all other domestic norms because of the Basic Law's status in the national legal order.

Obviously the practical salience of constitutional rights may differ, depending on the issue at stake. In ordinary courts competent for civil and criminal proceedings, basic rights may be invoked to assert a violation of the right to fair trial or to raise a claim not necessarily foreseen by domestic civil law. In judicial proceedings within the administrative courts, basic rights may be invoked in asylum and immigration issues as well as in other areas such as police law. Equally, basic rights violations can be claimed in proceedings before the labour courts, the social courts and the tax courts. It must be highlighted that claiming violation of rights by the state need not only be based on the Basic Law, but can also be made in reference to the ECHR. The FCC has emphasised the evolving nature of the domestic human rights system and its interdependence with the European one, declaring that the domestic courts must take into account the provisions of the ECHR and the judgments of the ECtHR (particularly with regard to comparable case law).[6] As a result, litigants can already invoke the ECHR before domestic courts, which must conform to it, while they can deviate from it only as an exception.

The domestic and regional courts are organised in different states (*Länder*) by the state Ministries of Justice, and each branch (such as the civil or administrative courts) ultimately leads to a final remedy in one of the federal courts, such as the Federal Court of Justice for civil law proceedings. This differentiated system of judicial review, with different bodies within each court branch and the respective federal court at the top, provides a first level of human rights protection. The FCC complements the domestic rights protection highly efficiently. Its task is to act as a supervisory body for the correct understanding and effective execution of the Basic Law in implementing the protection of basic rights.[7] This position should not be misunderstood with regard to the five branches mentioned above. Although the FCC has the discretion to nullify single court decisions, it does not revisit the merits and the legal interpretation of the appellate court's decision. It focuses only on the norms of the Basic Law and reviews how these are interpreted and adopted in the decisions issued by other courts.

The FCC is vested with the power to decide in the event of disputes concerning the powers of a supreme federal body,[8] and to scrutinise any federal law or state law on application by the federal government, a state government or members of the Federal Parliament.[9] Finally, the petition procedure can be initiated by any person alleging that a public authority has infringed his or her basic rights.[10] Such a complaint can be made with regard to administrative orders, court judgments or even legislative acts, if they directly affect the litigant.

This broad competence of the FCC explains the popularity of its complaint procedure. Although the number of the FCC's judgments which find a violation is relatively low, the mechanism is powerful. Complainants can even contest legal acts adopted by state parliaments or the Federal Parliament. It can be assumed that the broad discretionary power of the FCC leads to many complaints before it, as it has the competence to quash a legal act, revoke an administrative order or nullify a court decision. Once the FCC has declared an individual complaint admissible, it is not restricted to the basic rights originally claimed to be violated, but it can probe into any possible violation. Additionally, it may judge on the constitutionality of the applicable state or federal law underlying the judgment or the administrative order. In doing so, it reviews particularly the legislative procedure of the law in question. In the case of a violation of basic rights, the FCC's judgments have legal norm qualities of their own,[11] and they can amend a given legislative act, overruling the legislator.

What influence does the individual constitutional complaint structure have on litigation in the ECtHR originating in Germany? The capacity of the FCC to overrule any act of a public authority and its generally balanced rulings explains its broad acceptance in Germany. If it finds an act of any public authority wrongful, the court is entitled to scrutinise and even quash federal law. Essentially, a single person can alter domestic legislation through a constitutional complaint. Compared to the competence of the ECtHR, the FCC has a much greater discretionary power. Unlike the FCC, the ECtHR is only entitled to declare that a state authority has violated the ECHR, and it cannot alter the domestic legal order, although, to be sure, the Strasbourg Court has developed a more direct approach in the pilot judgments that prescribe in more detail the necessary measures.

Considering the FCC's broad competences and powerful mandate, one might assume that most complaints would be lodged with the FCC and only occasionally with the ECtHR as a last resort. Interestingly, this is not the case. After applicants make their claims before the FCC based on the Basic Law, they generally move on to pursue their claims before the ECtHR. In the past few years, the ECtHR registry has recorded an annual increase in applications stemming from Germany from 1,572 (in 2008) to 1,754 (in 2011).[12] In total, by 2011 some 3,000 applications from Germany were pending before the ECtHR.[13] The number of applications does not, however, correspond with the number of judgments finding a violation. In 2010, the ECtHR delivered twenty-nine adverse judgments, which found at least one violation of the ECHR, against Germany and in 2011 it delivered thirty-one.[14] These numbers have to be placed in a broader context: nineteen of the cases in 2011 related to Article 6 ECHR, concerning the length of domestic court procedures,[15] while in 2010, more than 1,500 applications stemming from Germany were either declared inadmissible or struck off the list.[16]

The relatively low number of adverse judgments against Germany can be seen as a direct corollary of the FCC's individual complaint procedure. In 2010 and 2011, the number of cases in which the FCC found no violation increased. The relatively small number of adverse Strasbourg Court judgments is also due to the fact that the basic rights are already taken into account by domestic ordinary courts, reflecting the salience of the judicial rights review system in Germany. Furthermore, there are other means of resolving a human rights claim before a court comes to a decision. For example, the administration can adapt to the required standards and the domestic legislature can amend existing law to rectify any incompatibilities. Even after the case is lodged with the ECtHR the government can take action in order to avert an adverse final judgment. In 2011, 5,744 individual complaints were decided by the FCC. Out of this caseload, the court found a violation of at least one article of the Basic Law in only ninety-three cases.[17] The numbers clearly demonstrate how the domestic complaints system already prefilters many cases and rectifies many of the infringements caused by state authorities. In sum, the judicial review system, especially the FCC, plays a very important role in protecting basic rights in Germany.

THE DOMESTIC IMPLEMENTATION SYSTEM OF ADVERSE STRASBOURG COURT JUDGMENTS

States are responsible for executing the ECtHR's judgments within their legal structure.[18] As the member states of the Council of Europe have not recognised the competence of the Court to nullify legal acts of domestic state authorities, implementation is dependent on the cooperation of each state under the supervision of the Committee of Ministers (CoM). This underscores the interrelated nature of the ECtHR's judgments and the domestic legal order. The binding effect of the ECtHR's judgments derives in Germany from Article 46 ECHR in conjunction with the domestic legislation approving the ECHR and the rule of law. In this regard, the FCC adopted an important decision in the *Görgülü* case in 2004.[19] It declared that 'the binding effect of statute and law also includes a duty to take into account the guarantees of the Convention and the decisions of the ECtHR as part of a methodologically justifiable interpretation of the law'.[20]

What does the FCC mean by taking the decisions of the ECtHR into account? This doctrine has two aspects tailored to fit into the legal culture in Germany, which has the Basic Law as its core. First of all, the judgments of the ECtHR bind all responsible bodies of any state authority in general directly within the framework of the Basic Law.[21] In the words of the FCC:

> The binding effect of a decision of the ECtHR extends to all state bodies and in principle imposes on these an obligation, within their jurisdiction and without violating the binding effect of statute and law (Article 20.3 of the Basic Law), to end a continuing violation of the Convention and to create a situation that complies with the Convention.[22]

This can require the judiciary to reopen a case in accordance with the existing rules of procedure. The legislature may be obliged to amend any impugned law within the legal framework of the Basic Law. The administration may be called on to revoke a wrongful administrative order, in accordance with the relevant rules of procedure. Especially in cases in which a third party is involved, such as in civil law claims or in law claims concerning neighbours, the competent state authority has to strike the right balance between redressing the violation and the interests of the third party.[23]

As the Basic Law does not cede state sovereignty to the ECHR, the Strasbourg Court's judgments have to be taken into account, but they are not executed automatically. At the same time, the authorities can deviate from the ECtHR's judgments only exceptionally when the execution of a judgment would imply a violation of the Basic Law.[24] The similar scope of the basic rights of the German Basic Law and the ECHR excludes almost completely any possible situation in which a deviation might be justifiable. This leads to the conclusion that all state authorities (legislator, administrative bodies and the judiciary) are obliged to execute the ECtHR's judgments within the legal framework of the Basic Law.

The implementation system in Germany is not composed of a single entity mandated to execute the adverse judgments of the ECtHR. While the Federal Ministry of Justice is charged with supervision and has partial execution powers, a diffused structure of implementation is in place, in which the officially designated institutions along with a host of other actors are involved. Looking at the federal government, the Federal Ministry of Justice supervises the execution of the judgments in cases where other state authorities are responsible. Where the government can act on its own, the ministry itself will execute the Strasbourg Court's decisions. The federal government's commissioner for human rights matters in the Ministry of Justice is responsible for addressing individual measures: ordering the payment of just satisfaction, pecuniary damage and costs, regardless of whether the infringement of the ECHR has been the result of a federal law or a state law. As Germany is a federal nation composed of sixteen states, each state and the federal government itself have their own budgets. If the federal government transfers the money stipulated in the judgment to the applicant in cases where the violation originated in an act of a state authority, the states have to reimburse the federal government.

Regarding the requisite general measures, these must be distinguished between those concerning state authorities and those concerning federal authorities. If a state authority is obliged to terminate an administrative practice or initiate a legislative procedure, the commissioner disseminates the judgments to all relevant state ministries of justice or, when deemed appropriate, ministries for the interior. The judgment is translated and accompanied with a letter stressing the necessity of adhering to the judgment and emphasising the measures that should be implemented. The federal ministry urges the state authorities to terminate the practice or to remedy the contested legislation in order to prevent repeated infringements.

One example from 2006 demonstrates this procedure. The Basic Law entitles states to exert police powers, including the competence to obtain evidence for criminal court proceedings. In a small number of states, the police were entitled to carry out the forcible administration of emetics to gain evidence from alleged drug dealers. This could be done if the person in question was suspected of swallowing narcotics to prevent police from confiscating them. The police then used the relevant evidence against the person in subsequent criminal proceedings. The ECtHR decided in an application stemming from Germany (see *Jalloh* v. *Germany*)[25] that this was a breach of Article 3 of the Convention and found that Germany had violated it. After the judgment was delivered, the state of Hamburg contested the binding force of the ECHR and of the *Jalloh* judgment, essentially arguing that it concerned only that single case and had no effect on comparable practices in other states of Germany.[26] The commissioner, however, informed the competent state authorities of the binding quality of the judgment. In the end, the Hamburg state authority abided by it and terminated the practice.[27]

If remedying measures must be executed by federal state authorities, the commissioner utilises other mechanisms. When the Federal Parliament has to implement an adverse judgment delivered by the ECtHR, because the violation can only be redeemed through a federal legislative procedure, different avenues exist. The legislative procedure can be initiated by any organ entitled by the Basic Law to do so. Bills may be introduced into the German Federal Parliament (*Bundestag*) by members of the parliament, the federal council (*Bundesrat*) or the federal government.[28] The *Bundestag* then has the capacity to adopt the bill[29] and may need the approval of the *Bundesrat*, depending on the bill's contents. In practice, the commissioner informs the appropriate committee in the *Bundestag* of the adverse judgment against Germany. This is one way of triggering the requisite legislative procedure. If the governing parties on the committees agree to pursue the amendments, they can initiate and prepare a bill to be adopted by Parliament itself. Additionally, the Federal Ministry of Justice may prepare a bill to be introduced into the legislative process by the *Bundestag*. Both routes can be used in Germany to file a motion in Parliament to adopt new legislation in response to the ECtHR's judgments. In 2009, for example, the federal government introduced a bill to amend the Criminal Code of Procedure in reference to the ECtHR's chamber judgment in *Mooren* v. *Germany*.[30]

Besides these concrete measures concerning adverse judgments, the commissioner has assumed various initiatives to foster general awareness of the ECHR and knowledge of the Strasbourg Court's case law. The translation and dissemination of adverse judgments against Germany is one tool. As the working language of the ECtHR is English or French, the language barrier has prevented the building of a common knowledge of the relevant case law in Germany. To overcome this barrier and establish a broad knowledge of a common corpus of ECtHR jurisprudence, the Federal Ministry of Justice provides the state ministries of justice with translations of adverse judgments and requests that they disseminate them to the appropriate courts. It has furthermore published annual reports in German on the judgments against Germany and the relevant implementation measures, as well as on related case law of the ECtHR against other states.[31] In addition to these reports, the Federal Parliament is informed bi-annually about the Council of Europe's related activities, including a brief overview of adverse judgments against Germany.[32] The commissioner also provides to the Human Rights Committee information concerning all relevant ECtHR case law. In doing so, the commissioner helps ensure a coherent knowledge of judgments in the federal and state ministries as well as in Parliament. This complementary work enables also members of Parliament to monitor the federal government. To reach all other actors – public authorities, legal practitioners and human rights organisations – the Ministry of Justice translates and publishes judgments concerning Germany on its website and co-finances the private publication of volumes containing a broader collection of judgments.

The Federal Foreign Office, particularly the permanent mission at the Council of Europe, and the representative of the federal government in the CoM, assumes another equally important role in the execution procedure. The federal government's representative functions as a liaison and information channel between the government and the CoM. As was outlined earlier, the ECtHR cannot revoke any state acts but it has to rely on the measures enacted by the member states. It is the responsibility of the CoM to scrutinise those measures and assess whether they redress the situation in the light of a judgment, and if necessary to supervise the execution of a judgment for many years.[33] What measures a member state must adopt to remedy the situation can vary widely and will depend on the individual circumstances of the case. It is the task of the CoM to decide whether these measures are sufficient to execute a judgment. The ECtHR may point out in its reasoning and final conclusions how to comply fully with the ECHR and what measures it may be necessary to take.[34] However, in the end it is the deliberations in the meetings of the committees which lead to a final resolution and thus terminate the supervision. Therefore, the arguments underpinning the position of the federal government and the information given by the state representative play a crucial role in pending cases of supervision.

What is the actual state of the relationship between the ECtHR and the federal legislator when a judgment implies the need for a change in federal law? In the past decades, the need to change existing law in the wake of a ECtHR's judgment has admittedly occurred only occasionally. Recently, for example, the Federal Parliament changed the provisions in the Criminal Code on preventive detention that the ECtHR had been found to be in violation of Article 7 ECHR in 2009.[35] The new legislation came into force in 2011.[36] It concerns the right of criminal courts to include preventive detentions in their verdicts on very serious crimes. Based on the old legislation, courts used this right retroactively, which triggered the applications before the ECtHR. Another example is the *Sürmeli* v. *Germany* case from 2006, in which the Strasbourg Court criticised the lack of an efficacious acceleration remedy for overlong court proceedings, and found it in violation of the

ECHR.[37] The legislation that was passed in response to this judgment[38] came into force in the end of 2011 and it is discussed in more detail below. Then in 2007, in the case of *Mooren* v. *Germany*,[39] the Federal Parliament adopted a bill revising the Criminal Code of Procedure in reference to the ECtHR's Grand Chamber judgment.[40] The access of the defendant's counsel to files in criminal proceedings was altered accordingly.

The first judgments requiring action by the federal lawmaker concerned the transfer of costs for interpreters in criminal court and regulatory offence procedures. In *Luedicke, Belkacem and Koç* v. *Germany*,[41] the ECtHR's judgment in 1978 found the impugned cost provision to violate the Convention, which was subsequently amended by the Federal Parliament in 1980.[42] In the case of *Öztürk* v. *Germany*,[43] regarding the costs for interpreters in regulatory offence procedures, the German legislator took five years to amend the law to comply with the judgment given in 1984.[44] The legislator took a long time because of the different understanding that national authorities had regarding the regulatory offence procedure. From the national point of view, this procedure was not part of a criminal procedure.[45] The ECtHR concluded, however, that there is no reason to differentiate between a criminal procedure and an offence procedure.[46] This divergent understanding led to procrastination and delayed the implementation of the judgment.

However, it is not clear in all parliamentary processes whether legislative amendments are caused by actual or by anticipated violations detected by the Strasbourg Court. For example, a new family law came into force in 1998[47] before the ECtHR's judgment in the *Elsholz* case in 2000.[48] In *Elsholz*, the ECtHR had found a violation of the previous legislation on custody for a child born out of wedlock. The federal legislator also proceeded to amend the law at issue in the *Garcia Alva* case in November 2000,[49] before the ECtHR judgment was delivered in 2001. The amendment concerned the Code of Criminal Procedure (Article 147) regarding access to file documents by the suspect's lawyer in a criminal investigation. Yet there was no reference to the *Garcia Alva* case in the justificatory report on the 1999 amendment of the Code of Criminal Procedure,[50] which came into force in 2000. The same can be said about the *Elsholz* case in the legislative procedure that amended the family law of 1998.[51] It is therefore not clear if in these amendments the legislator was engaging in preventive implementation. On the other hand, the FCC played a decisive role regarding the bill on family law[52] as well as in the amendments of the Code of Criminal Procedure.[53]

How then can we conceptualise the actual relationship between the German legislator and the ECtHR with regard to the implementation procedures? The little existing case law that prompted an amendment by the Federal Parliament and the few adverse judgments render it difficult to formulate an all-encompassing thesis. Nevertheless, some observations can be made. Because of the overall low number of adverse rulings by the ECtHR against Germany, there is a lack of practical training concerning the domestic execution of judgments. This can affect the attitude of members of Parliament towards adverse judgments, once the legislator is compelled to act. Furthermore, the constitutionality of legal acts is considered in relation to the Basic Law and the judgments of the FCC, which are the main point of reference in political debates. It is within this frame of the Basic Law and the FCC's decisions that EU legislation and the judgments of the Court of Justice of the EU are taken into account. The growing awareness regarding the EU can be seen in the form of the German Federal Parliament office in Brussels, set up in early 2007,[54] and the FCC's judgment on the Lisbon Treaty that strengthened the Federal Parliament's rights.[55] By contrast, the Council of Europe and the ECtHR do not bear the same level of influence as the EU. The ECtHR simply does not have an important role in the daily work of a member of Parliament. This limited consciousness of the salience of the ECtHR can influence the willingness to execute judgments and lead to their tardy implementation. When it comes to more structural changes in the domestic legal order, the governing parties in the Federal Parliament have shown a recalcitrant attitude, which stems not from the limited political salience of the ECtHR but from an unwillingness to amend the law. That might be the reason of the cumbersome execution in the *Sürmeli* and the *Öztürk* cases, in which the ECtHR essentially requires the legislator to amend a systematic flaw in the domestic court structure that is the product of a long-standing national tradition.

What are the repercussions of adverse judgments for state parliaments? Theoretically, all sixteen state parliaments or state assemblies are obliged by the framework of the Basic Law to abide by the judgments delivered by the ECtHR. It must be noted that during the time that Germany has been a signatory to the ECHR, only two judgments have pertained directly to state law. These were *Schmidt v. Germany*,[56] regarding the payment of a mandatory fire service levy (*Feuerwehrabgaben*), and *Stambuk v. Germany*,[57] concerning the public communication of medical professionals. In light of just these few cases, it is difficult to assess the influence of the ECtHR's judgments on the state parliaments and, even more so, the attitude of the members of state parliaments.

The ECtHR, however, is highly relevant to state administration, including its judgments against other contracting states, which then have to be taken into account for the interpretation of the ECHR, and for deciding comparable cases in Germany.[58] Several judgments against Germany were implemented by state authorities and they have important repercussions for future cases.[59] The reason for this can be found in the competencies and acts of the state administrations, which fall within the ambit of several ECHR provisions. The daily activities of the state police and the execution of domestic immigration law must be mentioned in particular. The work of the police may fall under Articles 3 and 5 ECHR. Furthermore, the administrative orders issued by the state authorities with regard to immigration law may interfere with the rights guaranteed in Articles 3 and 8 ECHR. This particularly applies in cases of expulsion orders. It took years for a common legal understanding to be reached in Germany and for the respective domestic courts and administration to adhere to the ECtHR's interpretation regarding Article 8 ECHR (respect for family and private life) and the legal status of immigrants.[60]

How do state authorities implement the ECtHR's adverse judgments against Germany? One option is simply to terminate a practice found to infringe the Convention, as exemplified in the forcible administration of emetics by the police.[61] When it comes to administrative orders, the authorities can revoke and replace final orders in accordance with the administrative rules of procedures. The case of *Yilmaz* v. *Germany* is a good example of this.[62] The applicant had received an indefinite expulsion order by a state authority, which was found by the Strasbourg Court to be in violation of Article 8 ECHR. As a result, the responsible state authority revoked the indefinite order and replaced it with a limited order, enabling the applicant to re-enter Germany.[63] If an adverse ECtHR judgment concerns a final decision by a domestic federal court in one of the five branches (such as the Federal Court of Justice), the respective code of procedure now includes a reopening provision that enables the applicant to initiate a new court procedure on the same issue. The Criminal Code of Procedure has allowed for reopening criminal court proceedings since 1998, while for all other judicial branches the law was amended in 2006. Once the successful applicant files a motion with the appropriate court, the court has to revise the judgment in view of the ECtHR's reasoning.

Aside from the procedural aspects concerning implementation, the attitude of the various institutional actors towards the judgments of the ECtHR is equally important. While generally the prevailing opinion is that the Convention and the control mechanism of the ECtHR are important for democratic developments and the establishment of a common European legal culture of human rights, there are some contentious issues. Due to the FCC's strong position, tensions between the two systems occur when the ECtHR questions one of the FCC's well-established doctrines. For instance, this happened in the wake of the *von Hannover* case,[64] in which the ECtHR deviated from the FCC's doctrine in redefining the balance between the rights of the media (freedom of the press) and the respect for private life. It found Germany to be violating the ECHR due to the FCC's very broad interpretation of who can be considered a person of public interest.[65] This judgment triggered a great deal of discussion and controversy about the relationship between the two courts, and revealed tensions between them.[66] In another instance, however, the FCC supported the implementation of a judgment issued by the Strasbourg Court and strengthened its position in the domestic legal order. In an unprecedented case, a higher regional court consciously decided to disregard a judgment of the ECtHR.[67] In this judgment, the Strasbourg Court found that the domestic court's refusal to grant visiting rights to the applicant's son violated Article 8 ECHR.[68] Following this ruling, the FCC adopted an important decision on the binding quality of the ECHR and the judgments of the ECtHR[69] and continued to press the responsible court to implement the *Görgülü* judgment.[70] So, while occasional tensions do occur, overall, mutual support between the FCC and the ECtHR predominates.

The FCC complements the execution of judgments and guarantees compliance from its own perspective of how the Basic Law and the ECHR interact. It has accepted that an individual constitutional complaint can be lodged if a domestic state authority did not take the judgments of the ECtHR into due consideration:

> Against this background, it must at all events be possible, on the basis of the relevant fundamental right, to raise the objection in proceedings before the Federal Constitutional Court that state bodies disregarded or failed to take into account a decision of the ECtHR. In this process, the fundamental right is closely connected to the priority of statute embodied in the principle of the rule of law, under which all state bodies are bound by statute and law within their competence.[71]

As the FCC cannot judge solely in reference to the ECHR, the claim must appeal to a parallel provision in the Basic Law.[72] The FCC reiterated in 2008 that a complaint can be brought to the court claiming that the case law of the ECtHR was disregarded or not taken into due consideration.[73] Even though this option of an individual constitutional complaint does not directly form part of the execution, it has an important role in guaranteeing full implementation and preventing national authorities from circumventing the full consequences of a judgment. It complements the obligation deriving from the ECHR and increases pressure to respect the ECtHR's judgments.

COMPLEMENTARY GOVERNMENTAL AND NON-GOVERNMENTAL MECHANISMS TO IMPLEMENT ADVERSE JUDGMENTS

The commissioner for human rights of the Federal Ministry of Justice does not only act as a representative for the German government before the ECtHR. He or she is also responsible for reviewing bills prepared and introduced by the federal government for compliance with the ECHR and the ECtHR's judgments. The drafting of new legislation requires the participation of the Federal Ministry of Justice, but often also the involvement of the Ministry for the Interior in legislation drafts relating to subjects in its portfolio.

Being part of the committee system in the German Parliament, the Committee of Interior Affairs and the Committee of Legal Affairs scrutinise bills originating in the federal government, the *Bundesrat* or the Parliament itself. Along with many other tasks, they also assess a bill against the back-ground of the Basic Law and occasionally in the light of the ECHR. As in many parliamentary systems, their final report on the draft legislation includes recommendations for Parliament and plays a decisive role in the legislation procedure. The Committee of Human Rights and Humanitarian Aid, however, does not have a similarly pivotal and influential position within the committee structure. While it is kept informed about relevant legislation procedures, it lacks the same political power when it comes to the final report and the recommendations for Parliament. Interestingly, it is the role of the opposition in Parliament to file motions referring to the ECtHR's judgments. For instance, in the current term (2009–13) of the Federal Parliament, the opposition introduced a bill after the judgment in *Heinisch v. Germany*[74] to protect whistleblowers through labour law,[75] and questioned the national asylum procedure practice[76] after the Strasbourg judgment of *M.S.S. v. Belgium and Greece*.[77] The same can be observed for the previous term (2005–9), during which the parties in the government coalition at the time adopted a resolution to strengthen the execution of the ECtHR's judg-ments in Germany in general.[78] During the same term, the opposition filed motions in reference to issues such as adoption rights for homosexuals and data protection.[79]

Does the preventive system within the legislative procedure stop federal and state legislators violating the Basic Law and the ECHR? Admittedly, no politician, member of federal or state government, civil servant or state employer would deliberately disregard the principles of the Basic Law. However, sometimes the prevailing political climate obfuscates a proper interpretation of the Basic Law. New interpretations can also be established as more appropriate to address the ever-changing circumstances of modern society. As a result, the FCC and the ECtHR continue to detect rights viola-tions of the Basic Law and the Convention respectively.

Bearing in mind the sophisticated and effective state system for imple-menting the ECtHR's judgments, the question arises as to whether non-state actors are influential at all. In fact, they do play an important role. Although no NGO works solely in the field of promoting and assisting the imple-mentation of the ECtHR's judgments, such organisations complement the implementation of the ECHR and its case law with their work in different areas. However, because of the robust mandate of the FCC, the main frame of reference for such organisations is still the German Basic Law, even as they increasingly incorporate the ECHR in their work.

In Germany, most of the NGOs in this field specialise in different human rights areas. A number of them have established a network with its own office in Berlin called Forum Menschenrechte.[80] The organisations that participate in the forum have sprung from different kinds of association including church organisations, political foundations, journalists' organisations, anti-racist organisations, groups promoting the rights of homosexuals and specialised human rights organisations working on immigration, asylum and questions of internal security and anti terrorism measures. In pursuing their particular objectives, these organisations promote a consciousness for human rights issues in Germany and sensitise public opinion, politicians and interested individuals, even without directly referring to the ECtHR. In short, they help create an indispensable environment for human rights to flourish.

Human rights organisations also monitor and point out possible short-comings or infringements during the development of legislation. This is generally done against the background of the Basic Law, but also with increasing reference to the Convention and the judgments of the Strasbourg Court. It must be noted that in the field of rights for asylum seekers and immigrants, the Convention is a more important frame of reference, mainly due to the interpretations of Articles 3 and 8 by the ECtHR, which provide broader legal protection than that enjoyed under the Basic Law. Finally, some organisations seek to promote and enhance compliance with court decisions by regularly monitoring the development of the case law stemming from the ECtHR and its implementation within the German legal order in their special field of interest. Their activities in this regard include contacts with members of the Federal Ministry of Justice and the provision of finan-cial support for individual litigants to pursue court proceedings, as well as launching information campaigns. Especially in the area of immigration and asylum law, their profound knowledge and their ability to collect informa-tion directly from the country of origin enable some of the human rights NGOs to provide valuable and sometimes decisive information to litigants petitioning domestic courts.

Another important actor is the German Institute for Human Rights, which was established in 2001. The institute's mandate is to promote awareness and a more advanced understanding of human rights protection through, inter alia, research on human rights topics as well as policy advice.[81] It does not have a designated role in the implementation of the ECtHR judg-ments. Yet, in a broader sense, it contributes to the execution of judgments by monitoring the ECtHR's case law with regard to the current human rights problems within Germany and the European Union. The institute regularly refers to the ECHR and its case law in statements and talks with members of the Federal Parliament and of federal ministries. In sum, the NGOs and the German Institute for Human Rights efficiently complement the execution of judgments in establishing the necessary public environment and exerting pressure upon public authorities to comply with them.

GERMANY'S JUDICIAL SYSTEM: THE REMEDY IN RESPECT OF LENGTHY COURT PROCEEDINGS

One area in which the implementation of the ECtHR's judgments has been marred by tensions and cumbersome legislative processes concerns the remedy in overlong court proceedings (the acceleration procedure). The majority of the adverse judgments against Germany, which are supervised by the CoM, concerns the length of court proceedings.[82] Three of them merit attention: the judgment of *Sürmeli* v. *Germany*,[83] in which the ECtHR found Germany to have violated Article 13 of the Convention because of the lack of a sufficient remedy for lengthy civil court proceedings; *Kirsten* v. *Germany*,[84] in which a similar violation was found with regard to lengthy proceedings before the FCC; and finally *Rumpf* v. *Germany*,[85] which is the first and so far the only pilot judgment against Germany concerning the same matter.

The abovementioned cases highlight an important legal issue: the lack of a domestic remedy whereby the litigant can enforce his or her right to a hearing. In *Sürmeli* v. *Germany* the applicant pursued a claim in a civil court procedure for damages and a monthly pension for injuries sustained in an accident. The ECtHR observed that the judicial procedure in Germany had lasted more than sixteen years, and found that the applicant could not have expedited the litigation process and the court proceedings. Consequently, the ECtHR concluded that the 'applicant did not have an effective remedy within the meaning of Article 13 of the Convention, which could have expedited the proceedings in the Regional Court or provided adequate redress for delays that had already occurred'.[86] In *Kirsten* v. *Germany* the applicant claimed the payment of a monthly allowance that had been suspended due to German reunification and filed an action with the domestic social court. The proceedings lasted almost ten years and ended with a constitutional complaint. Although the FCC's process within the overall time frame took only just over two years, the ECtHR found Germany to have violated Article 13 ECHR. It argued that several other complaints concerning the payment of public allowances affected by the reunification had already been pending for approximately six years when the case in question was referred to it, and it found that such a delay was disproportionately long.[87]

As a result, Germany is now faced with judgments finding a violation of Article 13 ECHR because of the lack of a domestic remedy. The first judgment was delivered in 2006, the second in 2007 and the pilot judgment in 2010. The execution of those judgments remains under supervision by the CoM.[88] It is debatable whether any kind of remedy in lengthy court proceedings can adequately redress the violation at issue. This does not alleviate the pressure to implement the judgments as Germany is obliged to do in accordance with Article 46 ECHR. The judgments clearly demonstrate a gap in the German domestic system in reference to Article 13 ECHR and do not leave much room for divergent interpretations.

What are the repercussions of the Article 13 adverse judgments against Germany? The Federal Ministry of Justice had already begun talks with state ministries of justice in 2002, after the judgment in *Kudla* v. *Poland*,[89] to introduce an acceleration remedy for all five judicial branches.[90] The ministry discerned a comparable structure (to that of Poland) in the German legal system and tried to avert an adverse finding by the Strasbourg Court by introducing a draft bill with a new remedy regarding inaction.[91] The bill contained a provision allowing the applicant to lodge a complaint with the respective court where the case was pending. If the court did not remedy the situation, the applicant could pursue his/her complaint in the appellate court in order to increase the pressure.

The above draft bill, though, was not adopted by the federal government, nor was it introduced into the legislation proceedings. According to its provisions, complaints claiming lengthy proceedings could be addressed to the court in question or an appellate court.[92] However, as a new parliament was elected in 2005 and a new government established, the process was delayed further. The ECtHR encouraged the federal government in the case of *Sürmeli* v. *Germany* to introduce such remedies and the Federal Parliament and the federal government had almost three years in the 2005–9 term to execute the judgment. Yet developments were slow and did not even reach the stage of a bill to be adopted by the federal government.[93] Admittedly, the federal government did not question the necessity to act,[94] but it was not able to come to an agreement with the governing parties in the Federal Parliament. During the current parliamentary term (2009–13), the federal government was faced with the pilot judgment (*Rumpf* v. *Germany*), in which the ECtHR stated that Germany had to adopt legislation by the end of 2011. In response, a bill was submitted to the Federal Parliament[95] and the legislation came into force in November 2011.[96] The law now allows for the payment of damages in cases of excessively lengthy court proceedings, but it does not provide a complaint procedure to address inaction as foreseen in the first bill. The newly adopted legislation also provides for payments in proceedings with the FCC.

What might be the reasons for the cumbersome and protracted legislative process, which had begun in 2002 and became more pressing following the judgment in *Sürmeli* v. *Germany* in 2006? The first reason that the relevant legal reform took a long time to adopt is the simple fact that such a reform presupposes changes to the entire system of judicial review. Unlike other cases, the remedy does not simply require a single authority to revoke a single administrative order. It has direct repercussions for the whole domestic judicial system, and for the judges who perceive such a remedy as implicitly criticising their overall work. Therefore, one should not be surprised that the judgment was received very controversially.[97] While the Federal Ministry of Justice underscored the need for an amendment, there was simply no majority in the Federal Parliament that would allow for its adoption. The first draft proposal caused a heated debate among practitioners, especially judges. To help reach a common understanding, the Federal Ministry of Justice organised a round table with legal experts on the issue in October 2007. Presumably the debates contributed to the adoption of the now applicable remedy to obtain damages. Overall, the problems that occurred during the execution of *Sürmeli* v. *Germany* suggest that judgments requiring change to an ingrained legal tradition trigger far-reaching controversy and often take a long time to be executed.

CONCLUSION

What are the important aspects to be highlighted regarding Germany, its domestic human rights protection system and its relationship with the ECtHR? The majority of human rights claims in Germany are addressed within the domestic confines. The Basic Law, with its human rights provisions by which all state powers must abide, and the FCC, which can be addressed by individuals alleging a violation of their rights, are highly conducive to promoting and protecting these rights. As such, violations are rectified mainly through the existing domestic mechanisms. This effective judicial review system has repercussions for the applications lodged with the ECtHR. Although many petitions claiming a violation by the German state authority are registered in Strasbourg, only few are declared admissible and even fewer lead to an adverse judgment. In 2011, thirty-one judgments were delivered, mainly concerning the length of court proceedings (Article 6 ECHR).

Once a judgment is delivered, the judicial and administrative systems generally function effectively and provide a range of execution mechanisms. This includes the prompt payment of just satisfaction and other costs, revocation of administrative orders, ending of an administrative practice, reopening procedures after a final domestic court judgment and the possibility of the Federal Parliament or the state parliaments amending existing legislation. Nevertheless, on rare occasions one can discern tensions between German state actors and the ECtHR. When these exist, they can result in delayed execution of a single case, such as in the case of interpreter costs in regulatory offence proceedings, or even lead to intentional disregard of the ECtHR's judgment by a higher regional court, as was evidenced in the wake of the *Görgülü* case.

The reasons for such recalcitrant implementation vary. Firstly and quite simply, the more actors involved, the longer it takes to execute a judgment. This applies especially to the legislative procedure. Secondly, if implementation of a judgment requires an overhaul of an entire part of the legal system, the legislator is likely to be confronted with a lot of criticism. This applies to the remedy for lengthy court proceedings, because it adds a significant remedy to the whole range of judicial codes of procedures. Thirdly, if an adverse ruling contests an aspect of the legal culture in Germany or an evolved interpretation of the domestic law, national authorities may be recalcitrant in implementing it. This occurred in the case concerning respect for private life and the publication of photographs of public persons. In particular, the ECtHR's judgments challenging the interpretations of the FCC were received controversially. Fourthly, if adverse judgments against Germany or if the interpretation of the Convention by the ECtHR challenge national sovereignty regarding immigration law, cumbersome procedures regarding residence permits for the immigrants concerned may be observed until the case law is fully adhered to.

The Convention and the rulings of the ECtHR have gained more importance over the past ten years. Far from being something outside the national context, they are part of a single and interrelated system of judicial protection, in which European human rights and domestic constitutional norms closely interact, despite national boundaries. An exclusive focus on the domestic system, though, can obfuscate awareness of the interrelated nature of both protection systems. It disregards the fact that at times the ECtHR can rectify single shortcomings not addressed by domestic judicial review. Instead, the interrelated and multi-level nature of rights protection that emerges from our study of the German case is premised on a broader understanding of a common European human rights legal order, a prerequisite for building European citizenship. Such an understanding has apparently come to prevail in Germany, and it underpins the effective implementation of the ECtHR's judgments in the country.

Notes

1. This chapter covers the ECtHR's adverse judgments against Germany up until March 2012.
2. European Court of Human Rights, *Annual Report 2007* (Strasbourg: Registry of the European Court of Human Rights, 2008), p. 142; European Court of Human Rights, *Annual Report 2008* (Strasbourg: Registry of the European Court of Human Rights, 2009), p. 130.
3. Based on the ECtHR annual reports, between 1978 and 1998 Germany was found to have violated the ECHR in fifteen cases.
4. European Court of Human Rights, *Annual Report 2010* (Strasbourg: Registry of the European Court of Human Rights, 2011), p. 150; European Court of Human Rights, *Annual Report 2011* (Strasbourg: Registry of the European Court of Human Rights, 2012), p. 156.
5. Hans-Jürgen Papier, 'Das Bundesverfassungsgericht als "Hüter der Grundrechte"', in Michael Brenner, Peter M. Huber and Markus Möstl (eds), *Der Staat des Grundgesetzes: Kontinuität und Wandel* (Tübingen: Mohr-Siebeck, 2004), pp. 411–29.
6. FCC, decision of 14 October 2004 (BVerfG, 2 BvR 1481/04), paras 38–46.
7. See Christoph Gusy, 'Die Verfassungsbeschwerde', in Robert Christian van Ooyen and Martin H. W. Möllers (eds), *Das Bundesverfassungsgericht im politischen System* (Wiesbaden: Verlag für Sozialwissenschaft, 2006), pp. 204–12.
8. Basic Law, Article 93, para. 1, subsection 1.
9. Basic Law, Article 93, para. 1, subsection 2.
10. Basic Law, Article 93, para. 1, subsection 4a.

11. Law of the Federal Constitutional Court, Article 31, para. 2.
12. European Court of Human Rights, *Annual Report 2011*, p. 162.
13. Ibid., p. 152.
14. European Court of Human Rights, *Annual Report 2010*, p. 150; European Court of Human Rights, *Annual Report 2011*, p. 156.
15. European Court of Human Rights, *Annual Report 2011*, p. 156.
16. European Court of Human Rights, *Annual Report 2010*, p. 148.
17. Available at http://www.bundesverfassungsgericht.de/organisation/gb2011/A-IV-2.html (last accessed 6 September 2012).
18. ECtHR, *Comingersoll SA v. Portugal* (no. 35382/97), 6 April 2000, para. 29.
19. ECtHR, *Görgülü v. Germany* (no. 74969/01), 26 February 2004.
20. FCC, decision of 14 October 2004 (BVerfG, 2 BvR 1481/04), para. 47.
21. Ibid., paras. 46–7.
22. Ibid., para. 30.
23. Piet van Kempen, 'Redressing Violations of the ECHR', in Theodora A. Christou and Juan Pablo Raymond (eds), *European Court of Human Rights: Remedies and Execution of Judgments* (London: British Institute of International and Comparative Law, 2005), p. 115.
24. FCC, decision of 14 October 2004 (BVerfG, 2 BvR 1481/04), para. 35. See Hans-Jürgen Papier, 'Gerichte an ihren Grenzen: Das Bundesverfassungsgericht', in Meinhard Hilf, Jörn Axel Kämmerer and Doris König (eds), *Höchste Gerichte an ihren Grenzen* (Berlin: Duncker & Humblot, 2008), p. 152.
25. ECtHR, *Jalloh v. Germany* (no. 54810/00), 11 July 2006.
26. See Kai von Appen, 'Zu spät für die Toten', *Taz Nord*, 13 July 2006, p. 21.
27. 'Endgültiger Verzicht auf Brechmittel', *Hamburger Abendblatt*, 2 August 2006.
28. See Basic Law, Article 76, para. 1.
29. Basic Law, Article 77, para. 1
30. Deutscher Bundestag, Drs. 16/11644, p. 13. ECtHR, *Mooren v. Germany* (no. 11364/03-Chamber), 13 December 2007. Upheld by the Grand Chamber: ECtHR, *Mooren v. Germany* (no. 11364/03), 9 July 2009.
31. Bundesministerium der Justiz, *Bericht über die Rechtsprechung des Europäischen Gerichtshofs für Menschenrechte und die Umsetzung seiner Urteile in Verfahren gegen die Bundesrepublik Deutschland im Jahr 2010*; Marten Breuer, *Bericht über die Rechtsprechung des Europäischen Gerichtshofs für Menschenrechte in Fällen gegen andere Staaten als Deutschland im Jahr 2010*.
32. For example: Deutscher Bundestag, Drs. 17/5987, 20 May 2011.
33. See Council of Europe Committee of Ministers, *Supervision of the Execution of Judgments and Decisions of the European Court of Human Rights: 5th Annual Report of the Committee of Ministers 2011* (Strasbourg: Council of Europe, 2012), pp. 46–8.
34. That was the case in *Görgülü v. Germany*, in which the ECtHR found a violation in respect to the refusal of visiting and custody rights. ECtHR. See further *Broniowski v. Poland* (no. 31443/96), 22 June 2004, which is known as a pilot case.
35. ECtHR, *M. v. Germany* (no. 19359/04), 17 December 2009.

36. *Gesetz zur Neuordnung des Rechts der Sicherungsverwahrung und zu begleitenden Regelungen* (Act to Reform the Law on Preventive Detention and on the Accompanying Provisions), 22 December 2010, BGBl. I, 2300.
37. ECtHR, *Sürmeli v. Germany* (no. 75529/01), 8 June 2006, paras 115–16.
38. *Gesetz über den Rechtsschutz bei überlangen Gerichtsverfahren und strafrechtlichen Ermittlungsverfahren* (Act on Legal Protection in the Event of Excessive Length of Court Proceedings and Criminal Investigation Proceedings), 24 November 2011, BGBl. I, 2302.
39. ECtHR, *Mooren v. Germany* (no. 11364/03-Chamber), 13 December 2007, paras 92ff. The judgment was upheld in this regard by the Grand Chamber in 2009. ECtHR, *Mooren v. Germany* (no. 11364/03-Grand Chamber), 9 July 2009, paras 124–5.
40. Deutscher Bundestag, Drs. 16/11644, 13; BGBl. I, 2274, 31 July 2009.
41. ECtHR, *Luedicke, Belkacem and Koç v. Germany* (no. 6210/73), 28 November 1978.
42. *Fünftes Gesetz zur Änderung der Gebührenordnung für Rechtsanwälte* (Fifth Act to Amend the Fee Regulation for Lawyers), 18 August 1980, BGBl. I, 1506–7.
43. ECtHR, *Öztürk v. Germany* (no. 8544/79), 21 February 1984.
44. The legislator rectified the law in 1989. See *Gesetz zur Regelung des Geschäftswertes bei land- oder forstwirtschaftlichen Betriebsübergaben und zur Änderung sonstiger kostenrechtlicher Vorschriften* (Act to Regulate the Fee Classification for the Transferences of Agricultural Businesses and to Amend Other Legal Cost Provisions), 15 June 1989, BGBl. I, 1083.
45. Olaf Kieschke, *Die Praxis des Europäischen Gerichtshofs für Menschenrechte und ihre Auswirkungen auf das deutsche Strafverfahrensrecht* (Berlin: Duncker & Humblot, 2003), p. 100.
46. ECtHR, *Öztürk v. Germany*, para. 53.
47. *Gesetz zur Reform des Kindschaftsrechts* (Act on the Reform of Family Law Concerning Children), 16 December 1997, BGBl. I, 2942.
48. ECtHR, *Elsholz v. Germany* (no. 25735/94), 13 July 2000.
49. ECtHR, *Garcia Alva v. Germany* (no. 23541/94), 13 February 2001.
50. Bundesrat, Drs. 65/99, 5 February 1999.
51. Cornelia Kopper-Reifenberg, *Kindschaftsrechtsreform und Schutz des Familienlebens nach Art. 8 EMRK: Zur Vereinbarkeit der deutschen Reform des Kindschaftsrechts mit der Europäischen Menschenrechtskonvention – eine kritische Analyse* (Baden-Baden: Nomos, 2001), p. 146.
52. Deutscher Bundesrat, Drs. 180/96, 22 March 1996, pp. 39–40; Kopper-Reifenberg, *Kindschaftsrechtsreform und Schutz des Familienlebens nach Art. 8 EMRK*, p. 30.
53. Deutscher Bundesrat, Drs. 65/99, p. 1.
54. Available at http://www.bundestag.de/bundestag/europa_internationales/eu/verbindungsbuero/index.html (accessed 7 September 2012).
55. FCC, decision of 30 June 2009 (BVerfG, 2 BvE 2/08 et al.)
56. ECtHR, *Karlheinz Schmidt v. Germany* (no. 13580/88), 18 July 1994.
57. ECtHR, *Stambuk v. Germany* (no. 37928/97), 17 October 2002.

58. As with the interpretation of Article 3 of the ECHR in expulsion cases: ECtHR, *Ahmed* v. *Austria* (no. 25964/94), 17 December 1996; ECtHR, *Chahal* v. *United Kingdom* (no. 22414/93), 15 November 1996.
59. ECtHR, *Keles* v. *Germany* (no. 32231/02), 27 October 2005; ECtHR, *Yilmaz* v. *Germany* (no. 52853/99), 17 April 2003.
60. See also Jan Bergmann, 'Aufenthaltserlaubnis auf Grund von "Verwurzelung"', *Zeitschrift für Ausländerrecht*, no. 4 (2007), pp. 128–31; Marion Eckertz-Höfer, 'Neuere Entwicklungen in Gesetzgebung und Rechtsprechung zum Schutz des Privatlebens', *Zeitschrift für Ausländerrecht*, no. 2 (2008), p. 41; Daniel Thym, 'Respect for Private and Family Life under Article 8 ECHR in Immigration Cases: A Human Right to Regularize Illegal Stay?', *International and Comparative Law Quarterly*, vol. 57, no. 1 (2008), pp. 87–112.
61. See ECtHR, *Jalloh* v. *Germany*.
62. ECtHR, *Yilmaz* v. *Germany*.
63. CoM, ResDH(2007)125 concerning the judgment of the European Court of Human Rights of 17 April 2003 in the case of Yilmaz against Germany, adopted on 31 October 2007.
64. Hans Prütting and Klaus Stern (eds), *Das Caroline-Urteil des EGMR und die Rechtsprechung des Bundesverfassungsgerichts* (Munich: C. H. Beck, 2005).
65. ECtHR, *Von Hannover* v. *Germany* (no. 59320/00), 24 June 2004, paras 74–81.
66. Papier, 'Gerichte an ihren Grenzen', pp. 149, 153–4.
67. OLG Naumburg, *Familienrechtszeitung* (2004), pp. 1510–12.
68. ECtHR, *Görgülü* v. *Germany*, paras 47, 51.
69. FCC, decision of 14 October 2004 (BVerfG, 2 BvR 1481/04).
70. FCC, decision of 10 June 2005 (BVerfG, 1 BvR 2790/04), paras 34–40.
71. FCC, decision of 14 October 2004 (BVerfG, 2 BvR 1481/04), para. 63.
72. FCC, decision of 14 October 2004 (BVerfG, 2 BvR 1481/04), para. 32. As an example see FCC, decision of 10 August 2007 (BVerfG, 2 BvR 535/06).
73. FCC, decision of 26 February 2008 (BVerfG, 1 BvR 1602/07, 1 BvR 1606/07, 1 BvR 1626/07), para. 98.
74. ECtHR, *Heinisch* v. *Germany* (no. 28274/08), 21 July 2011.
75. Deutscher Bundestag, Drs. 17/8567, 7 February 2012.
76. Deutscher Bundestag, Drs. 17/4635, 3 February 2011.
77. ECtHR, *M.S.S.* v. *Belgium and Greece* (no. 30696/09), 21 January 2011.
78. Deutscher Bundestag, Drs. 16/5734, 20 June 2007.
79. See Deutscher Bundestag, Drs. 16/8115, 13 February 2008; Drs. 16/8199, 20 February 2008; Drs. 16/8260; 20 February 2008.
80. According to its website, the Forum Menschenrechte is composed of fifty organisations: http://www.forum-menschenrechte.de/1/aktuelles/aktuelles-start.html (accessed 7 September 2012).
81. See the institute's website: http://www.institut-fuer-menschenrechte.de/de/das-institut/aufgaben.html (accessed 7 September 2012).
82. See CoM, DH-DD(2011)88, action plan concerning the Sürmeli group of cases, 8 February 2011.
83. ECtHR, *Sürmeli* v. *Germany*, paras 115–19.

84. ECtHR, *Kirsten v. Germany* (no. 19124/02), 15 February 2007, paras 56–7.
85. ECtHR, *Rumpf v. Germany* (no. 46344/06), 2 September 2010.
86. ECtHR, *Sürmeli v. Germany*, para. 116.
87. ECtHR, *Kirsten v. Germany*, paras 46, 49, 53ff.
88. CoM, DH-DD(2011)88, 1,128th meeting, 2 December 2011.
89. ECtHR, *Kudla v. Poland* (no. 30210/96), 26 October 2000.
90. Christine Steinbeiß-Winkelmann, 'Überlange Gerichtsverfahren – der Ruf nach dem Gesetzgeber', *Zeitschrift für Rechtspolitik*, no. 6 (2007), pp. 179–80.
91. ECtHR, *Sürmeli v. Germany*, para. 138.
92. Bundesministerium der Justiz, 'Mehr Rechte für Bürgerinnen und Bürger: Rechtsbehelf gegen überlange Verfahrensdauer', press release, 26 August 2005.
93. Deutscher Bundestag, Drs. 16/7655, 28 December 2007, para. 2.
94. Deutscher Bundestag, Drs. 16/7655, para. 12.
95. Deutscher Bundestag, Drs. 17/3802, 17 November 2011.
96. BGBl. I, 2302, 24 November 2011.
97. See Steinbeiß-Winkelmann, 'Überlange Gerichtsverfahren', p. 180.

Chapter 2

Between political inertia and timid judicial activism: the attempts to overcome the Italian 'implementation failure'

Serena Sileoni

The Italian legal system, as in every contemporary state, is not an isolated system, impervious to international and supranational legal rules. Far from it, it is part of a complex and broader legal community, where international institutions, in relation to their competences, play an influential role within the domestic system. Regarding the protection of human rights, the most important international regime bearing sustained influence on the Italian system is the European Convention on Human Rights (hereinafter ECHR), which has introduced an indirect system of control over national law. To be sure, the European Union, in whose foundation Italy played a central role, has also created a very strong system of rights protection following the jurisprudence of the Court of Justice of the EU (including the introduction of new rights, such as those concerned with the environment and privacy, that do not expressly appear in the Italian Constitution). In spite of its restricted competence on economic matters, the importance of the EU as a system that also protects human rights in a wider sense has been growing. Nonetheless, the revolution in the review of human rights for Italians is directly linked to the ECHR and its jurisprudence. In fact, the individual right to petition to the European Court of Human Rights (ECtHR) introduced to the Italian system the potential for individuals to directly address a rights review court. Nevertheless, the impact of the ECHR has been somewhat ambiguous and unclear, and its application by the domestic judiciary has not been immediate or uniform.

Institutional actors (Parliament, government, and judiciary, including the Constitutional Court as 'judge of the laws'[1]) have played a central role in integrating the ECHR system into the national context and in conferring to it a quasi-constitutional value. Against this background, we will examine in this chapter the domestic consequences of the ECtHR's judgments in the most problematic areas that have generated a large volume of case law against Italy, such as fair trial and length of proceedings, property rights, and the right to family and private life. We will analyse their impact on legislative change in the respective policy areas, but also their consequences for domestic structures and processes of implementation. The chapter argues that the ineffective and delayed implementation of the ECtHR's judgments in Italy has been due to factors concerning the legal system as well as the cultural attitude of Italian politicians and civil society. Although the Italian authorities still display a failure to undertake effective legal and judicial reform in response to the major violations of the ECHR (like those regarding Article 6), we witness over the past couple of years an effort to implement the state's obligations emanating from the Convention and an increasing sensitivity towards it. Especially important has been the role of the higher national courts, which have sought to partly counterbalance the political inertia to enforce Strasbourg Court judgments, even if they do so by exercising substantial self-restraint.

In the first section of the chapter, we focus on the historical path of this integration, from the initial conception of the ECHR as an ordinary law, to the most recent interpretation of it as a fundamental instrument for the protection of human rights, with a direct effect in the national context and the rank of a quasi-constitutional norm. In the second section, we explore the ECtHR's case law against Italy related to Articles 6 and 8 and Protocol 1, Article 1 of the ECHR, and the reforms attempted or carried out in order to bring national law in line with this case law. The focus of analysis is on categories of cases in which Italy has most frequently and systematically been found to violate the ECHR. It must be noted that in recent years, one can see a more variegated set of claims before the Strasbourg Court against Italy, which attests to the ECHR's growing legal culture among Italian lawyers.[2] In the third section, we examine the general measures taken by the Italian authorities to execute the ECtHR's judgments. And in the fourth section, we explore the actions of the government and the judiciary and the role that they have played in transferring the ECHR's legal culture into the national context.

THE INTEGRATION OF THE ECHR INTO THE DOMESTIC SYSTEM

Italy was among the ten countries that founded the Council of Europe (CoE) in 1949. The ECHR was signed by the Republic of Italy on 4 November 1950 and ratified on 25 October 1955. Since 1973, when Italy made declarations under Articles 25 and 46 of the Convention, acknowledging the right to individual petition to the ECtHR, an impressive number of applications against Italy have been deposited at the Court. The vast majority of these have focused on the administration of justice. But the actual impact of the ECHR was for a long time confined to a limited number of issue areas, such as the administration of justice, the due process guarantees, the protection of property rights and the right to privacy and family life. As late as 2005 it was not far from the truth that 'in Italy . . . very few people [were] familiar with the Strasbourg Court's case-law. Not only did public opinion ignore it, but also judges and national agents theoretically affected by it often [did] not care to know about it.'[3]

The first reason for the limited impact of the ECHR in Italy was its problematic role in the internal legal system. The Italian Constitution does not provide for the automatic reception of international treaties and does not specify the status they acquire, once ratified, in the internal hierarchy of norms. International agreements cannot be applied domestically until they are introduced into internal law by means of a specific Act of Parliament authorising the ratification of the treaty and containing an 'order of execution' of its provisions. Therefore, and prior to two Constitutional Court judgments of November 2007 (which we subsequently discuss), it was deemed that such agreements assume in the domestic system the same rank as the legislative acts which provide for their ratification and execution. For this reason, the ECHR was considered as a common international agreement that, just like any other, carried the force of ordinary law.[4] In this way, since its ratification and execution (through Law No. 848 of 4 August 1955) the ECHR has constituted an integral part of the Italian legal system, where it obtains, at least in theory, the force of an ordinary law.

The Italian courts, however, have for a long time been reluctant to apply the Convention, considering its provisions as merely programmatic. Only in 1988 did the Supreme Court of Cassation (SCC) acknowledged the direct and immediate applicability of a number of ECHR norms as self-executing, or binding in all their elements.[5] Notwithstanding the importance of this decision, it was undermined by the fact that the SCC recognised a self-executing quality only in those Convention provisions that are so detailed and complete that there could be no doubt about their effectiveness.[6] As they are recognised by Italian judges, self-executing rules are only those external (to the national system) ones that do not require any implementation by the Italian legislator. Yet the self-executing test is quite strict. For example, the SCC did not recognise the direct effectiveness of Article 5(3) ECHR, which states:

> Everyone arrested or detained in accordance with the provisions of paragraph 1(c) of this article shall be brought promptly before a judge or other officer authorised by law to exercise judicial power and shall be entitled to trial within a reasonable time or to release pending trial.

The presumed vagueness of the ECHR principles in comparison to the Italian constitutional provisions has been often used by common judges to deny the substantial effectiveness of the Convention. This position has also been supported by those legal scholars who consider the ECtHR's case law to have 'scarce or non-existent relevance among Italian judges'.[7]

Yet, over time, national jurisprudence has increasingly tended to give the Convention primacy over ordinary law, implicitly recognising its 'quasi-constitutional' rank, albeit with an ambiguous meaning.[8] Given that the

Convention does not per se possess primacy over ordinary legislation, the question has arisen whether it is subject to the rule *lex posterior derogat legi priori* and whether its provisions can be derogated by subsequent statutory norms. Both the Constitutional Court and the SCC resolved the question stating expressly that the Convention's provisions, because of their nature, cannot be derogated or abrogated by means of subsequent ordinary laws.[9] In 1993, in the case of *Medrano*,[10] the SCC recognised in the Convention's provisions a 'particular force of resistance' with respect to ordinary subsequent laws, due to their quality as 'general principles of the legal system'. According to the SCC, the particular nature of the ECHR can be deduced from the Italian Constitution itself as well as from the jurisprudence of the Court of Justice of the EU, which recommends that national courts apply the ECHR's provisions as part of the communitarian law.[11] In the same year, the Constitutional Court issued its Judgment No. 10, where in an *obiter dictum* it expressed a similar opinion. It stated that the Convention's provisions derive 'from an atypical competence of the State, and as such, they are not subject to being abrogated or modified by means of ordinary law'.[12]

While the above interpretation has not been confirmed by successive case law of the Constitutional Court or by other national judges, over the past couple of years, a number of factors have led to upgrading the domestic status of the Convention. Firstly, the introduction of the 'Pinto law' (which is discussed below) increased the confidence of common judges in the ECHR. A second factor that boosted the status of the Convention was the importance given to it in the European Community debate, and the reference to the ECHR in Article F of the Maastricht Treaty and in the Nice Treaty. Pointing to such a reference, some judges declined to apply domestic law that was in conflict with the ECHR principles.[13] Even the SCC affirmed that the ECHR provisions found their basis as general principles contained in Article F of the Maastricht Treaty (*Medrano* case, 26 January, no. 1340).[14] Further evidence of this evolution in the perception and understanding of the ECHR among Italian judges is provided by a judgment issued by the SCC on March 2004, declaring that Strasbourg Court jurisprudence has a homogenising role as living law[15]. Moreover, in a decision of 25 January 2007, the same court said that the effects of the ECtHR's decisions are constitutive: they generate rights and obligations even within the national system. That means that judges must decide in conformity with the Strasbourg Court's jurisprudence, even when this implies reopening proceedings that have already been concluded.

Notwithstanding the importance of the abovementioned national courts' decisions[16] for the domestic reception of the Convention, it seemed that, at the beginning of the twenty-first century, the Italian judiciary was still in search of interpretative criteria to affirm the primacy of the Convention vis-à-vis ordinary legislation. The 2001 reform of the Italian Constitution (the most important one since its entry into force), along with the Constitutional

Court's judgments nos. 248 and 249/2007, have provided an answer to this quandary. In conformity with the 2001 constitutional reform, the 2007 judgments have clarified once and for all the relation between the ECHR and national law. The constitutional reform of 2001 amended, among others, Article 117 of the Constitution, which stipulates that the legislator must act in compliance with constraints deriving from international legal norms and obligations. In reference to this amendment, the Constitutional Court has changed its traditional view and has attributed a constitutional significance to the Convention's norms. It must be noted that the Constitutional Court already had on a previous occasion dealt with the new Article 117 of the Constitution, but it had avoided interpreting it.[17]

Finally, with its judgments nos. 348 and 349/2007 the Constitutional Court has definitely settled the hierarchical position of the Convention. In a highly controversial interpretation, it established that, since the entry into force of the revised Article 117, any international agreement occupies a median position between the Constitution and ordinary legislation.[18] It also stated that the ECtHR is the only judicial authority legitimated to interpret Convention provisions, but the Constitutional Court remains the guardian of the supreme principles of the national system. The two judgments are very relevant because they offered the Constitutional Court the first opportunity to clarify the value of Article 117 as the only constitutional norm that allows the transposition of international law. They also put an end to the contradictory and ambiguous jurisprudence of the ECHR within the domestic system.

Apart from the difficulty in establishing the ECHR's status within national law, there is another legal reason for its ambiguous role. This is its overlap with the established and reasonably efficient system of domestic human rights protection. As already noted, there is a generalised belief that fundamental rights are regulated in greater detail in the Italian Constitution, while they are more abstractly addressed in the ECHR.[19] In general, the perception of legal professionals is that Italy already has a high level of protection of human rights. On this subject, even the Constitutional Court recently noted with regard to proceedings in absentia that 'the European Convention of Human Rights does not recognise higher guarantees than Art. 111 Const'.[20] A theoretical consequence of such an opinion is that the majority of the ECHR provisions, as they refer to rights already protected by the Italian Constitution, are a useful instrument to specify, integrate and clarify the value of such rights. Such a consideration is in line with the subsidiary role of the ECtHR, and it is reinforced by the legal issues that have come under the scrutiny of the ECtHR. Italian cases before the ECtHR concern areas where there is a gap in the Italian system and there is a systematic violation of rights that are not provided for or are weakly protected in the Italian Constitution (such as length of proceedings, expropriations, administration of justice, right to privacy).

INFRINGEMENTS OF THE ECHR BY ITALY

Italian case law at Strasbourg focuses on violations which reflect structural deficiencies of the domestic legal system – such as the length or fairness of proceedings (Article 6 ECHR) or property rights (Article 1, Protocol 1 ECHR) – and which are therefore difficult for local courts to address.[21] The volume of these violations is so large that in 2006 the first governmental report to Parliament on the implementation of the ECtHR's judgments took into account only the cases of expropriation, the length of proceedings and fair trial. Another Convention provision that is often claimed by Italian litigants is Article 8 ECHR on the right to privacy, a right that is not expressly provided for in the Italian Constitution.

The vast majority of applications are related to the reasonable length of proceedings implicitly guaranteed by Article 6 ECHR. In the *Capuano* case,[22] compensation was awarded to the applicant in consequence of the violation of Article 6. This case inaugurated an interminable series of judgments delivered against Italy,[23] which finally led to the configuration of an 'Italian problem' within the Convention system.[24] Indeed, and risking collapse due to an inundation of complaints presented against Italy under Article 6, the ECtHR declared in 1999 that 'excessive length of proceedings were incompatible with the Convention'.[25] It was also stated that the persistent phenomenon of the excessive length of proceedings was compromising the qualification of the Italian state as *état de droit*.[26]

The question of the length of proceedings has also been examined by the Constitutional Court. It is worth noting that on this occasion the ECtHR and its case law have been used by the Constitutional Court in a hermeneutic sense, as pillars for its reasoning and judgments. While in 1985 the Constitutional Court said that the 'question of the length of proceedings [. . .] is not raised by the Constitutional Charter',[27] a decade later it used Article 6 ECHR to elucidate in a new way Article 24 of the Constitution, which gives every citizen the right to take legal action in the courts to protect his or her rights and interests. The Constitutional Court has understood the protection of Article 24 to require a reasonable length of proceedings.

Apart from the excessive length of proceedings, observance of Article 6 ECHR has also been questioned before the Strasbourg Court with respect to the right to an effective remedy[28] and to proceedings in absentia (*processo in contumacia*).[29] Another infringement of Article 6 has been found in relation to parliamentarian immunities.[30] In this regard, it is worth noting the attitude of the Constitutional Court. After the *Cordova*[31] and *De Jorio*[32] cases the Italian Constitutional Court changed its jurisprudence on the ability of a third party to intervene in the proceedings having as object a conflict between Parliament and judges in cases of parliamentary immunity. In 2004, it departed from its previous approach and found admissible the intervention of a third party. It justified this overturning through a direct reference to the

ECtHR jurisprudence,[33] with the goal of making 'more acceptable in front of the ECtHR the entire domestic system of immunities'.[34] Nonetheless, the Strasbourg tribunal and the Italian Constitutional Court are still in conflict over the meaning of parliamentary immunity and its limits, as the *Cofferati* case shows.[35]

In the past few years contentious cases involving Italy have concerned a diverse set of issues that extend well beyond Article 6 ECHR. A rising number of petitions relating to property rights question the lawfulness of the practice of constructive expropriation (*occupazione acquisitiva* or *accessione invertita*) and its conformity to the Convention. This practice has permitted the Italian public administration to take possession of lands without respecting the formal procedure for expropriation. Respect for property rights is also consistently invoked before the Strasbourg Court in relation to the procedure of enforcement of evictions following the expiry of a lease (*sfratto per finita locazione*). In the pilot case of *Spadea and Scalabrino*,[36] the ECtHR rejected the applicants' view that the government's housing policy reflected a breach of Protocol 1, Article 1 of the ECHR, since the 'means chosen were appropriate to achieve the legitimate aim pursued'. On the other hand, in subsequent similar cases, the Court did find violations of the Convention (Art. 1 Prot. 1 and Art. 6), not due to the measures of suspension and the staggering number of evictions per se, but in consideration of the excessive length of enforcement procedures and of the difficulties for the landlords in accessing justice.[37]

In a large number of cases, the Strasbourg Court has also found violations of Article 8 of the Convention. In part, these cases pertain to the restrictions imposed on prisoners' correspondence under the law on administration of prisons and in accordance with the Prison Administration Act (Law No. 354/1975).[38] The Court also found violation of Article 8 when the censorship of correspondence was applied only to prisoners prosecuted for or convicted of specific offences – such as in those linked to Mafia activities – empowering the judge to suspend the application of the ordinary prison regime in whole or in part (in accordance with Article 41 bis of Law No. 354/1975).[39] However, the vast majority of cases filed under Article 8 ECHR relate to an alleged violation of the right to respect the privacy of correspondence and/or family life in connection with the applicants' involvement in bankruptcy procedures. Applicants contested the conformity of the Bankruptcy Act (Royal Decree No. 267 of 16 March 1942), which regulated this procedure on two different grounds: censorship of correspondence and alleged violation of privacy, which in turn derive from the civil incapacities and the deprivation of certain individual rights connected with bankruptcy status.

Another group of cases includes claims of violation of Article 8 in circumstances where children need to be fostered when the parents are deemed unable to perform their parental obligations (*affido di minori*), as well as in cases of child custody resulting from divorce or separation. Starting with the case of *Scozzari and Giunta* (and following with *Bronda, Roda and Bonfatti* and *Covezzi and Morselli*)[40] the ECtHR has stated that the removal of children from their home is not unlawful if carried out in the interest of the child. However, it may entail a breach of Article 8 whenever authorities fail to supervise families and communities fostering children, to facilitate contact visits between children and their parents, or to involve parents in the decision-making concerning their children.

In two cases (*Guerra and others, Giacomelli*),[41] Article 8 and the right to respect for home, private and family life have been invoked in relation to environmental issues. Considering that 'severe environmental pollution may affect individuals' well-being and prevent them from enjoying their homes in such a way as to affect their private and family life adversely', the state's omissions were on that occasion found to constitute an interference with the private and family life of the applicants.

Apart from a few pivotal cases, most of the judgments concerning Article 8 raise similar problems. Some others concern the proper value of privacy, such as the prohibition against disclosing aspects of a person's private life into the public domain.[42] The recurrent recourse of applicants to Strasbourg with Article 8 complaints is due to the fact that the Italian Constitution lacks a specific and clear norm regarding private life. Although there are provisions about respect for home, correspondence or family life, privacy is not expressly constitutionalised. So in cases involving bankruptcy or a special regime of detention, there is no constitutional guarantee for respecting privacy. The wide and generic definition of the notion of private life under the ECHR fills this gap in the Italian catalogue of rights. The *Guerra and others* case exemplifies this, as it concerns a lack of information on health risks. The ECtHR found a violation of the respect of family life in the government's failure to provide the local population with information about risk factors, as well as information on what to do in the event of an accident at a nearby chemical factory.[43] Neither the right to family life nor the right to a healthy environment is expressly protected in the Italian Constitution or explicitly recognised in the national legal system.

LEGAL REFORMS PROMPTED BY ECtHR CASE LAW AND ONGOING CHALLENGES

The ECHR and its case law have exercised a considerable impact on the domestic legal system. A number of legal changes and normative solutions have been adopted under pressure from Strasbourg institutions and the judgments issued by the Court. Nevertheless, Italy has encountered many difficulties in the execution of the Court's judgments, particularly when they concern structural and historical deficiencies in the domestic legal system which require substantial and radical reforms. Indeed, with regard to the execution of the ECtHR's judgments, the Strasbourg organs have denounced the grave state of non-compliance by Italy, noting, for example, that 60 per cent of cases pending for execution before the Committee of Ministers (CoM) in 2005 concerned this country.[44]

As we have stressed more than once, the vast majority of judgments under the Strasbourg Court's scrutiny are concentrated in a few specific areas (due process, length of proceedings, infringements of property and privacy rights). Until now, the CoM has concentrated on monitoring the execution and implementation of judgments relating to the excessive length of proceedings and the functioning of the judicial system in Italy.[45] Other judgments against Italy under the supervision of the CoM concern the unfairness of criminal proceedings,[46] inadequate guarantees to secure the lawfulness of emergency expropriations and excessively restrictive compensation rules,[47] and the infringement of flat owners' rights to peaceful enjoyment of their possessions due to the failure to enforce judicial eviction orders. This last category of cases has been the least problematic, with all ECtHR judgments having been executed and the applicants having been able to take possession of their property. Judgments that remain under the supervision of the CoM can be divided into two categories. First, there are isolated cases, in which the CoM has mainly insisted on *restitutio in integrum* or a just compensation. Secondly, there are repeat violations of the ECHR, in which the CoM requires legislative or administrative reforms as general measures.

Regarding violations of Article 8 ECHR relating to the secrecy of correspondence in the regime of detention,[48] in 2004 Law No. 95 entered into force. It reformed Law No. 354/1975 on the penitentiary system and provided major guarantees for the secrecy of detainees' correspondence, as requested by the ECtHR. The new provision was also extended to the special regime of detention mentioned earlier.[49] It stated more clearly the conditions that justify monitoring prisoners' correspondence, such as the necessity to prevent the perpetration of crimes, to guarantee prison security and to preserve the secrecy of investigations. It also entirely prohibited censoring correspondence with lawyers and international human rights organisations.

Regarding the application of the special detention regime (Art. 41 bis, Law No. 354/1975), the ECtHR has affirmed its compatibility with a democratic system.[50] At the same time, it has condemned the Italian state for violation of not only Article 8, but also of Articles 3, 6, and 13 of the ECHR, because of the existence of restrictive measures regarding the conditions of detainees.[51] In an interim resolution in 2005 the CoM noted with concern that the right to an effective remedy against monitoring of prisoners' correspondence and other restrictions on prisoners' rights remained insufficiently guaranteed.[52] Therefore it called upon the Italian authorities to rapidly adopt legislative and other necessary measures. Until now, only the courts have brought their jurisprudence in conformity with the CoM European recommendations.[53] Regarding prison conditions (Art. 3 ECHR), the legislator replaced existing provisions (Art. 41 bis) with Law No. 279/2002, specifying the prerequisites for the application of the special detention regime and clarifying the system of impugnment.

The other judgments finding violation of Article 8 mainly pertain to the right to respect correspondence, privacy and family life in connection with applicants' involvement in bankruptcy procedures. Following a resolution of the CoM,[54] Italy finally adopted a legislative decree containing measures aimed at speeding up the procedure. The same law also aimed to remove the rights restrictions imposed upon individuals in bankruptcy procedures (Law No. 5 of January 2006), such as limitations to electoral rights, freedom of circulation and secrecy of correspondence, restrictions which are provided for in the law on bankruptcy procedure (Articles 48 and 49). Following this legislative reform, the CoM ended its supervision of this category of cases with its Final Resolution No. (2005)55, considering that, after this amendment, respect for correspondence and freedom of movement had improved.

Property rights have also come under the scrutiny of the Strasbourg Court. The ECtHR has found violations of Protocol 1, Article 1 of the Convention in cases in which the public administration expropriates property from individuals, such as in the case of the so-called *occupazione acquisitiva* or *accessione invertita*. In the Italian system, this is legitimate, because the Italian Constitution defines property not as an absolute right, but as an instrumental right having a 'social function' in order to promote a general welfare (*ex* Art. 42 Const.) Moreover, in reference to the 'social function' of property, the Italian system does not recognise full indemnification subsequent to the expropriation. As far as the first aspect is concerned, a general measure undertaken was the reform of the code on expropriation (Legislative Decree No. 327/2001), restricting the range of legitimate cases of indirect expropriation. The purpose of such reform was expressly the need to make Italian law conform to the Strasbourg Court's view on property rights, as the Council of State noted in its opinion on the respective bill.[55] Moreover, the budget of 2007 for the first time gave local administrations direct responsibility to compensate for damages resulting from an expropriation.

In spite of these general measures, there are still lingering incompatibilities between the national system and the European human rights system concerning property rights, especially in the amount of indemnification. The recent Constitutional Court mentioned above do not solve the problem, because they confirm the view of property as a right that is not absolute, in divergence from Protocol 1, Article 1 of the ECHR as interpreted by the Strasbourg Court. Even though the Constitutional Court has demanded that any indemnification should be more proportionate to the market value of the expropriated property, compensation of the former owner for its full value is still not required.

But the vast majority of petitions against Italy pertain to the judicial system, as already noted. There are numerous new norms which have been

introduced to bring the administration of justice into line with the decisions
of the Strasbourg Court. At the constitutional level, the principles of due
process are now guaranteed by the Constitution's new Article 111, which
contains practically all the judicial guarantees safeguarded in Article 6 of
the Convention. Concerning judicial guarantees, a sensitive issue that is
still pending is the need to reopen judicial proceedings in criminal trials as
a consequence of a judgment by the ECtHR. On the other hand, different
procedures have been adopted over the years to facilitate the quick resolution of proceedings. Measures have included an increase in the number of
magistrates with the creation of 'justices of the peace' (*giudici di pace*) and
of honorary judges competent for minor civil and criminal litigations (Law
No. 374/1991); the restructuring of the judicial offices of the court of first
instance; the introduction of so-called abridged sections (*sezioni stralcio*,
special, temporary sections created in order to handle the large volume of
proceedings); the extension of special and quicker procedures in a larger
spectrum of cases (Law No. 80/2005); and a faster issuing of rulings for
some administrative proceedings (Law No. 205/2000). Moreover, in the past
few years, the comprehensive reform of civil and criminal proceedings has
been under discussion. Successive governments have sought to adopt such
a reform, but so far with little success. In spite of the various reforms and
initiatives, judicial proceedings remain much too lengthy.

The 'Pinto law' (Law No. 89/2001), involving 'measures for speeding up
judgments and expectations for fair compensation in case of violation of the
reasonable length of proceedings', cannot be seen as a good solution either.
Adopted under pressure from the ECtHR's case law and the CoM's resolutions, it introduced a compensatory remedy, providing the option to appeal
to national courts – specifically the competent court of appeal – in order to
obtain a just compensation in cases of excessive length of proceedings. Since
its entry into force, appeals before the Court in Strasbourg have decreased.
Still, such a law cannot be seen as a permanent solution, given that monetary
compensation represents an excessive cost for the state and does not solve
the problem of length of time. More recently, Parliament has considered
legislative measures aimed to introduce temporal limits for proceedings,
with the explicit purpose of harmonising the national system with Article
6 ECHR. One bill contains measures for reducing the excessive length of
proceedings;[56] another bill introduces a broader reform of the criminal and
civil proceedings.[57] The latter also provides for the reopening of proceedings
after a judgment of the ECtHR and for compensation following the violation
of reasonable length of proceedings.

The 'dialogue' among national judges and the ECtHR has been very
important in order to define the criteria that determine a violation of Article
6(1) of the Convention. Such a 'dialogue' has also been stimulated by the
'Pinto law', which refers to the ECHR and its interpretation by the ECtHR.[58]
Article 2 of the 'Pinto law' introduces in a compelling way the Article 6

jurisprudence of the ECtHR into the Italian system. Yet, far from being clear and unambiguous, the reception of the ECtHR's interpretation of Article 6(1) among ordinary judges has been controversial, with major points of conflict between Strasbourg case law and domestic jurisprudence. In fact, initially the Court of Cassation denied that Italian judges were obliged to respect the interpretation of Article 6 of the Convention advanced by the ECtHR.[59] The conflict culminated in the *Scordino* case, where the ECtHR found the 'Pinto law' inadequate to solve the problem of excessively lengthy proceedings.[60] After this important case, which the ECtHR examined together with 100 Italian cases, the Italian Court of Cassation revised its view to conform to the Strasbourg Court's interpretation.[61] For the first time, the Court of Cassation stated that the Italian judges have to follow the ECtHR's jurisprudence on the excessive length of proceedings, and that they are not free to interpret this clause in ways other than the one prescribed by the Strasbourg tribunal.

The reforms presented in this section show that the Strasbourg Court's jurisprudence has significantly influenced Italian law and policy. It has prompted substantial legislative and administrative reforms in the field of due process, length of proceedings, infringements of property rights, bankruptcy and the regime of special detention. These reforms have in most cases been stimulated by the judicial activism of the Supreme Court of Cassation and the Constitutional Court. While in full respect of the legislator, the Supreme Court's systematic and strong jurisprudence has encouraged legislative reforms in order to bring Italian law in conformity to ECtHR case law and to improve protection of individual rights in several areas of law and administrative practice.

Between domestic judicial initiatives on the one hand, and the CoM's resolutions and the ECtHR's condemnations on the other, Italian governmental and political elites in the past couple of years have grown more sensitive about the 'Italian implementation failure'. They have promoted institutional reforms to improve domestic implementation mechanisms. The harmonisation of the Italian system has not been easy or complete, as we see in the case of the excessive length of proceedings, which continues to represent the most significant failure before the ECtHR. In other matters, though, legislative initiatives seem to have provided effective solutions, such as in the case of prison conditions and bankruptcy.

Enhanced national attention to the execution of the ECtHR's judgments has not yet had a direct effect, though, on the number of applications lodged in Strasbourg or on the number of violations found by the ECtHR.[62] The largest number of applications, as well as of violations, continue to concern Article 6 ECHR, in particular the excessive length of proceedings, as well as protection of property (Art. 1 Prot. 1 ECHR).[63] Ongoing delays in the delivery of justice continue to represent the main reason for Italy's failure. Apart from this, though, the introduction of some broad reforms across different categories of infringement demonstrates the significant attempts of Italian political elites to promote the execution of Strasbourg judgments, which we discuss in the next section.

NATIONAL ACTORS AND INSTITUTIONS INVOLVED IN IMPLEMENTATION

Generally speaking, the responsibility for the execution of the ECtHR's judgments is held primarily by the Prime Minister's Office (especially for violations of Art. 1, Prot. 1 ECHR) and the Ministry of Justice (especially for violations of Art. 6), and to a lesser extent by the Ministry of the Interior and other ministries. In this frame, the most determined effort of the Italian government to promote the implementation of the ECtHR's judgments was the entry into force of the 'Azzolini law'.[64] This act can be seen as a comprehensive effort to establish coordination between the different branches of the Italian administration in implementing the ECtHR's case law. It designates the Prime Minister as the main actor responsible for implementation, while the department of legal and legislative affairs within the Presidency of the Council of Ministers is responsible for the practical execution of judgments. Such an initiative had, above all, a strong symbolic meaning. Assigning direct responsibility to the Prime Minister and his office signals the high priority that the Italian government assigns to compliance with the ECtHR's judgments.

The 'Azzolini law' establishes a new information channel between the Prime Minister, who is responsible for foreign affairs and the representative of the Italian state before the ECtHR, and Parliament, the main actor involved in implementing international obligations on human rights. The law defines the Prime Minister's tasks and states that he is now responsible for initiating action on the part of the government: communicating judgments to Parliament in a timely fashion, so that they can be examined by the competent parliamentary commissions, and presenting annually a report on the state of implementation of judgments.[65] The law also enables Parliament to be regularly informed about the judgments and to rapidly adopt legislative measures as they become necessary.

Apart from the crucial role of the Prime Minister and his office, other institutional actors involved in Italy are the Ministry of the Economy, the Ministry of Justice and the two parliamentary chambers as well as their permanent committees (the Italian Parliament does not have a formal committee on human rights). Moreover, since 2005 a permanent body scrutinising the judgments of the ECtHR has been established within the lower chamber of Parliament, the Chamber of Deputies. Since 2006 this organ has regularly monitored judgments delivered against Italy and has given legal support both to the Italian delegation to the Parliamentary Assembly of the CoE and to the competent bodies in the Italian Parliament. Concerning the role of

Parliament, it is worth noting that three letters from the Speakers of both chambers (published between 2005 and 2006) underscored the obligation to evaluate the compatibility of every new law with the ECHR. The Directorate General for Litigation and Human Rights, a department of the Ministry of Justice, is charged with collecting information for each judgment issued by the ECtHR against Italy and to act as intermediary between Italian institutions and the permanent representation of Italy in Strasbourg. It informs Italian jurisdictional institutions about judgments and communicates systematic violations to the legislative office of the Ministry of Justice.

Of course a prominent role is played by the ordinary courts, which are obliged to judge in a manner consistent with the ECtHR's jurisprudence, and they can potentially counterbalance the legislators' inertia. Moreover, in order to guarantee the quality of information between the actors involved in implementing the ECtHR's decisions, the Court of Cassation and the Constitutional Court are developing a database for public consultation of the Strasbourg Court's judgments. The Supreme Counsel for the Administration of Justice in Italy has a relevant training role, which has grown in the past few years. It decided to include the subject of human rights and the ECtHR's case law in the curricula of all initial training courses for junior judges, and in the annual programme of in-service training. Furthermore it has promoted the organisation of seminars, both at national and local level, aimed at training people working in the field of family law on the requirements of the ECHR, as interpreted in the Strasbourg Court's case law in this field.

The more open attitude of the higher Italian courts towards the Convention system is confirmed by recent national case law. We have already quoted the two Constitutional Court judgments on the role of the ECHR in the Italian system (nos. 348/2007 and 349/2007), but we also find that a growing number of its decisions quote the ECtHR's jurisprudence (such as nos. 89/2008, 129/2008 and 254/2007). Both administrative and ordinary judges are more familiar with the Convention and more frequently refer to its provisions, as well as to the case law of the ECtHR. In the first half of 2008, the Court of Cassation referred to the Convention and the ECtHR's judgments in at least twelve decisions,[66] while administrative judges did so at least twice.[67] By contrast, in 2007 there were four relevant decisions from the Court of Cassation quoting the ECHR principles,[68] and only one from an administrative judge.[69]

The role of judges has been fundamental during these past few years. First of all, as we have already discussed, they have compensated for the lack of clarity regarding the role of the ECHR. Secondly, they have been progressively more open to judge in a manner that is consistent with the ECHR, giving greater importance also to the judgments of the ECtHR. Once the Constitutional Court clarified the Convention's role within national law, national judges became more confident in using the ECHR norms as quasi-constitutional parameters. The higher Italian courts seem to have taken the lead and initiative in this process of upgrading domestic implementation and

Italian compliance with the Convention, in comparison with the executive and parliamentary institutions. The latter are more cautious and at times reluctant – for political reasons – to adopt the measures necessary to bring Italian law in line with the ECHR provisions and the Court's case law.

Besides the clarification of the status of the Convention within the national legal hierarchy, which encouraged national judges to appeal to its provisions, there is another important reason that prompted the Italian higher courts to embrace the ECHR and its jurisprudence. It relates to the political failure to improve compliance with the ECtHR's judgments, which has most likely stimulated the judiciary to take a proactive role and show willingness to act in the place of the legislator. As the *Dorigo* judgments issued by the Constitutional Court and the Court of Cassation show, the judiciary has encouraged the legislator to adapt the national law to the ECHR's principles, although a gap remains regarding the knowledge of the Convention system among ordinary judges (especially those acting in the lower courts) as against the highest courts. It is quite difficult still to find references to the ECHR system at the lower level of jurisdiction, because of linguistic barriers among other things.

CONCLUSIONS

The preceding analysis shows that over the past couple of years, the Italian government has assigned a much higher priority to the domestic implementation of the ECtHR's judgments than it did in the past. It is unclear whether the Italian government's enhanced efforts at compliance are motivated by the attempt to avoid pecuniary condemnations, or if they are driven by a genuine and wholehearted intent to conform to the ECHR. At a political level, in spite of a rough distinction between conservatives (who are wary of international legal regimes such as the ECHR) and liberals (who appear more open to them), there are no identifiable differences between political parties towards implementation of the ECtHR's judgments. Parties of both the left and the right agree about the need to reduce the length of proceedings and to reform the procedural rule in trials. Declared intentions apart, the reforms necessary for the Italian legislation to conform to the ECtHR's judgments have been endorsed by both liberal and conservative governments under pressure from European institutions like the CoM. Nonetheless, the main structural problems that lie at the root of recurrent infringements are still in place.

From a jurisdictional perspective, the traditional reluctance on the part of the judiciary towards the Convention may be partly explained by the fact that the ECHR's provisions overlap to a great extent with the fundamental human rights already protected by the Italian Constitution. At the same time, the efforts of the Court of Cassation and the Constitutional Court over the past few years to integrate the Convention into the domestic system and to assign it a higher position from ordinary law have generated a deeper awareness of its importance among judges. National judges are now more willing to derogate national norms, when they are in conflict with the ECHR, and to apply the Convention principles as interpreted by the Strasbourg Court. These principles do in fact have a binding value for national courts.

Furthermore, the Court of Cassation and the Constitutional Court have pushed Parliament to assume full responsibility for implementing the ECtHR's judgments by means of general measures, when they show a patent and recurrent violation of the same rights. The fact that the judiciary has been more willing than Parliament and the government to follow the ECtHR's jurisprudence and to integrate this international system into the national one is quite understandable. It is understandable if one considers the difficulty involved in adopting comprehensive legislative reforms, such as the reform of the administration of justice that Italy has needed for many years now, in order to conform to the ECtHR's case law. Generally speaking, it is easier for a single judge to apply the ECHR's principles in single cases than for a legislator to adopt a wide and costly reform that challenges ingrained but deficient practices of the national administration and the justice system.

The differing attitudes of judges and the government towards the Convention and the Strasbourg Court's case law can be clearly illustrated by the *Dorigo* case. In 1998 the European Commission on Human Rights established a violation of Article 6 of the Convention for unfair trial in a case concerning sentencing to imprisonment on the basis of evidence collected when the accused was unable to defend himself.[70] The judgment was issued in response to a claim brought by Paolo Dorigo, a person convicted of terrorism on the basis of testimony that was not confirmed during the criminal hearing. Problems arose in the execution of the Strasbourg judgment, because the Italian system lacks any provision for reopening proceedings following an infringement of the ECHR. This Italian shortcoming has been repeatedly denounced by the ECHR's institutions as a violation of Article 46 ECHR.[71]

Both the Court of Cassation and the Constitutional Court have already issued two judgments on the *Dorigo* case. Following the ECtHR condemnation, Dorigo claimed unfair imprisonment and illegal detention before the Court of Cassation. The judgment subsequently issued by the latter has made a major contribution to the definition of Italian obligations with regard to the ECHR system.[72] Overturning the decision of the lower court judge, the Court of Cassation stated that judges may reopen proceedings when the Strasbourg Court finds a violation of the right to a fair trial, even if the legislator has not introduced specific means to reopen the trial. In the opinion of the Court of Cassation, the lack of a legal provision for the reopening of proceedings could be considered as violating Article 46 of the Convention. Such a bold declaration is a signal of the willingness of judges to counterbalance

Parliament's inertia, if this is necessary to comply with the obligations deriving from the Convention.

Meanwhile, the court of appeal in Bologna was asked by Dorigo to reopen the trial on the basis of the ECtHR's judgment. This court referred to the Constitutional Court the question of compatibility of Article 630 of the Criminal Code[73] with the Convention and the Strasbourg Court's case law.[74] The judgment of the Constitutional Court, though, was rather surprising and unexpected: it rejected the claim that the absence of a special provision to reopen proceedings was against the ECHR and stated that the constitutional parameters invoked are erroneous. According to the Constitutional Court, the lack of a provision in the Italian system that allows for the reopening of proceedings in response to a Strasbourg judgment must be solved by the legislator, and not by the judiciary.

Instead of issuing a judgment on the substantive issue, the Constitutional Court preferred to leave the problem to the legislator, and did no more than stress the urgency of a legislative reform of the Criminal Code. What we see here is an example of judicial self-restraint that is in contrast with the more activist approach of the Court of Cassation on the same issue. This is probably linked to the wide discretion in choosing the most appropriate mechanism for reopening proceedings, which suggests the need for legislative reform more than a corrective intervention by the judges. A further reason could be the fact that more than one bill on this issue was pending in Parliament at the time, with the last one submitted by the government in September 2007 (Bill No. AS1797). However, the new Parliament that was formed after the election of 2008 abrogated all the relevant bills that were pending.

In conclusion, the analysis of this chapter on the changing attitudes of the judicial branch toward the ECHR shows an improvement and greater receptiveness of the ECHR culture in the domestic system, which affects all branches of the state. The involvement of Parliament and the government is exemplified by the entry into force of the 'Azzolini law'. Besides its symbolic meaning, the 'Azzolini law' was valuable in introducing the annual report on the execution of the ECtHR's judgments. This represents a strong instrument of control and transparency that can be used not only by governmental agents, but also by citizens and individuals, who for the first time realise how serious the efforts of the Italian institutions in implementing ECHR obligations are.

Notes

1. Enzo Cheli, *Il giudice delle leggi: la Corte costituzionale nella dinamica dei poteri* (Bologna: Il Mulino, 1996).
2. See in particular the increasing importance of cases concerning immigrants' issues in the 2008 and 2009 reports of the Italian government to the Parliament

Esecuzione delle pronunce della Corte europea dei diritti dell'uomo nei confronti dello Stato italiano (Presidenza del Consiglio dei Ministri).

3. Antonio Cassese, *I diritti umani oggi* (Rome and Bari: Laterza, 2005), p. 134.

4. Italian Constitution, Article 72.

5. Cass. Sez. Un., 23 November 1988, *Polo Castro*. The court reiterated the same opinion in the judgment of 22 November 1991, *Vierin*.

6. In this context see also Cass. Sez. I, 16 April 1996, *Persico*; Cass. Sez. III, No. 254, 12 January 1999; Cass. Sez. I, No. 8503, 14 June 2002.

7. Andrea Guazzarotti, 'La CEDU e l'ordinamento nazionale: tendenze giurisprudenziali e nuove esigenze teoriche', *Quaderni costituzionali*, no. 3 (2006), pp. 492–93.

8. See Roberto Bin et al. (eds), *All'incrocio tra Costituzione e CEDU: il rango delle norme della Convenzione e l'efficacia interna delle sentenze di Strasburgo* (Turin: Giappichelli, 2007).

9. This has been called '*teoria della specialità*' of the ECHR. See Benedetto Conforti, *Diritto internazionale*, 5th ed. (Naples: ESI, 1997), p. 316.

10. Cass. Pen. Sez. I, 10 July 1993. See also Cass. Sez. Un., No. 7762, 10 July 1992.

11. Especially after the inclusion of Article F within the Maastricht Treaty (1992) – now Article 6, para. 2 of the Amsterdam Treaty on the European Union (1997).

12. The *obiter dictum* remained isolated, but highly quoted by ordinary judges. On this point, see Guazzarotti, 'La CEDU e l'ordinamento nazionale', p. 492.

13. See among others Trib. Genova, 4 June 2001; Comm. Trib. Reg. Milano, 19 September 2000; Corte d'Appello Roma, Sez. Lavoro, 11 April 2002.

14. But some do not agree with this opinion. See Enzo Cannizzaro, 'Gerarchia e competenza nei rapporti fra trattati e leggi interne', *Rivista di diritto internazionale*, no. 2 (1993), p. 351.

15. Cass. Civ. Sez. Lav., No. 6173, 27 March 2004.

16. Other recent decisions of the Court of Cassation confirm this view: Cass. Civ. Sez. I, No. 10542, 19 July 2002; Cass. Civ. Sez. I, No. 28507, 23 December 2005.

17. For instance, in judgment no. 224/2005, the Constitutional Court denied that Article 10 of the Italian Constitution makes reference to the ECHR, but avoided speaking Article 117.

18. There is a lively debate in the Italian legal scholarship on the issue. For instance, see Giuseppe G. Floridia, who stated that 'it is easy – yet not easy! – to imagine what consequences [Article 117] will have for the role of the Constitutional Court' (Giuseppe G. Floridia, 'Diritto interno e diritto internazionale: profili storici e comparatistici', in *Percorsi storici di un giurista: scritti di Giuseppe G. Floridia in prospettiva storica e comparata (1986–2005)* (Turin: Giappichelli, 2008), p. 109). A very different opinion is expressed, among others, by Paolo Caretti. See his book *Stato, regioni, enti locali tra innovazione e continuità: scritti sulla riforma del Titolo V della Costituzione* (Turin: Giappichelli, 2003), p. 61.

19. See Alessandro Pace, 'La limitata incidenza della CEDU sulle libertà politiche in Italia', *Diritto pubblico*, no. 1 (2001).

20. Corte Cost. No. 89/2008.

21. ECHR statistics show that 1,648 judgments were delivered against Italy in the years from 1999 to 2006 and 1,264 violations found: 923 related to length of proceedings, 255 to property rights and 192 to the guarantees of a fair trial. See more at http://www.echr.coe.int/ECHR/EN/Header/Reports+and+Statistics/Statistics/Statistical+data/ (accessed 7 September 2012).
22. ECtHR, *Capuano* v. *Italy* (no. 9381/81), 25 June 1987.
23. Among these, see ECtHR, *Ciricosta and Viola* v. *Italy* (no. 19753/92), 4 December 1995. While the Court did not find a violation of Article 6 in this case, it elaborated a set of criteria to determine the reasonable length of proceedings and just compensation.
24. See Vitaliano Esposito, 'Il ruolo del giudice nazionale per la tutela dei diritti dell'uomo', in Claudio Zanghì and Karel Vasak (eds), *La Convenzione europea dei diritti dell'uomo: 50 anni di esperienza. Gli attori e i protagonisti: il passato e l'avvenire* (Turin: Giappichelli, 2000), p. 223.
25. ECtHR, *Bottazzi* v. *Italy* (no. 34884/97), 28 July 1999; *Di Mauro* v. *Italy* (no. 34256/96), 28 July 1999; *Ferrari* v. *Italy* (no. 33440/96), 28 July 1999.
26. CoM, 'Length of Civil Proceedings in Italy: Supplementary Measures of General Character', ResDH(1997)336, adopted on 27 May 1997.
27. Corte Cost. No. 202/1985.
28. See ECtHR, *Artico* v. *Italy*, (no. 6694/74), 13 May 1980, where the Court condemned Italy for failing to guarantee the effectiveness of the right to free legal assistance (*gratuito patrocinio*).
29. Such a trial is held when the accused, after being duly summoned, does not appear at the hearing and neither requests nor agrees that it takes place in his or her absence. ECtHR, *Colozza* v. *Italy* (no. 9024/80), 12 February 1985 is the leading case on the subject.
30. ECtHR, *Ielo* v. *Italy* (no. 23053/02), 6 December 2005; ECtHR, *Patrono, Cascini and Stefanelli* v. *Italy* (no. 10180/04), 20 April 2006.
31. ECtHR, *Cordova* v. *Italy* (No. 1) (no. 40877/98), 30 January 2003; *Cordova* v. *Italy* (No. 2) (no. 45649/99), 30 January 2003.
32. ECtHR, *De Jorio* v. *Italy* (no. 73936/01), 3 June 2004.
33. In its judgment no. 154/2004, the Constitutional Court stated: 'The right to access to justice and to a fair trial [. . .] derives from Arts. 24 and 111 Const., and it is protected also by Art. 6 ECHR, as applied by the ECtHR.'
34. Sergio P. Panunzio, 'I diritti fondamentali e le Corti in Europa', in Sergio P. Panunzio (ed.), *I diritti fondamentali e le Corti in Europa* (Naples: Jovene, 2005), p. 103.
35. ECtHR, *CGIL and Cofferati* v. *Italy* (no. 46967/07), 24 February 2009. The ECtHR found an infringement of Article 6 on the grounds that the Italian Parliament had granted immunity to a parliamentarian who was charged with defamation. The Constitutional Court had upheld the parliamentary decision (judgment no. 305/2007).
36. ECtHR, *Spadea and Scalabrino* v. *Italy* (no. 12868/87), 28 September 1995.
37. ECtHR, *Immobiliare Saffi* v. *Italy* (no. 22774/93), 28 July 1999.
38. ECtHR, *Calogero Diana* v. *Italy* (no. 15211/89), 15 November 1996; *Domenichini*

v. *Italy* (no. 15943/90), 21 October 1996; *Rinzivillo* v. *Italy* (no. 31543/96), 21 December 2000; *Di Giovine* v. *Italy* (no. 39920/98), 26 July 2001; *Madonia* v. *Italy* (no. 55927/00), 6 July 2004, *Messina* (No. 3) v. *Italy* (no. 33993/96), 24 October 2002.

39. ECtHR, *Labita* v. *Italy* (no. 26772/95), 6 April 2000; *Ospina Vargas* v. *Italy* (no. 40750/98), 14 October 2004; *Argenti* v. *Italy* (no. 56317/00), 10 November 2005; *Bastone* v. *Italy* (no. 59638/00), 11 July 2006; *Leo Zappia* v. *Italy* (no. 77744/01), 29 September 2005; *Moni* v. *Italy* (no. 35784/97), 11 January 2000; *Musumeci* v. *Italy* (no. 33695/96), 11 January 2005; *Salvatore* v. *Italy* (no. 42285/98), 6 December 2005.

40. ECtHR, *Scozzari and Giunta* v. *Italy* (nos. 39221/98, 41963/98), 13 July 2000; *Bronda* v. *Italy* (no. 22430/93), 9 June 1998; *Roda and Bonfatti* v. *Italy* (no. 10427/02), 21 November 2006; *Covezzi and Morselli* v. *Italy* (no. 52763/99), 9 May 2003.

41. ECtHR, *Guerra and others* v. *Italy* (no. 14967/89), 19 February 1998; *Giacomelli* v. *Italy* (no. 59909/00), 2 November 2006.

42. See ECtHR, *Craxi* (No. 2) v. *Italy* (no. 25337/94), 17 July 2003; *L.M.* v. *Italy* (no. 60033/00), 8 February 2005.

43. ECtHR, *Guerra and others* v. *Italy*.

44. Committee on Legal Affairs and Human Rights, AS/Jur (2005) 35, 20 June 2005.

45. See among others ResDH(2000)135, concerning excessive length of judicial proceedings in Italy, general measures, adopted on 25 October 2000; ResDH(2005)114, concerning the judgments of the European Court of Human Rights and decisions by the CoM in 2,183 cases against Italy relating to the excessive length of judicial proceedings, adopted on 30 November 2005; ResDH(2007)2, concerning the problem of excessive length of judicial proceedings in Italy, adopted on 14 February 2007.

46. See among others CoM, ResDH(2005)85, *Dorigo* v. *Italy* (violation of the right to a fair trial) (application no. 33286/96), interim resolutions DH(1999)258, DH(2002)30, DH(2004)13, adopted on 12 October 2005; Parliamentary Assembly, resolution (2006)1516, regarding the implementation of judgments of the ECtHR, adopted on 2 October 2006.

47. CoM, ResDH(2007)3, concerning systemic violations of the right to the peaceful enjoyment of possessions through 'indirect expropriation' by Italy, adopted on 14 February 2007.

48. See CoM, ResDH(2001)178, concerning monitoring of prisoners' correspondence in Italy – measures of a general character, adopted on 5 December 2001; ResDH(2005)55, concerning monitoring of prisoners' correspondence in Italy and the right to an effective remedy, adopted on 5 July 2005.

49. *ex* Art. 41 bis, Law No. 354/1975.

50. ECtHR, *Natoli* v. *Italy* (no. 26161/95), 9 January 2001.

51. ECtHR, *Labita* v. *Italy*; *Rinzivillo* v. *Italy*; *Messina* v. *Italy* (No. 2) (no. 25498/94), 28 September 2000; *Indelicato* v. *Italy* (no. 31143/96), 18 October 2001; *Ganci* v. *Italy* (no. 41576/98), 30 October 2003; *Musumeci* v. *Italy*; *Bifulco* v. *Italy* (no. 60915/00), 8 February 2005; *Argenti* v. *Italy*.

52. CoM, ResDH(2005)56, concerning monitoring of prisoners' correspondence in Italy and the right to an effective remedy, adopted on 5 July 2005.

53. See the new perspective affirmed by the Court of Cassation in the judgment *Zara*, Cass. Sez. I, 26 January 2004. See also, more generally, the Constitutional Court's judgment no. 192/1998.

54. See CoM, ResDH(2002)58 on application no. 22716/93, *P.G. II v. Italy*, adopted on 16 April 2002.

55. Council of State, Adunanza Generale, Prot. Norm. No. 124/2000, Gab. No. 4/2001, 29 March 2001. In the same way, see also Council of State, judgment of 29 April 2005, no. 2.

56. Bill No. AC3137, approved by the Senate on 20 January 2010, and now under discussion in the Chamber of Deputies.

57. Bill No. AS1444, pending in the Senate.

58. Since the entry into force of the 'Pinto law', ordinary judges have often used the criteria set by the ECtHR on Article 6.1. See among others Rome Court of Appeal, decision of 10 July 2001; Turin Court of Appeal, decision of 19–25 June 2001.

59. Cass. Sez. I, no. 11573, 2 August 2002; Cass. Sez. I, no. 5664, 10 April 2003.

60. ECtHR, *Scordino and others* (No. 1) v. *Italy* (no. 36813/97), decision on admissibility, 27 March 2003.

61. See Cass. Sez. Un., no. 1338/2004, 27 November 2003; Cass. Sez. Un., no. 11350/2004, 17 June 2004; Cass. Sez. Un., no. 17139/2004, 27 August 2004.

62. The number of applications against Italy allocated to a judicial formation has continued to increase since 2008 (1,824) to reach 4,733 in 2011. In 2011, Italy accounted for 9.1 per cent of the total cases pending before the ECtHR, coming third after Russia and Turkey. See European Court of Human Rights, *Annual Report 2011* (Strasbourg: Council of Europe, 2012), pp. 153, 162.

63. Ibid., p. 156.

64. Law No. 12/2006: Disposizioni in materia di esecuzione delle pronunce della Corte Europea dei Diritti dell'Uomo (Rules on the execution of the judgments of the ECtHR).

65. Art. V, para. 3, Law No. 400/1988 as modified by Law No. 12/2006.

66. Judgements nos. 14, 3 January; 677, 16 January; 1354, 22 January; 3927, 23 January; 6026, 31 January; 3716, 14 February; 4428, 21 February; 4603, 22 February; 17408, 22 February; 5172, 27 February; 9328, 10 April; 9152, 8 April.

67. TAR Cagliari (Sardinia), no. 83, 31 January; Consiglio di Stato, no. 303, 4 February.

68. Judgments nos. 15887, 17 July; 23844, 19 November; 7319, 7 December; 5136, 18 December.

69. TAR Brescia (Lombardy), no. 466, 8 June.

70. ECommHR, *Dorigo* v. *Italy* (no. 33286/96), 9 September 1998.

71. CoM, ResDH(2002)30, adopted on 19 February 2002; ResDH(2004)13, *Dorigo* v. *Italy*, application no. 33286/96, interim resolutions DH(99)258 of 15/04/99 (finding a violation) and DH(2002)30 of 19/02/02, adopted on 10 February 2004;

ResDH(2005)85, adopted on 12 October 2005; Parliamentary Assembly, resolution (2006)1516, adopted on 2 October 2006, 11.1.
72. Cass. Pen. Sez. I, no. 2800, 1 December 2006.
73. This article states the conditions that justify the reopening of trials, but the existence of a judgment by the ECtHR is not included among them.
74. Bologna Court of Appeal, Decision No. 337/2006, 22 March 2006.

Chapter 3

The reluctant embrace: the impact of the European Court of Human Rights in post-communist Romania

Dragoş Bogdan and Alina Mungiu-Pippidi

Romania's politics after its 1989 'entangled revolution'[1] can be roughly divided into two phases. The first phase was one of democratisation, following the only 'revolution' in central and eastern Europe which did not bring about a victory for anti-communists in the subsequent elections. Ion Iliescu, a former communist leader, and his populist National Salvation Front (NSF), which campaigned with slogans against party politics and Western capitalism, won an overwhelming victory after the first free but unfair elections in May 1990. The second phase was one of consolidation, which started with the peaceful departure from power of Iliescu in 1996, after he lost the elections to a coalition formed by anti-communists and deserters from his own party. The transition in the period 1990–6 saw highly contentious politics in Romania, as well as considerable civil unrest. The emerging civil society contested Iliescu, who in turn resorted to the help of vigilante miners to keep his opponents in check.

Following on from the legacies of the Ceausescu regime, this early contentious transition only increased the challenges to human rights protection. In the early 1990s Romania had the worst Freedom House scores of all former Warsaw Pact countries other than the former Soviet Union. In 1991, however, a Constitution was adopted, which reconfirmed Romania as a fused unitary and strongly centralised state. It included, however, an important limitation to the principle of sovereignty in connection with human rights. Article 20 enshrined the pre-eminence of relevant international law over domestic law with respect to treaties to which Romania is a party: 'Where inconsistencies exist between domestic laws and the covenants and treaties on fundamental human rights to which Romania is a party, international regulations shall prevail.' A Constitutional Court was also set up to enforce the new fundamental law. The 1991 Constitution endured until 2003 when a number of modifications were made and approved in a referendum.

During the transitional period, the question of human rights protection was first dealt with in the context of accession to the Council of Europe (CoE). Romania became a member of the CoE in 1993, and, on 20 June 1994, it ratified the European Convention of Human Rights (ECHR). Being accused of nationalism and human rights abuses by his opponents and a very critical Western media, Iliescu was keen to redeem his regime's image in the West. Meanwhile, the country's politics changed markedly after Romania applied for EU membership in 1995 and, furthermore, after it was granted candidate status in 1999. The Copenhagen criteria, which the EU's European Council adopted in 1993, explicitly mentioned respect for human rights as a condition that candidate states had to fulfil in order to qualify for accession to the EU. Following Romania's application for EU membership, every government and most political elites domestically, including Iliescu and his party (the NSF, then subsequently the Social Democratic Party or SDP) started to display acceptance of European standards.

During the accession process, compliance with human rights requirements was evaluated in the country progress reports as a distinct chapter, and as a decisive condition for accession it strongly influenced the Romanian authorities. The European Council meeting in June 2004 in Brussels made a commitment to accept Bulgaria and Romania as members of the Union in January 2007 if they met the Copenhagen criteria. The political criteria for accession stipulated that these countries must first achieve 'stability of institutions guaranteeing democracy, the rule of law, human rights and respect for and protection of minorities'. With the entry into force of the Treaty of Amsterdam in May 1999, the political criteria defined at Copenhagen were enshrined as constitutional principles in the Treaty on the EU.[2] By requiring fulfilment of these conditions, the accession process opened the door to a new type of political change domestically, a change pushed from below but taking advantage of external conditionality. The drive behind this was the overwhelming support of the Romanian public for EU accession, which has always been at over 80 per cent, meaning that governments and parties which were perceived as underperforming on EU accession risked paying an electoral price.

At the same time, the importation of a growing body of case law concerning fundamental political rights and civil liberties from the European Court of Human Rights (hereafter ECtHR or the Court) found the Romanian judiciary, still largely unchanged from communist times, unprepared. The Romanian judiciary operates on the basis of the 1991 Constitution, revised in 2003, and the Judiciary Law of 1992, revised in 1997, 2004 and 2006. The High Court of Cassation and Justice ensures the consistent interpretation and application of the law by the national courts. For most of the transition, however, the General Prosecutor, appointed by the state President, enjoyed and abused the right to extraordinary appeals to final sentences of the High Court. Hundreds of such appeals were lodged each year, creating an environment of high uncertainty.

During the first few years after the ratification of the Convention, the Romanian judiciary did not respond to ECtHR case law. In part, this was due to the total lack of information concerning the ECtHR's judgments; human rights, and especially the Court's case law, were not studied in law schools.

Romanian magistrates were not trained on or informed about human rights. There were no available books or studies which could explain in an accessible manner to Romanian lawyers and judges the main principles, institutions and notions of the Convention and the Court's jurisprudence. Furthermore, state authorities (high judiciary officials and government representatives) refused to take fully into account the judgments of the Court, which at times asked directly for a change in essentially outdated practices such as the powers of the prosecutors (see *Vasilescu v. Romania* and *Brumărescu v. Romania*). One key heritage of communism was a system where the policeman was stronger than the prosecutor, who, in turn, had more powers than the judge. Reversing this needed years of efforts on top of constitutional and procedural changes.

Progress was slow and gradual. In the late 1990s, information on the Convention and the Court's case law became available, and since then the awareness of the judiciary has increased. In 1999, the National Institute of Magistracy, the sole national institution entrusted with the training of magistrates, introduced in its curricula the study of the Strasbourg Court's case law. A few analyses were published on the Court's jurisprudence and, in 2005 the first books on the subject became available on the market. Most importantly, the numerous cases lost by the Romanian state following *Brumărescu*[3] and the large amounts of damages which the government had to pay[4] received wide media coverage. This, in turn, increased the pressure on the judiciary, who became more and more aware of the importance of the Strasbourg Court's case law and the need to apply it.

With wide access to mass-media coverage of the Strasbourg Court, but also unaware of its actual nature, the public at large began to perceive it as a 'supreme court' where all the misdoings of the national judicial system could be undone, some kind of panacea for all dissatisfactions related to the functioning of national courts. As a result, more and more applications were lodged before the Court. According to the 2011 annual report of the Court, at the end of that year Romania's applications accounted for 8.1 per cent of the 151,600 allocated applications pending before the Court, the fourth largest number among European countries.[5]

Most of the cases where the ECtHR found a violation of the Convention are linked with the country's communist past. Some of them reflect old mentalities, challenged by new democratic values: cases concerning freedom of expression,[6] the powers of the prosecutors[7] or the powers of the secret services.[8] The issues at stake in other cases reveal the fear of a new democracy faced with the shadow of the past,[9] or they are related to difficulties in the restitution of land and houses confiscated by the communist regime.[10] An analysis of the Court's judgments against Romania shows that some communist institutions and practices survived the fall of communism, such as the lack of democratic accountability of the secret services or the limitation of freedom of the media where high-ranking officials are concerned. Also, the lengthy and contentious process of restitution of property confiscated by the communists put under strain the relations between the judiciary and the executive at central and local levels. In some cases the executive refused to comply with final judgments of the national courts. In others, the powers of the prosecutors to challenge a final judgment undermined legal certainty.[11]

The authority of the ECtHR has grown over the years due to the process of EU accession. The regular reports of the European Commission made up the main monitoring mechanism pushing for enforcement of the Court's decisions. Between 1998 and 2005, the Commission's reports on Romania reviewed the human rights problems it had identified: supervisory reviews (extraordinary appeals by the General Prosecutor against final sentences of the Supreme Court), discrimination against the Roma population, freedom of expression for journalists, the refusal to restitute nationalised property, and the persecution of homosexuality, were, among others, extremely important issues addressed by these reports.

Intense political pressures from the EU led the Romanian authorities to take important reforming measures in these fields. The frequent references made by the Commission to the decisions of the ECtHR and to the ECHR reveal the common agenda of the European Commission and the CoE. The problems addressed by the ECtHR's judgments (supervisory review procedure, freedom of expression for journalists etc.) were taken over in the European Commission's monitoring reports in view of accession, which thus became important sources of pressure for their implementation. Due to this linkage, it is difficult sometimes to separate the impact of the Court from the impact of the European Commission. The four main fields in which the ECtHR has had the greatest impact that has translated into a change of policy concern prosecutorial powers, freedom of expression, nationalised property and the powers of the secret services. We shall review them in turn.

DOMESTIC IMPLEMENTATION AND POLICY IMPACT I: POWERS OF THE PROSECUTORS

During communist times, the prosecutor as an institution (*prokuratura*) was a powerful instrument of the state and its main legal arm.[12] Prosecutors had the power to control the legality of any activity in society even without a lawsuit being brought before a court, and to apply sanctions. In particular, they had the power to challenge final and binding judicial decisions without any time limitation both in civil and criminal trials, to arrest, to intercept phone calls, and to order and conduct body and home searches, among other things. Their decisions in any of these matters, as well as any decision taken during the preparation of a case (a seizure, for instance), were not under the control of an independent authority, such as a judge, and there the individual under investigation had no legal recourse to contest any such steps. After

1989, these powers remained unchanged and although constitutionally qualified as 'magistrates', the prosecutors were still perceived as an instrument in
the hands of the government.[13]

The ECtHR's judgments have strongly challenged the powers of the
Romanian prosecutors. In the first judgment concerning the prosecutors'
powers, *Vasilescu*,[14] the Court tackled the problem of access to a court
with the purpose of contesting seizures ordered by a prosecutor and concluded that prosecutors were not independent. The immediate practical
consequences of this judgment were limited because some of the measures
ordered by the prosecutors had already been challenged by the Romanian
Constitutional Court.[15] However, the ECtHR's decision boosted the civil
society's advocacy campaign regarding the prosecutors' independence.

The second judgment, *Brumărescu*,[16] condemned the extraordinary appeal
powers of the General Prosecutor, who had the right to request that a final
court judgment be quashed, even if he or she was not a party to the proceedings. Before *Brumărescu*, the Code of Civil Procedure had been modified
by introducing a six-month period in which the General Prosecutor could
lodge the supervisory review.[17] The Romanian authorities were trying to
defend the extraordinary appeal by setting this temporal limitation (later
increased to a year) and were not ready to accept that its principle was actually wrong. In fact, the modification of the Code of Civil Procedure in 2000
increased the degree of discretion of the General Prosecutor to file a '*recours
en annulation*' and to request the repeal of a final court judgment. Despite
the discomfort expressed by the European Commission[18] and continued
condemnations from the ECtHR, the legal provision granting the General
Prosecutor the extraordinary appeal powers in civil matters endured in the
Code of Civil Procedure up until 2003 (and in the Criminal Code until 2004)
when it was finally abolished under pressure from the EU. However, in 2003,
a judicial interpretation of the reform reduced its scope because the Supreme
Court decided that the General Prosecutor could still oppose all final judgments adopted before the abrogation. As a result, at the beginning of 2006,
the Supreme Court was still admitting supervisory reviews lodged by the
General Prosecutor in 2004.

Following *Vasilescu*, it was obvious that the Romanian legislation concerning arrests was contrary to the Convention because of the lack of independence of the prosecutor and the lack of an obligation to present the person
arrested to a judge in less than 102 hours. But the Romanian authorities
preferred to ignore the various criticisms coming from legal practitioners[19]
and civil society or pressures from the EU[20] until the express condemnation
by the Court in the *Pantea* case. The *Pantea* judgment concerned the power
of arrest, the nucleus of the prosecutor's powers,[21] and was widely discussed
and commented in the media.[22] Furthermore, after the judgment on just
satisfaction in *Brumărescu* in January 2001, and numerous condemnations in
identical cases in 2002 and 2003, which were amply covered in the press, the

ECtHR began to be widely perceived by the public as an independent and just international forum.

In June 2003, a judiciary scandal concerning a judge, who was accused of corruption and arrested by a prosecutor, gave the opportunity to the Supreme Court to decide, based on *Pantea*,[23] that the prosecutor could not arrest people at all. Some journalists presented the decision of the Supreme Court as a 'war of the robes' between judges and prosecutors,[24] prompting a shift in judicial powers from the prosecutors, an instrument of the government, to the judges, who were perceived as being more independent. This resulted in confusion for several days, as it was not clear who could sign preventive arrest warrants (and, as a result, in several regions the prosecutors did not proceed with pending arrests).[25] The General Prosecutor issued an internal regulation requiring prosecutors to bring an arrested person before a judge within three days of arrest[26] and in the same month, a law to this effect was introduced.[27] The system was definitively changed in October 2003, when the prerogative to decide on preventive custody was transferred to a judge through an amendment of the Constitution itself.[28]

After the first condemnations in *Vasilescu* and *Brumǎrescu* that targeted the powers of the prosecutor, the *Pantea* judgment was the one which completely shifted the organisation of the criminal judicial system by transferring competences from the prosecutors to the judges. Only a few days after the issuing of the *Pantea* judgment, Parliament decisively changed the Criminal Code.[29] It also modified other important issues regarding the role of the prosecutor, which had not been touched by the Court's judgments. First, the new law allowed any party to challenge the prosecutors' decisions before a court.[30] This provision was subsequently considered by the Court as an effective remedy in *Stoica v. Romania*, and had been a response, after almost five years, to the ECtHR's condemnation in *Vasilescu*. The same law permitted the interception of communications or home searches only with the prior authorisation of a judge, with warranties in accordance with the ECtHR's standards. In the same month, through an emergency ordinance, the government abrogated the Civil Procedure Code provisions concerning the infamous extraordinary appeal, renouncing this supervisory review procedure.[31] In 2004, this procedure was removed from the Criminal Code, although there was no ECtHR judgment that specifically condemned such supervisory review in criminal matters. An attempt to reintroduce it under a different name in criminal matters was blocked with reference to the ECtHR and in view of the fact that it would have affected the accession negotiations with the EU.[32] As it was stated by APADOR-CH, a human rights watchdog group:

> The year 2003 led to the official recognition of discrepancies between the Romanian criminal legislation and the European standards as set by the European Convention on Human Rights and Fundamental Freedoms and its Five Protocols,

as they are interpreted by the European Court of Human Rights in Strasbourg [. . .] The ECtHR's judgments were the latest – and strongest – impulse for a substantial modification of the criminal legislation, which domestic and international NGOs, as well as European governmental and non-governmental institutions had constantly demanded over the years.[33]

DOMESTIC IMPLEMENTATION AND POLICY IMPACT II: FREEDOM OF EXPRESSION

After fifty years of absence, freedom of speech emerged in Romanian society in the revolutionary days of December 1989. During communism, any criticism of the party and the state administration was impossible. Insult and calumny were criminal offences that carried a prison sentence (Articles 205 and 206 of the Criminal Code) and journalists were obliged to prove the truth of their allegations (Art. 207 – proof of truth). Furthermore, insult and calumny of civil servants were separate criminal offences (Art. 238, concerning offence against authority, and Art. 239, concerning verbal outrage).

Following the transition to democracy, the existing Romanian media did not immediately liberalise. At the same time, though, a new press appeared overnight alongside the old communist press, stimulating changes in the latter, which gradually improved. The new Romanian media operated freely without any censorship but also without any standards of impartiality at all. In an attempt to prevent it from operating, miners were employed in 1990 to attack some newspapers' headquarters. Born in such a revolutionary way, in the direct passage from totalitarianism and full control to complete freedom, the new media was wildly partisan, inaccurate and frequently libellous. Building a set of ethical standards for the democratic exercise of this new freedom proved an extremely difficult process. There were excesses both in expressing and in repressing free speech and, as a result, many libel suits were brought against journalists who were condemned under the provisions mentioned above. This prompted the Parliamentary Assembly of the Council of Europe (PACE) to request the Romanian government, under Resolution No. 1123, to amend those provisions in order to align national legislation on press offences with European standards.[34] Romania subsequently went through a period of monitoring, which ended in April 2002.

Aligning national legislation with European standards of free speech has been a long battle which is still unfinished. On one side, domestic NGOs, with the help of international establishments such as the ECtHR, other bodies from the CoE and the European Commission, pressured the Romanian authorities to decriminalise insult, calumny, offence against authority and verbal outrage. Essentially such pressures for change aimed to remove the burden of proof from journalists criticising the government, and were initiated in 1997 with a public campaign involving ten NGOs led by APADOR-CH.[35] In a November 1997 press release, APADOR-CH declared, among other things, that it 'wishes to draw attention to the fact that the present wording of Arts. 205, 206, 238 (offence against authority) and 239 (outrage) runs counter to Art. 10 of the ECHR and to the case-law of the ECtHR'.

In 1998 the Chamber of Deputies rejected a draft bill for the modification of the Criminal Code that would have abolished prison sentences for insult and libel and eliminated the 'offence against authority' and 'verbal outrage'. This rejection provoked a public protest from APADOR-CH, which again drew support from the ECtHR's case law. In 1999, the ECtHR made a groundbreaking ruling in favour of a journalist who had been given a suspended prison sentence for calumny in 1994 (*Dalban* v. *Romania*).[36] The ECtHR found that the decisions of the Romanian courts violated Article 10 ECHR. As was stated in a report from the US Department of State, 'domestic media supported the [*Dalban*] ruling and defined it as precedent-setting for the many libel and calumny suits'.[37]

In late June 2000, on the recommendation of the CoE,[38] the Romanian Chamber of Deputies adopted a draft bill which repealed Articles 238 and 239 of the Criminal Code and lowered the prison sentence for insult and defamation. As shown in an APADOR-CH Report, in order to bring the five articles of the Criminal Code in line with the demands of the CoE,[39] the Senate had to take a vote. In spite of strong international pressure, the Senate had delayed voting on this issue until the elections in November 2000.[40] It must be noted that the European Commission's progress report for that year highlighted that 'laws penalising "offences against authorities" and "verbal outrage" can inhibit the freedom of expression'.[41] In spite of this, in 2001 ex-President Ion Iliescu's SDP, winner of the 2000 elections, sought to cancel the amendments to Articles 205, 206, 238 and 239 of the Criminal Code, which had been voted by the Chamber of Deputies in June 2000.

The government's resistance triggered a furious public protest from civil society organisations such as APADOR-CH, which was well argued on the basis of the ECtHR's case law that had urged for the decriminalisation of insult and libel.[42] APADOR-CH's position was cited in the European Commission's report.[43] As a result of the criticisms put forward both by civil society and by European organisations, the government's proposal was withdrawn. Instead, in May 2002, the government modified through an emergency ordinance[44] some of the provisions mentioned: the crime of offence to authorities was repealed, the crime of insult was no longer punishable with a prison sentence, and the maximum prison terms for calumny against private persons and calumny against officials were reduced. Still these modifications were considered insufficient by NGOs, which initiated another public protest to demand the decriminalisation of insult and calumny, on the basis, among others, of the *Dalban* v. *Romania* judgment of the ECtHR. Their position and arguments also echoed the views expressed by the European Commission.[45]

Under such pressure from European organisations and civil society, Iliescu, who had earlier stated that insult and calumny must be penalised in some form,[46] returned the ordinance to the Romanian Parliament, asking that the prison penalty for calumny be dropped. In June 2004, a new Criminal Code was adopted by Parliament. It repealed 'insult' and removed the possibility of a prison sentence for slander, thereby aligning requirements on the burden of proof with those of the ECHR.[47] The code never entered into force as in 2005 a new Minister of Justice, Monica Macovei, preferred to draft an improved new version. These developments, however, showed that the political class had finally given in to pressures from civil society, the EU and the CoE, accepting democratic standards for freedom of expression.

Even so, it was only after elections in 2004, when the SDP lost to a centre-right alliance, that the old Criminal Code, which was still in force, was finally amended: the prison sentence was also eliminated for calumny and the offence of outrage was repealed.[48] In 2006, nearly a decade after the first explicit international criticism by the CoE,[49] insult and calumny were also repealed.[50] Yet this breakthrough was short lived. In 2007, in a strongly contested decision, the Romanian Constitutional Court (RCC) declared unconstitutional the law decriminalising 'insult and defamation'.[51] It decided that previously existing provisions in the Criminal Code criminalising insult and defamation should be reinstated. Interestingly, the RCC also invoked the ECtHR's case law on Article 13 ECHR, stating that according to this provision there has to be an effective remedy for interference in the private life or reputation of individuals. Domestic media organisations criticised that decision. The Organization for Security and Co-operation in Europe representative for press freedom also expressed concern, calling the ruling a setback in achieving a free press and a more favourable working environment for the media.[52]

In parallel with this protracted legislative battle, in which the ECtHR's case-law was invoked mainly (but not only) by freedom of expression advocates, there were many individual judicial battles in which journalists based their defence solely or mainly on the ECtHR's case law. Since the first invocation of Article 10 of the Convention in a 1997 national court decision,[53] the domestic courts' original reluctance had dissipated. They increasingly started to resort to the ECtHR's case law to acquit journalists in freedom of expression cases, as the Committee of Ministers (CoM) of the CoE acknowledged.[54] Experienced journalists also agree that this major shift has taken place and that it appears to be more visible among the younger judges.

DOMESTIC IMPLEMENTATION AND POLICY IMPACT III: NATIONALISED PROPERTY

State policies aimed at correcting property abuses of the communist period in central and eastern Europe have followed two distinct models: the restitution model and the compensation model.[55] The restitution model is based on the actual return of the confiscated property. In exceptional cases, where restitution is not possible, the government offers compensation. This model was applied in its purest form in Czechoslovakia and in a modified version – with elements of both restitution and compensation – in East Germany. The compensation model includes the physical return of property only in a limited number of cases, while in most cases former owners receive compensation for their property loss. This can take the form of cash, bonds, stocks or vouchers. Hungary offers the prime example of the compensation model. Both models recognise the property rights of former owners and their right to compensation for the injustice suffered in the communist period; however, their effects are different both for former owners and for the state's resources. Romania hesitated for most of the first decade of the transition on which policy to adopt. Ion Iliescu, President of Romania between 1990 and 1996, was not in favour of any restitution. The anti-communist parties acted as representatives of former owners. Beyond the legal problems, property restitution posed serious social problems as the communist state had relocated hundreds of thousands of tenants in confiscated houses.

The absence of a clear restitution policy drove former owners to pursue individual claims in the courts. Many succeeded in claiming exceptions from the nationalisation laws. The rapid increase of such cases led Iliescu to make a public pronouncement that the courts were not competent to rule on cases concerning nationalised property. After this speech the General Prosecutor resorted to the extraordinary appeal procedure, and the Supreme Court was forced to judge again in each case ruling that the courts were not competent to judge claims concerning nationalised property issues.[56] As was publicly recognised by its ex-president, the Supreme Court's decisions on nationalised property were politically influenced in 1995.[57] Between 1990 and 1998, when a broader restitution law was finally passed, the situation became ever more complicated. In the framework of a 1995 law that made possible sales to tenants even when lawsuits were pending, many politicians bought houses at prices significantly below the market value.[58] Between 1995 and 1998, statistics of the ex-owners' association showed that, out of 115,000 houses sold, 90,000 had been sold to their tenants.[59]

Following the 1996 elections, won by a right-wing coalition which was in favour of the restitution of nationalised properties, the Supreme Court again changed its case law: in 1998, it allowed courts to judge ex-owners' claims to nationalised houses. The courts' competence to determine claims regarding such homes was further confirmed by a new property law in November 1998.[60] A second wave of lawsuits followed, causing chaos in the courts' case law as there were no clear legal provisions, a situation which was also highlighted in the European Commission's 2000 report.[61] The European Court of Human Rights later condemned these wide policy shifts, which, combined with the lack of legislative coherence, created a general climate of legal insecurity.[62]

This policy incoherence and the oscillation between *restitutio in integrum* versus sale to the tenants prompted the creation of two competing advocacy groups: the ex-owners who tried to recoup their nationalised property and the former tenants who had bought the houses from the state. Both of these groups organised themselves as associations[63] and became a constant presence in Romania's political and social life, seeking to defend their interests. The right-wing parties were in favour of the ex-owners, while the left-wing parties were in favour of the tenants. This distinction is somewhat blurred by the fact that some important right-wing politicians had also bought nationalised houses and therefore their personal interests coincided with those of the tenants.[64]

In these circumstances, the ECtHR delivered its landmark *Brumărescu* judgment in 1999. Following this case, between 2001 and 2003, the Court delivered a large number of judgments in similar cases, condemning Romania and ordering payment of important compensatory damages. These judgments were widely covered by the press.[65] As a result of this media frenzy, the general public began to understand and sympathise with the ex-owners of nationalised houses. The ex-owners began to use the *Brumărescu* decision in pursuit of their interests, perceiving it as a support of their cause by the ECtHR. To be sure, the Court's judgment in *Brumărescu* mainly concerned the power of the General Prosecutor to lodge extraordinary appeals in civil matters. It was only incidental that in that case, the appeal concerned a nationalised house. Despite the fact that the case primarily pertained to the powers of the General Prosecutor, ex-owners (and the press alike) regarded the Court's judgment as providing strong support for the restitution of property in kind. Subsequently, they advocated their *restitutio in integrum* claim on the basis of the ECtHR's case law. As a result of this campaign, the media and the rest of the public began to misinterpret the ECtHR's case law, seeing it as creating an obligation for the Romanian state to restitute all the properties confiscated by the communists.[66]

The ECtHR's case law added to existing external pressures on the Romanian government to change the property restitution law. Already in 1997, PACE had requested the Romanian government to 'amend the legislation relating to the return of confiscated and expropriated property [. . .] so as to provide for the restitution of such property *in integrum* or fair compensation in lieu'.[67] Despite pressures from the European Commission and the ECtHR's decisions, a new law was not adopted until 2001, due to a lack of political consensus. The European Commission monitoring report stated that the new law went 'considerably further than the requirements of the European Convention on Human Rights by covering almost all confiscations made under the Communist regime'.[68]

The abovementioned 2001 law had a number of drawbacks while

subsequent reforms of the compensation legislation continued to be at odds with the Convention. Although the 2001 law set the principle of *restitutio in integrum* (in kind), this principle was not followed. In cases where a house had already been sold, the ex-owners were to receive compensation instead. But, as the European Commission observed, 'the administrative procedures for calculating and awarding compensation were not adequately defined [. . .] this issue will be covered by future legislation; there has been slow progress in preparing such legislation.'[69] Most importantly, the new law created a new (third) wave of lawsuits between former owners and tenants, allowing ex-owners to challenge the tenants' sale contracts. An additional 2005 law enabled ex-owners to receive shares in a mutual fund set up by public assets transfer (worth about €4 billion), which they could sell on the stock exchange. In 2007, ongoing condemnations from the ECtHR led to yet another change to the compensation mechanism, allowing just satisfaction in cash up to €125,000 and in shares for sums exceeding this.[70] The case law of the ECtHR, however, has continued to rule that the compensation mechanism is not efficient, leading to more than 100 condemnations of the Romanian government in Strasbourg. Compensation was finally granted by the Central Commission for Establishing Compensation on the basis of Law No. 247/2005 on compensation rights and sums were paid, exclusively in equivalent shares, to the state-established Property Fund (FP). By mid-2011, though, at the height of the economic crisis, payments were again suspended. FP was endowed with assets and entrusted to the private management of Franklin Templeton.

Throughout this time, the Romanian government failed to adopt any substantial reforms to redress the problems of property restitution, even though more than 250 nearly identical restitution cases had resulted in Convention violations since 2005. This was reaffirmed in the case of *Maria Atanasiu and others* v. *Romania*, on which the ECtHR issued a final judgment on 12 October 2011. The ruling is no different from previous ones concerning property restitution, except that it uses the pilot procedure and gives a detailed exposition of the problems and their potential solutions. The ruling condemned Romania's systematically flawed restitution system – and demanded that the national authorities reform it within eighteen months. The Strasbourg Court suspended the other 644 Romanian cases related to restitution in the interim. The most significant measure taken by the Romanian authorities in the aftermath of the *Atanasiu* judgment was listing FP on the stock exchange in January 2011. This was an important step in making Romania's compensation mechanism more effective, as it ensured that shares in FP could be sold immediately at market prices.

By August 2011, a shortage of resources undermined FP's viability, threatening once again to derail implementation of the restitution process. The Romanian state had only €150 million left to disburse from the funds and it had not yet announced any new sources of compensation. In addition, low

FP share prices have created a de facto 50 per cent cap on compensation for earlier claimants, resulting in lawsuits. As a consequence, the deadline of July 2012 that was set for the Romanian government to finally ensure compensation for all remaining claimants with the *Atanasiu* judgment appeared unlikely to be met. The existing fund was already exhausted by this date, and the government started negotiating an extension of at least six months. The latest draft law proposes the limitation of compensation to 15 per cent of the value of the properties, payable in 10–12 years, and a suspension of restitution payments in kind. But as Romania has had a very contested political year in 2012 (two falls of government, an impeachment of the President, and two rounds of elections), it is unlikely that the political will to tackle this delicate issue can be found.

DOMESTIC IMPLEMENTATION AND POLICY IMPACT IV: ACCOUNTABILITY OF SECRET SERVICES

Post-communist Romania inherited Ceaușescu's fearsome secret services and a society which was governed by surveillance. In 1990 the miners' invasion of Bucharest showed that the secret services still remained heavily involved in Romanian politics. As a consequence of this entrenched legacy, the ECtHR's decisions in this area had little impact. The *Rotaru* case[71] has been under the CoM's supervision since 2000 and there has not yet been a change of legislation beyond drafts of new laws. The case concerns a breach of the applicant's right to respect for his private life. It is based on the claim that the relevant national legislation does not contain sufficient safeguards against abuse of the powers of the Romanian Intelligence Service (SRI), the domestic intelligence service, in gathering, keeping and using information. The ECtHR has concluded that the storage and use by SRI of information on the applicant's private life were not 'in accordance with the law' within the meaning of the Convention (violation of Art. 8 ECHR).

Through an interim resolution in 2005 the CoM called upon the Romanian authorities to rapidly adopt legislative reforms in response to the *Rotaru* judgment concerning the gathering and storing of information by the secret services. The committee noted with regret that more than five years after the date of the judgment, several shortcomings identified by the European Court had still not been remedied.[72] By October 2007, the CoM expressed its concern that seven years after the judgment, no execution measures had yet been adopted and insisted on the need to fully and immediately execute this judgment. To this day, the core power of the secret service – the system of gathering and storing information – remains unreformed.

In the *Popescu* (No. 2) judgment,[73] the powers of the prosecutor to order phone interceptions were challenged. The prosecutors could order secret surveillance measures on the basis of the Criminal Code or on the basis of the law on national security (these latter surveillance measures were executed by the secret services). According to the statistics of the General Prosecutor's office, between 1991 and 2002, some 14,267 such orders were given by the prosecutors on the basis of the law on national security. By comparison, only 5,849 orders were given on the basis of the (now modified) Criminal Code.[74] After successive modifications in 2003 and 2006, in line with the judgment of the ECtHR, the Criminal Code now contains many safeguards concerning the interception and transcribing of telephone calls, the storage of relevant information and the destruction of information which is not relevant. Yet, even after the entry into force of these Criminal Code reforms, the public prosecutor still has powers to order surveillance measures to the secret service under the law on national security.

The reform of the Criminal Code, which seemed to be in line with the Court's judgment, did not touch at all upon the powers that the secret service had and still has on the basis of the unreformed law on national security. As a consequence, given the special status of the law on national security and its very wide area of application, the same secret service practices condemned by the ECtHR are still possible under the same terms.[75]

Other judgments pertaining to less sensitive issues have been partially implemented by the national authorities. In the *Lupsa* and *Kaya* cases[76] the Court found a breach of Article 8 ECHR in reference to the problem of deportation of aliens on the ground of being a threat to national security and to the more general problem of secret service interference in the private life of individuals. The authorities provided the applicants with neither any reason for their deportation nor an order declaring their presence to be undesirable. In the respective judgments the ECtHR held that the legislation on the basis of which the deportation was ordered was incompatible with the Convention: it did not require the authorities to justify their decisions to deport people, nor did it subject such decisions to judicial review.

The ECtHR attached weight to the fact that the Bucharest Court of Appeal confined itself to a purely formal examination of the order of deportation. The public prosecutor's office did not provide the Court of Appeal with any details regarding the offence of which the applicants were suspected. The court in turn did not examine the assertions of the public prosecutor in order to verify that the applicants really did represent a danger to national security or public order. It is clear that the applicants did not enjoy even a minimum degree of protection against arbitrariness on the part of the authorities. The Court concluded that the interference with their private life was not in accordance with law and therefore did not satisfy the requirements of the Convention. In response to these two judgments, a new law was adopted in March 2003 to address the questions raised by the Court in its judgment. However, compliance with the Court's decision has only been partial, as the new law does not appear to guarantee adversarial proceedings.[77]

PARTIAL IMPLEMENTATION AND FACTORS INFLUENCING IT

According to CoM statistics, Romania is not good at executing the ECtHR's judgments. Romania accounts for 7 per cent of the leading cases that are not executed.[78] This figure has not changed much over the years and has kept Romania among the top five worst executors.[79] How can this poor performance in the implementation of the ECtHR's judgments be explained? In the first place, opposition on the part of the elites obstructs the implementation of those ECtHR judgments that confront the well-established mentality of the elites, whether they be in the legislature, the executive or the judiciary. This is for instance evidenced in cases concerning the powers of the secret services. No new laws have been adopted by the legislature or the executive (through a government ordinance) over the past eight years, nor have existing laws been reformed through judicial interpretation.[80] In addition, the scope of the reforms which have been undertaken is severely limited, and the most important powers of the security services have until now remained untouched. Likewise, legislative reform in response to adverse ECtHR judgments concerning freedom of expression took about eight years, following intense pressures from civil society and the European Commission. The process was again halted by another RCC decision which practically recriminalised libel and insult, invoking through twisted reasoning the ECtHR's case law.[81]

Restrictive implementation can also be seen in the ECtHR's judgments related to the General Prosecutor's powers to lodge supervisory reviews. After an insufficient change in legislation in 2000 – an instance of 'contained compliance'[82] – the legal provision granting the General Prosecutor extraordinary appeal powers in civil matters was finally abolished under pressure from the EU in 2003. However, as a consequence of a judiciary interpretation the General Prosecutor continued to lodge supervisory review applications during 2004 as well. In all these cases, there seems to be a well-established mentality, common to the legislative and judiciary powers, which seems to be characterised by widespread resistance to the ECtHR's decisions. The legislature has always showed an unwillingness to revise legislation to comply with the ECtHR's judgments, while Romania's higher courts have in turn limited the scope of the reforms that have been undertaken.

There are also cases in which the positions of the legislative and judiciary powers in relation to the ECtHR's case law diverge, for instance, regarding the power of prosecutors to arrest. As described earlier, Parliament, particularly when dominated by communist successor parties, was unwilling to change the national legislation that allowed prosecutors to arrest without judicial control. Yet a highly controversial situation prompted the Supreme Court to abolish this power completely, on the basis of the judgment in *Pantea v. Romania*. After this powerful response from the judiciary and following intense pressure from the European Commission and civil society, the relevant legislation was modified through a reform that was wide in scope and changed the existing balance within the judiciary.

In other cases, the lack of political consensus on the measures to be adopted halted or delayed the reform. For instance, regarding the problem of nationalised property, the mechanism for compensation was to be defined in 2001 and implemented quickly. However, it was only in 2005 that such a mechanism was established, and in 2008 it was changed in order to comply, as much as possible, with the ECtHR's rulings. In other situations, the political will to drive the reform process was simply lacking. The political class did not seem sufficiently interested in the issue, there was little pressure from the EU or civil society, and domestic implementation was greatly delayed. For instance, this occurred in cases concerning prisoners' right to correspondence, in which a change of legislation took place some four years after the Court's decision, and the relevant cases were closed by final resolution in 2007.[83] Throughout the post-1990 period, except for Monica Macovei, a human rights lawyer who had previously worked for the CoE, who held the post of Minister of Justice in 2004–7, there has been no government member who is a champion of human rights reform.

CONCLUSIONS AND THE ROLE OF THE EU

Over the past few years, the general public and the media in Romania have perceived the ECtHR as a 'supreme arbiter' in issues related to human rights and democratic values. Despite the high place of the Court from the viewpoint of Romanians, Romania is a bad executor of the ECtHR's judgments. Leaving aside technical problems and infrastructure shortcomings – such as the lack of personnel or efficient inter-institutional communication – one possible explanation for such a restrictive implementation could be the fact that the ECtHR's judgments have touched upon sensitive issues related to the country's communist past. These pertain to the powers of the secret service, freedom of expression, balance of power in the judiciary and the restitution of nationalised properties. In this conflict between old mentalities and new democratic values, there has been huge domestic resistance to the latter. Nonetheless, the domestic implementation of the ECtHR's judgments has not proved sufficient in producing sustainable results in the absence of sustained political will and motivated agents of change domestically.

Accession to the EU and constant monitoring by the European Commission have together provided the principal driving force in pushing implementation of the ECtHR's decisions, particularly in areas pertaining to broader issues of judicial independence and human rights implementation. Without its monitoring and pressure, many necessary changes would not have taken place. As has been described, the European Commission's reports not only made references to major Court judgments against Romania, but they also often concurred with the position of domestic civil society on important human rights issues. In this way, they created a huge pressure on Romanian officials to reform the system. It is too early to provide an assessment of the implementation of the ECtHR's rulings since Romania's accession to the EU, but, as shown in the interim reports of the Commission, the pace of the reforms has slowed down.[84]

Progress on the implementation of the Court's case law was only achieved due to cross-pressures from grassroots civil society in tandem with pressure from the European Commission. To be sure, though, while civil society has had an important role in applying pressure for reforms in some issue areas, there has been limited public mobilisation, possibly a reflection of a lack of a widespread human rights culture. At the same time, the media seems to focus more on the aspects related to the heavy financial obligations for the state and treats rather superficially the aspects related to the merits of a case.

Following the onset of the EU accession process in 2000, the regular annual reports of the European Commission monitored Romania's progress on political criteria, economic criteria and the implementation of the *acquis communautaire*. Most of the reforms were assisted by the EU through advice, monitoring, pre-accession funds and assistance from member states through twinning programmes. Negotiations on justice and home affairs, one of the EU's main pillars, were closed at the beginning of December 2004 in order for Romania to sign the accession treaty in 2005. Issues such as the independence of the judiciary were covered by the Copenhagen political criteria and encompassed areas of reform upon which the ECtHR's judgments often also touched. During negotiations with the EU, soft *acquis* issues such as reforming the judiciary and fighting corruption became important issues. New laws had to be passed in these fields, sometimes even constitutional amendments.

Despite the fact that the EU did not have an *acquis* in regard to the judicial system and to the fight against corruption, the Commission, with the help of other international organisations, including the CoE and the ECtHR, invested in a considerable amount of assistance, monitoring and coaching. Conditionality was also strong, particularly for laggards such as Romania: action plans on justice and home affairs submitted in 2005 before the signing of the accession treaty of Romania and Bulgaria became mandatory (under the penalty of a safeguard clause which could have denied these countries entry to the EU in case of non-compliance). The main instrument of monitoring was the regular Commission report, issued twice a year.

Despite their effectiveness as triggers of substantial domestic reform in human rights and the rule of law, the EU accession process and the obligation to implement the ECtHR's judgments have shown their limits in this regard. While Romania progressed considerably in 2005–6 in human rights reform during the tenure of Monica Macovei as minister, subsequently, following its accession in the EU, it tended to fall back on old practices. A 2009 report by the Centre for European Policy Studies concluded that the

Romanian authorities 'have become very apt at mimicking progress in the areas they consider important for the EU with the consequence that changes are introduced not for the country's benefit in the long term but rather to please Brussels. This is a dangerous development that can ossify the current corrupt structures and make the judiciary even less effective in administering justice than it is today.'[85]

Notes

1. Nestor Ratesh, *Romania: The Entangled Revolution* (Boulder, CO: Praeger, 1991).
2. They were emphasised in the Charter of Fundamental Rights of the European Union, which was proclaimed at the Nice European Council in December 2000. See Wojciech Sadurski, 'The Role of the EU Charter of Rights in the Process of Enlargement', in George Bermann and Katharina Pistor (eds), *Law and Governance in an Enlarged European Union* (Oxford: Hart, 2004), pp. 61–95.
3. ECtHR, *Brumărescu v. Romania* (no. 28342/95), 28 October 1999; *Brumărescu v. Romania* (Article 4) (no. 28342/95), 23 January 2001.
4. For instance the government was obliged to pay some €700,000 in ECtHR, *Falcoianu v. Romania* (no. 32943/96), 9 July 2002, and €900,000 in ECtHR, *Popescu Nasta v. Romania* (no. 33355/96), 7 January 2003.
5. European Court of Human Rights, *Annual Report 2011* (Strasbourg: Council of Europe, 2012), p. 13.
6. For instance, ECtHR, *Cumpănă and Mazăre v. Romania* (no. 33348/96), 17 December 2004; *Sabou and Pîrcălab v. Romania* (no. 46572/99), 28 September 2004.
7. ECtHR, *Pantea v. Romania* (no. 33343/96), 3 June 2003; *Brumărescu v. Romania*; *Vasilescu v. Romania* (no. 27053/95), 22 May 1998.
8. ECtHR, *Rotaru v. Romania* (no. 28341/95), 4 May 2000; *Lupsa v. Romania* (no. 10337/04), 8 June 2006; *Kaya v. Romania* (no. 33970/05), 12 October 2006.
9. ECtHR, *Partidul Comunistilor (Nepeceristi) and Ungureanu v. Romania* (no. 46626/99), 3 February 2005. The case concerns the refusal by the Romanian courts in 1996 to register as a political party the 'Party of Communists', on the grounds that its aims as reflected in its constitution and political programme were contrary to the constitutional and legal order of Romania.
10. ECtHR, *Păduraru v. Romania* (no. 63252/00), 1 December 2005.
11. There are also other judgments in which the Court examined the different aspects of the power of the prosecutor, such as the power to arrest in *Pantea v. Romania*, and the lack of judicial control over any decision of the prosecutor in *Vasilescu v. Romania*.
12. Ondine Ghergut, 'Magistratii-securisti, formati la scoala de la Bran', *România Liberă*, 11 March 2008.
13. 'Înscrierea Alianței, atacata de revoluționarii lui Iliescu si ai PSD', *Evenimentul Zilei*, 13 January 2004; 'Robe contra robe', *Evenimentul Zilei*, 23 June 2003; 'Mai sunt șanse pentru justiția romana', *Evenimentul Zilei*, 21 June 2003.
14. ECtHR, *Vasilescu v. Romania*.

15. Already in 1997, the Constitutional Court (Decision No. 486/1997, *Monitorul Oficial*, 6 March1998) had significantly rectified the problem which was at the source of this violation. It did so by interpreting the Code of Criminal Procedure so as to provide for a judicial appeal against the acts of prosecutors (see IR(99)676). Judicial practice has subsequently changed and, as a result, courts now accept appeals against prosecutors' acts.

16. ECtHR, *Brumărescu* v. *Romania*.

17. Law No. 17/1997, *Monitorul Oficial*, no. 26, 18 February 1997.

18. European Commission, *2001 Regular Report on Romania's Progress towards Accession* (Brussels: European Commission, 2001), p. 20. Available at http://crib. mae.ro/upload/docs/9402_2001_Regular_Report.pdf (accessed 10 September 2012). See also European Commission, *2002 Regular Report on Romania's Progress towards Accession* (Brussels: European Commission, 2002), p. 24, available at http://ec.europa.eu/enlargement/archives/pdf/key_documents/2002/ro_en.pdf (accessed 10 September 2012).

19. For instance, Dumitru Radescu, 'The notion of "magistrate" in Romanian legislation and some contradictions with European Regulations', *Justiție*, vol. 2, no. 4 (2000), p. 137.

20. European Commission, *1999 Regular Report from the Commission on Romania's Progress towards Accession* (Brussels: European Commission, 1999), p. 17. Available at http://ec.europa.eu/enlargement/archives/pdf/key_documents/1999/ romania_en.pdf (accessed 10 September 2012).

21. ECtHR, *Pantea* v. *Romania*.

22. For instance, between 6 and 26 June 2003 there were eighteen articles on this subject in the newspaper *Adevărul*. Other newspapers also covered the subject in the same way. See, for instance, 'Nici o ancheta la Bihor', *Evenimentul Zilei*, 7 June 2003; 'Ministerul Justiției se vede învins de arestații preventive', *Evenimentul Zilei*, 6 June 2003; 'Dosarul Pantea zguduie serios Justiția Romana', *Evenimentul Zilei*, 5 June 2003; 'La Strasbourg, încolonarea', *Evenimentul Zilei*, 5 June 2003; 'Foști deținuți despăgubiți cu 44.000 de euro', *Evenimentul Zilei*, 4 June 2003.

23. One press article mentions that the Supreme Court judges waited for five hours for a translation of the ECtHR's judgment into Romanian. See 'Cine ordonă arestările în România?', *Evenimentul Zilei*, 11 June 2003.

24. 'Robe contra robe'.

25. 'Avocații timișoreni trimit deținuții la CEDO', *Evenimentul Zilei*, 12 June 2003; 'Justiția în pană', *Evenimentul Zilei*, 12 June 2003; 'Cine ordonă arestările în România?'; 'Efectul Ciucă: haos în Justiția română', *Adevărul*, 21 June 2003.

26. 'Curtea Suprema bate obrazul PNA: "Probe insuficiente"', *Evenimentul Zilei*, 12 June 2003.

27. Law No. 281 of 26 June 2003, *Monitorul Oficial*, no. 468, 1 July 2003.

28. Emergency Ordinance No. 109/2003, *Monitorul Oficial*, no. 748, 26 October 2003, followed by the amendment of the Constitution on 30 October 2003.

29. Law No. 281/2003, *Monitorul Oficial*, 1 June 2003.

30. 'Paul Florea, forțat să se judece singur', *Evenimentul Zilei*, 27 June 2003.

31. Emergency Ordinance No. 58/2003, *Monitorul Oficial*, no. 460, 28 June 2003,

quoted in ECtHR, *SC Maşinexportimport Industrial Group SA* v. *Romania* (no. 22687/03), 1 December 2005, para. 22.

32. 'Reprezentanţii opoziţiei si ai societăţii civile acuza: Recursul in anulare, recuperat pe uşa din dos', *Evenimentul Zilei*, 2 October 2004.

33. *2003 Report* (Bucharest: Association for the Defence of Human Rights in Romania – the Helsinki Committee, APADOR-CH, 2003), available at http://www.apador.org/en/index.htm (accessed 10 September 2012).

34. Committee of Ministers, ResDH(1997)1123 on the honouring of obligations and commitments by Romania, 24 April 1997. Available at http://assembly.coe.int/Mainf.asp?link=/Documents/AdoptedText/ta97/ERES1123.htm (accessed 11 September 2012).

35. *Human Rights Developments in Romania: The Activities of the Romanian Helsinki Committee – 1997 Report* (Bucharest: Association for the Defence of Human Rights in Romania – the Helsinki Committee, APADOR-CH, 1997). Available at http://www.apador.org/en/index.htm (accessed 11 September 2012).

36. ECtHR, *Dalban* v. *Romania* (no. 28114/95), 28 September 1999.

37. Bureau of Democracy, Human Rights, and Labor, *Country Reports on Human Rights Practices: Romania* (US Department of State, 1999). Available at http://www.state.gov/g/drl/rls/hrrpt/1999/354.htm (accessed 11 September 2012).

38. Bureau of Democracy, Human Rights, and Labor, *Country Reports on Human Rights Practices: Romania* (US Department of State, 2000). Available at http://www.state.gov/g/drl/rls/hrrpt/2000/eur/881.htm (accessed 11 September 2012).

39. Committee of Ministers, ResDH(1997)1123.

40. *Human Rights Developments in Romania: The Activities of the Romanian Helsinki Committee (APADOR-CH) – 2000 Report* (Bucharest: Association for the Defence of Human Rights in Romania – the Helsinki Committee, APADOR-CH, 2000) Available at http://www.apador.org/en/index.htm (accessed 11 September 2012).

41. *2000 Regular Report from the Commission on Romania's Progress towards Accession* (8 November 2000), p. 21. Available at http://ec.europa.eu/enlargement/archives/pdf/key_documents/2000/ro_en.pdf (accessed 9 October 2012).

42. *Human Rights Developments in Romania: The Activities of the Romanian Helsinki Committee (APADOR-CH) – 2001 Report* (Bucharest: Association for the Defence of Human Rights in Romania – the Helsinki Committee, APADOR-CH, 2001), available at http://www.apador.org/en/index.htm (accessed 11 September 2012).

43. European Commission, *2001 Regular Report on Romania's Progress towards Accession*, p. 26.

44. Emergency Ordinance No. 58/2002, *Monitorul Oficial*, no. 351, 27 May 2002.

45. 'The amendments are limited and maintaining calumny against officials as a specific offence with a higher penalty than a similar offence against non-officials contradicts the case law of the European Court of Human Rights.' (European Commission, *2002 Regular Report on Romania's Progress towards Accession*, p. 32.)

46. Bureau of Democracy, Human Rights, and Labor, *Country Reports on Human Rights Practices: Romania* (US Department of State, 2002). Available at http://www.state.gov/j/drl/rls/hrrpt/2002/18387.htm (accessed 11 September 2012).

47. European Commission, *2004 Regular Report on Romania's Progress towards*

Accession (Brussels: European Commission, 2004), p. 25. Available at http://ec.europa.eu/enlargement/archives/pdf/key_documents/2004/rr_ro_2004_en.pdf (accessed 11 September 2012).

48. Law No. 160/2005, *Monitorul Oficial*, no. 470, 2 June 2005.
49. Committee of Ministers, ResDH(1997)1123.
50. Law No. 278/2006, *Monitorul Oficial*, no. 601, 12 July 2006.
51. RCC Decision No. 62/2007, *Monitorul Oficial*, no. 104, 12 February 2007.
52. Bureau of Democracy, Human Rights, and Labor, *Country Reports on Human Rights Practices: Romania* (US Department of State, 2007). Available at http://www.state.gov/g/drl/rls/hrrpt/2007/100580.htm (accessed 11 September 2012).
53. Bucharest Regional Court, Decision No. 284/A/24.03.1997.
54. See Council of Europe Press Division, 'Committee of Ministers assesses reforms adopted by Romania to comply with a European Court judgment concerning freedom of expression', Press Release 061(2005), 9 February 2005. Available at https://wcd.coe.int/ViewDoc.jsp?id=834855&Site=COE (accessed 9 October 2012).
55. G. Douglas Harper, 'Restitution of Property in Cuba: Lessons Learned from East Europe', in Association for the Study of the Cuban Economy, *Cuba in Transition*, vol. 9 (Silver Spring, MD: Association for the Study of the Cuban Economy, 1999), pp. 411–12.
56. See the Supreme Court's Decision No. 1/2.02.1995, which was adopted with a very slim majority (21 to 20).
57. 'Statul roman nu respecta întotdeauna hotărârile CEDO?', *Evenimentul Zilei*, 30 April 2003.
58. 'Pelerinajul românilor la Strasbourg', *Evenimentul Zilei*, 24 July 2003; 'Despăgubirile pentru casele naționalizate, amânate', *Evenimentul Zilei*, 29 December 2002.
59. *The Restitution of Properties Abusively Confiscated by the Romanian State: Legislation and Case-law* (Bucharest: Association for the Defence of Human Rights in Romania – the Helsinki Committee, APADOR-CH, 2001).
60. Law No. 213/1998, *Monitorul Oficial*, no. 448, 24 November 1998.
61. See *2000 Regular Report from the Commission on Romania's Progress towards Accession*, p. 22.
62. ECtHR, *Păduraru v. Romania*.
63. See, for instance, the website of Asociatia Proprietarilor Deposedati Abuziv de Stat at http://www.apdas.ro (accessed 11 September 2012).
64. According to the *Cotidianul* newspaper (10 August 1999), 100 parliamentarians (among whom 42 were from the right-wing party) had bought nationalised houses. *Evenimentul Zilei* also published a list of high-ranking officials who bought nationalised houses ('Proiectul Stan-Iorgulescu', 5 April 2000).
65. See, for instance, 'Ambițiile imobiliare ale lui Iliescu încep sa afecteze vistieria tarii', *Evenimentul Zilei*, 3 February 2001; 'Magistrații care ne-au dat in primire la CEDO', *Evenimentul Zilei*, 18 December 2002; 'Statul roman, bun de plata 200.000 de dolari', *Evenimentul Zilei*, 22 January 2001; 'România, condamnata la

plata a 916.523 de euro!', *Adevărul*, 8 January 2003; 'Unsprezece judecători de la CSJ i-au păgubit pe romani cu 4.293.786 de euro', *Gardianul*, 7 August 2003.

66. See, for instance, 'CEDO solicită autorităţilor române să restituie averile naţionalizate', *Adevărul*, 23 October 2002; 'Pelerinajul românilor la Strasbourg'; 'Acasa, la Strasburg', *Evenimentul Zilei*, 19 July 2003; 'La "Calendele grecesti", banii de pe case', *Evenimentul Zilei*, 29 December 2002.

67. CoM, ResDH(1997)1123.

68. European Commission, *2002 Regular Report on Romania's Progress towards Accession*, p. 27.

69. Ibid.

70. On the influence of the ECtHR's judgments, see 'Tăriceanu si-a adus aminte de Fondul Proprietatea, după ce i-a atras atenţia CEDO', *Gândul*, 1 February 2007; 'România continua sa fie condamnata de CEDO pentru ca nu restituie proprietăţile', *Gândul*, 22 November 2006; 'Jongleria Fondul Proprietatea denunţata de CEDO', *Gândul*, 24 July 2006; 'Fondul Proprietatea, "piaţa" titlurilor de despăgubire', *Jurnalul Naţional*, 8 February 2007; 'Fondul Proprietatea reclamat la Bruxelles şi la Washington', *Cotidianul*, 23 May 2007; 'Vlădescu, somat să deblocheze Proprietatea', *Jurnalul Naţional*, 31 January 2007.

71. ECtHR, *Rotaru v. Romania*.

72. These concerned the procedure to be followed so that SRI would take over access to the archives from the former secret services (other than 'the Securitate'), the absence of a specific regulation concerning how long information could be stored by the authorities, and the lack of any possibility to contest ongoing storing of this information. See Committee of Ministers, ResDH(2005)57, concerning the judgment of the ECtHR of 4 May 2000 in the case of *Rotaru v. Romania*, available at https://wcd.coe.int/ViewDoc.jsp?id=878271&Site=CM (accessed 11 September 2012).

73. ECtHR, *Dumitru Popescu v. Romania* (No. 2) (no. 71525/01), 26 April 2007.

74. 'Mii de telefoane, ascultate degeaba', *Evenimentul Zilei*, 12 December 2003.

75. 'Anticoruptie cu timpanul', *Evenimentul Zilei*, 28 September 2007.

76. ECtHR, *Lupsa v. Romania*; *Kaya v. Romania*.

77. The Authority for Aliens was reorganised by Emergency Ordinance No. 63/2003 then approved by the Romanian Parliament as Law No. 604/2003. According to the new provision, upon receiving a claim from a public prosecutor, the Bucharest Court of Appeal is entitled to pronounce on the undesirability of an alien. The data and information providing the basis of such declarations shall be placed at the disposal of the judicial authority and the judicial authority shall inform the alien of the facts forming the basis of the submission. Clarification is needed as to whether the amendments also guarantee adversarial proceedings.

78. According to the CoM, 'leading cases' are those which reveal a new systemic/general problem in a respondent state and which thus require the adoption of new general measures, more or less important according to the case(s). See Council of Europe Committee of Ministers, *Supervision of the Execution of Judgments of the European Court of Human Rights: 1st Annual Report 2007* (Strasbourg: Council of Europe, 2008), p. 205, available at http://www.coe.

int/t/dghl/monitoring/execution/Source/Publications/CM_annreport2007_en.pdf (accessed 11 September 2012).

79. Council of Europe Committee of Ministers, *Supervision of the Execution of Judgments of the European Court of Human Rights: 4th Annual Report 2010* (Strasbourg: Council of Europe, 2011), available at http://www.coe.int/t/ dghl/monitoring/execution/Source/Publications/CM_annreport2010_en.pdf (accessed 11 September 2012).

80. See RCC Decision No. 53/2007, *Monitorul Oficial*, no. 134, 23 February 2007, in which the court allowed prosecutors and security services to continue the 'surveillance policy' which led to the surveillance of 14,267 people without any procedural warranty between 1991 and 2002.

81. RCC Decision No. 62/2007, *Monitorul Oficial*, no. 104, 12 February 2007.

82. Lisa Conant, *Justice Contained: Law and Politics in the European Union* (Ithaca, NY: Cornell University Press, 2002), p. 58.

83. ECtHR, *Petra v. Romania* (no. 27273/95), 23 September 1998; *Cotleţ v. Romania* (no. 38565/97), 3 June 2003.

84. European Commission, *Interim Report from the Commission to the European Parliament and the Council on Progress in Romania under the Co-operation and Verification Mechanism*, 14 February 2008.

85. Susie Alegre, Ivanka Ivanova and Dana Denis-Smith, *Safeguarding the Rule of Law in an Enlarged EU: The Cases of Bulgaria and Romania* (Brussels: Centre for European Policy Studies, 2009), p. 82.

Part II

LEGAL MOBILISATION AND THE POLITICAL CONTEXT OF IMPLEMENTATION

Chapter 4

European human rights case law and the rights of homosexuals, foreigners and immigrants in Austria

Kerstin Buchinger, Barbara Liegl and Astrid Steinkellner

After regaining its full sovereignty through the Austrian State Treaty in 1955, Austria joined the Council of Europe (CoE) as its fifteenth member state on 16 April 1956. Accession to the European Convention for the Protection of Human Rights and Fundamental Freedoms (ECHR or the Convention) was politically undisputed and perceived as a mere act of European solidarity. Both the government and the judiciary were of the opinion that fundamental rights were already sufficiently guaranteed within the domestic legal order. Therefore, the ratification of the Convention was not considered to have any substantial consequences. It came as a surprise when soon afterwards, a relatively large number of applications were lodged against Austria before the European Court of Human Rights (ECtHR or the Court).[1]

Austria was the first state to fully incorporate the ECHR into its constitutional legal order. This created a high level of awareness of the legal and practical implications of the Convention within Austrian society, as well as the influence exerted by the Strasbourg Court. From 1985 to 2007 about ninety decisions and judgments of the ECtHR were issued against Austria that pertained to the core civil and political rights of members of marginalised groups, including foreigners, ethnic or religious minorities and homosexuals. These comprised rulings on Articles 8 to 11 and 14 of the ECHR as well as judgments on the rights of the abovementioned groups under the other provisions of the Convention. A little less than one third of these cases were launched by non-nationals, and they involved proceedings on residence prohibitions after criminal convictions, unfair trial and discrimination on grounds of foreign citizenship or language. One out of ten judgments dealt with discriminatory treatment based on sexual orientation. Altogether, the ECtHR established violations in twenty-two out of a total of thirty-seven judgments, that is, in almost 60 per cent of all judgments against Austria concerning non-nationals and individuals from other marginalised groups. The remaining cases were either declared inadmissible, resolved in a friendly settlement, or not found to involve any violation of the Convention.

In Austria human rights in general are seen as primarily protecting the socially disadvantaged. The number of applications to the ECtHR stemming from marginalised groups, homosexuals and non-nationals is relatively high and the applicants' reasons for taking recourse to the Court are manifold. The most plausible explanation for these applications is linked to restrictive legal provisions affecting the human rights of these groups. For instance, Austria's longstanding practice of criminal prosecution of male adults who have homosexual contacts with persons under age has been the subject of a significant amount of complaints lodged. These complainants were opposed to a section of the Criminal Code (now abolished) that stipulated different ages of consent for male and female homosexuals. Several attempts to have the provision abolished by the Austrian Constitutional Court had failed until a considerable number of complaints, which were backed by civil society initiatives, were pending before the ECtHR and started to exert effective leverage and pressure on the Austrian authorities.

By contrast, civil society mobilisation on behalf of non-nationals has long been limited. To be sure, NGOs representing various interests of non-nationals and migrant organisations have gained influence over the past fifteen years. Still, immigrants and people representing their views are hardly involved in politics, where Austrian law and policy concerning foreigners and asylum seekers are discussed in a politically heated atmosphere.[2]

The following analysis explores ECtHR case law referring to the rights of homosexuals and concerning the legal situation of foreigners and immigrants. In the first part of this chapter, a brief description of the relevant Court judgments provides an overview of the main issues, controversies and challenges posed to Austrian case law, law and policy. In this context, the importance of judgments, that is their relevance for the substantive rights of these marginalised groups (as opposed to merely procedural issues) is addressed. Subsequently, the domestic implementation and impact of ECtHR case law are examined. Following a brief presentation of the individual and general measures adopted in response to the judgments, their relevance for Austrian law and policy is discussed. Has their implementation promoted the rights of homosexuals and of foreigners and immigrants? And has the Court's jurisprudence been more effective in one law and policy area than in the other?

By comparing the two sets of cases, this chapter seeks to identify the conditions under which judgments prompt legislative and other reforms of Austrian laws and policies, and the factors that account for divergent patterns of state compliance. Why have the ECtHR's judgments played a central role as triggers of domestic legislative and policy change in some areas but not in others? On the basis of this analysis, we argue that societal and political factors such as civil society mobilisation, power relations between political parties and the attitude of the judiciary bear a substantial, even if variable, influence on the different categories of cases. The concluding section summarises the conditions under which ECtHR judgments can promote significant social and political reform with regard to homosexuals, foreigners and immigrants in Austria.

LITIGATION RELATED TO MARGINALISED GROUPS, DISCRIMINATION AND EQUAL TREATMENT

While labour migration became established during the late 1960s, Austria has always been a country of immigration.[3] Subsequent governments and the trade unions had agreed on the so-called 'rotation principle', indicating that migrants would only stay for one to two years. However, in the 1970s family reunification started and since then, migrants have been considered immigrants.[4] In the following two decades the immigrants' countries of origin diversified. While the first immigrants predominantly came from Turkey and the former Yugoslavia, later on they also came from various eastern European countries, Africa and Asia. In 2001, when the last census was conducted, about 9 per cent of the population were foreigners and 13 per cent were foreign born.[5] All third-country nationals are subject to the Settlement and Residence Act (formerly called the Aliens' Act), to the Aliens' Police Act and the Aliens' Employment Act,[6] regulating entry into the country, residence status and access to the labour market, respectively.[7]

Most of the cases that have been taken to Strasbourg by non-nationals fall within the scope of Articles 6 and 8 of the ECHR. The applications alleging violations of the right to a fair trial (Article 6) have raised general questions about the Austrian justice system. These concern the lack of access to a court, the failure to hold a hearing, insufficient interpretation during trial, the failure to have the defendant appear before court, the failure to publicly pronounce judgments and excessive length of proceedings. Some of the cases in which the Strasbourg Court established a violation of Article 6 ECHR were followed by fairly quick legislative changes due to the fact that they touched upon widely accepted issues, mainly concerning procedural matters. One such example is the establishment of the Independent Administrative Tribunals as courts of appeal in administrative matters. In this area, the national authorities undertook fundamental reforms that entailed a redefinition of policy frameworks in a direction that was fully in line with the principles of the ECHR.

By contrast, judgments regarding the rights of third-country nationals, like residence prohibitions imposed after criminal or administrative offences, deportations, duration of detention and refusals to issue a visa, did not have such an impact. For instance, in the early 2000s Austria was condemned for having violated Article 8 in relation to residence rights in four cases, three of which affected foreigners who had been criminally convicted by Austrian courts (judgments in *Jakupovic*, *Radovanovic* and *Yildiz*).[8] According to the domestic authorities, the need to preserve public order and safety outweighed the respect for the right to private and family life invoked by the non-Austrians and justified the residence prohibitions imposed on them.

Despite the ECtHR's rulings, similar cases, such as *Maslov*, followed.[9]

In this case the applicant was a second-generation immigrant from Bulgaria who was sentenced to imprisonment twice for committing several criminal offences. A ten-year residence ban was imposed on him and he was deported after he reached majority. The authorities did not take into account the applicant's lack of social and cultural ties to his home country, or the long period of time he had been living in Austria without any convictions. Again, the Court found a violation of Article 8 on grounds that the exclusion order was a disproportionate measure. A residence ban was also issued in an instance of illegal employment of a non-national in the case of *Moser*,[10] where the applicant was deprived of the custody of her newly born son. The ECtHR established a violation of Article 6, because the applicant had been denied a public hearing. The Court also found a violation of Article 8 in view of the fact that the national court had not explored any alternative solutions while it relied on insufficient reasons to justify such a serious interference with the applicant's right to family life.

A very important case with regard to asylum seekers was *Ahmed*,[11] on which the ECtHR ruled in 1995. The applicant was a Somali refugee within the meaning of the Geneva Convention. He lost his asylum status due to an attempted robbery and therefore was to be deported to his country of origin (Somalia), where he would have been at risk of being tortured by non-state actors. Even though the Strasbourg Court had decided that his upcoming deportation amounted to a violation of Article 3 ECHR, the Austrian authorities would not grant him any subsidiary protection. In sheer desperation the applicant committed suicide in Platz der Menschenrechte (Human Rights Square) in the city of Graz.[12]

Occasionally, petitions involving foreigners were the result of strategic litigation, as they were clearly taken to the ECtHR in order to achieve domestic legislative change and an improvement in the employment and social situation of immigrants in Austria. The first of these cases was launched by a Turkish national who was refused emergency assistance. The ECtHR found a violation of Article 14 ECHR in conjunction with Article 1 of Protocol 1 to the Convention. The authorities' refusal of emergency assistance had been exclusively based on the fact that the applicant did not have Austrian nationality and it was not corroborated by any 'objective and reasonable justification'.[13] The relevant legal provisions were a stumbling block in this case, because they prohibited non-Austrians from having equal access to emergency allowances. Their unconstitutionality was therefore obvious to legal experts. This opinion, however, was not shared by the Constitutional Court. Entitlement of foreigners to emergency assistance for an indefinite period of time was not seen as necessary; considered as 'guest workers', they were expected to return to their country of origin eventually. Moreover, a legal reform of the unemployment insurance system had not been a pressing issue on the political agenda, at least not before the ECtHR delivered its judgment in 1997.

Another applicant of foreign origin, Mümtaz Karakurt, turned to the

ECtHR to challenge Austrian law preventing non-nationals from becoming works council members.[14] He had been elected as employee representative to the workers' council of an NGO, but was later deprived of his membership in the council on the grounds that he was not eligible to stand for election due to his Turkish nationality. The NGO intervening on behalf of the applicant in front of the ECtHR wanted to achieve a legislative change that would enable non-nationals to adequately represent their work interests. Yet this endeavour was not supported by the decision delivered by the ECtHR: the case was struck out of the list, because the Court held that a workers' council could not be considered an 'association' within the meaning of Article 11 ECHR. After a total of eight years of unsuccessful court proceedings both in Austria and in Strasbourg, the UN Human Rights Committee finally took a favourable decision in April 2002.[15] It adopted the view that stripping the man of his mandate violated Article 26 of the International Covenant on Civil and Political Rights. However, it was only in 2006, after the Court of Justice of the EU decided that Austria had failed to fulfil its obligations under the association agreement between the European Economic Community and Turkey,[16] that the legislator undertook the necessary legal amendments to the Labour Constitution Act and the Chamber of Labour Act by finally removing the discriminatory provisions.[17]

Even though not launched by foreigners, two other strings of cases had an indirect impact on the situation of immigrants and asylum seekers. The first concerned the Aliens' Employment Act and led to the ECtHR's judgments in *Jancikova* and *Jurisic and Collegium Mehrerau*.[18] In these, the Court found that domestic administrative procedures for dealing with complaints about the refusal to issue employment permits were of excessive length and rather opaque. It also found that the existing law did not provide any legal protection against the failure to reach a decision within due time in administrative penal proceedings. The second string of cases pertained to the issues of freedom of the press and public debate (see for example the cases of *Oberschlick* and *Unabhängige Initiative Informationsvielfalt*)[19] and clustered around xenophobic tendencies within the right-wing Austrian Freedom Party (FPÖ).[20] Journalists criticising statements and actions by this party as racist agitation were repeatedly convicted by Austrian courts for defamation or insult. These rulings deterred those who publicly opposed racism to protect members of minorities from constant racist abuse.

The ECtHR's judgments on behalf of homosexuals' rights all touched upon key issues. The primary cause for complaints was the former Section 209 of the Criminal Code, which made consensual homosexual contacts between male adults (over eighteen years of age) and minors (males under eighteen) a punishable offence.[21] On average, sixty criminal proceedings based on Section 209 were opened in Austria per year, a third of which resulted in convictions. A term of imprisonment, usually exceeding three months, was imposed in 65 to 75 per cent of the sentences. Numerous applications were filed with the Strasbourg Court which led to a considerable number of judgments against Austria.

The ECtHR issued its first judgment on the issue in the case of *L. and V.* in 2003.[22] It held that the different 'age of consent' in the Criminal Code that applied to homosexual men in comparison to homosexual women and to heterosexuals discriminated against the applicant under Article 14 in conjunction with Article 8 ECHR. In consequence of this and several subsequent rulings,[23] Austria had to pay more than €350,000 to ten persons who had successfully sought redress before the Strasbourg Court. Litigation in Strasbourg had been part of a broader campaign by civil society and certain political actors who were pressing for the abolition of the respective provision. The ensuing verdicts as well as the abolition of Section 209 were comprehensively covered by the press.[24] Interestingly, Section 209 was repealed before the ECtHR finally pronounced itself on the issue, but clearly in anticipation of the Court's judgment.

Another major issue concerning homosexuals' rights was the lack of an option for same-sex partners living together to enter into a tenancy agreement. It was picked up by the ECtHR in the case of *Karner*,[25] based on a complaint over discriminatory treatment on the grounds of sexual orientation and an interference with the right to family life. The applicant had been living together with his homosexual partner in an apartment rented by his partner from 1989 until the latter's death in 1994. Although the applicant was his partner's designated heir, proceedings were brought against him by the landlord to clear the apartment. Both the Court of First Instance as well as the Court of Appeal dismissed the lawsuit since they found that the right of succession into a tenancy for family members under the Rent Act[26] was also applicable to persons in same-sex relationships. Unexpectedly, however, the Austrian Supreme Court reversed their decision, arguing that the respective provision had to be interpreted according to the legislator's intention back in 1974 (when the law had been passed), which did not include persons of same sex within the meaning of the notion 'life companion'. The ECtHR arrived at the conclusion that the protection of the traditional family unit (that is, heterosexual couples) should not exclude homosexuals from the scope of legislation. In doing so, the Supreme Court had infringed the principle of proportionality.

A recent Court judgment showing support for freedom of expression in relation to homosexuality was *Kobenter and Standard Verlags GmbH*.[27] The applicants had published an article in an Austrian daily newspaper (*Der Standard*) that harshly criticised a domestic court judgment and the judge who had pronounced it, for supporting homophobic attitudes. In this latter case the author of an article published in a church newspaper had described homosexuals as 'rats (crawling) out of their holes'[28] who should be subjected to 'Nazi methods'.[29] The contribution in *Der Standard* criticised not only the acquittal of the author, but also how this judgment depicted homosexuality in reference to practices in the animal world. In their article, the applicants compared these court proceedings to medieval witch trials, and they were convicted of defamation. The ECtHR ruled in favour of the applicants, claiming a violation of their rights under Article 10 of the Convention.[30]

ASSESSING THE IMPACT OF THE ECtHR'S JUDGMENTS

In exploring the impact of the Strasbourg Court's case law, one has to look into the variable patterns of domestic implementation, that is, the specific individual and general measures undertaken (or not undertaken) in response to the ECtHR's rulings in different areas of rights claims, law and policy. Significant factors have been identified in the issue and policy areas under study, which might have facilitated or, conversely, hindered implementation. In the first place, it often makes a difference whether the issue at stake concerns mere procedural questions or substantive concerns of members of marginalised groups. Secondly, multiple condemnations on the same issue over time generate more support and political pressure to take action.

Domestic implementation processes following the ECtHR's rulings are highly institutionalised in Austria. However, the steps taken in response to a particular judgment depend on the field of law or policy on which a particular ruling touches. The main actors in charge of implementing Strasbourg Court judgments include the Federal Chancellery, the Constitutional Court and the relevant ministries. They act jointly so as to effectively put judgments into practice. The concrete measures to be adopted are determined separately for each single case. Normally, a few obstacles arise, as the implementation process involves open discussions among the different actors, in which conflicting opinions may exist on how to proceed in a particular case. Even though the department in the Chancellor's office in charge of developing and reporting on the implementation steps is an administrative organ rather than a proactive player with political weight, it can still exert policy influence over implementation, depending on the personal engagement of the individuals involved.

The resolutions issued by the Committee of Ministers (CoM) of the CoE give a clear picture of the changes and reforms undertaken by the Austrian authorities as a consequence of the Court's judgments. In terms of individual measures providing redress to the applicants for the discomfort suffered, the sums for compensation awarded by the Court (or otherwise agreed on in a friendly settlement) are usually paid in full and promptly. According to CoM statistics, Austria respected the payment deadlines for just satisfaction awards in almost 96 per cent of cases in 2007, missing the deadline in only one case out of the twenty-three heard that year.[31] In following years the proportion declined: 73 per cent of the payments were made on time (in eight out of eleven cases) in 2008 and 67 per cent (in eight out of twelve cases) in 2009.[32] However, in 2010 the number of timely payments rose slightly, to 71 per cent (ten out of fourteen cases) and did so again in 2011, to 78 per cent (seven out of nine cases).[33]

Apart from compensation payments, however, additional individual measures are fairly rare and mostly consist in the reopening of domestic criminal proceedings following the applicant's request. In other fields of law, the Austrian authorities provided an individual remedy to the applicant apart from monetary compensation in only one case. This involved the decision to revoke a deportation order that violated Article 3 ECHR (*Ahmed*),[34] the implications of which are discussed further below.

In providing redress in response to unfavourable judgments of the ECtHR, the domestic authorities appear to be much more active concerning the adoption of general measures in order to prevent future condemnations in similar cases (see Table 4.1 below). According to the analysis of the CoM's final resolutions, legislative amendments rank first in the judgments on which this study focuses. In most of the cases in which domestic laws and regulations did not comply with the Convention, the necessary modifications have been undertaken.

Those ECtHR judgments which raised issues of unequal treatment of immigrants and other non-nationals residing in Austria, as well as of gay and lesbian people, cluster around various legal and policy fields. The relevant policy areas range from labour market and social policies (e.g. *Gaygusuz*, *Karakurt*) to anti-discrimination (e.g. *Karner*, *L. and V.*) and to migration and asylum policy (e.g. *Ahmed*, *Jakupovic*, *Moser*). In order to understand the different patterns of implementation, we must examine the specific actions and initiatives undertaken by governmental, legislative, judicial and administrative authorities, as well as their significance for the individuals involved and for the broader area of law and policy concerned. Legislative reforms and responses by the judiciary resulted at times in important and comprehensive

Table 4.1 *General measures applied in the Austrian cases pertaining to foreigners' and homosexuals' rights (1985–2007)*

Article	Type of general measure						
	LEG	EXE	JP	ADM	PRACT	DISS/PUB	Total
3	1	0	1	0	0	1	3
5	1	0	0	0	0	0	1
6	5	2	0	0	0	3	10
8	9	0	0	0	0	2	11
14	1	0	1	0	0	1	3
Total	17	2	2	0	0	7	28

Abbreviations: LEG: parliamentary legislation; EXE: executive action in the form of regulations, circulars or changes of practice; JP: changes of jurisprudence; ADM: administrative measures; PRACT: practical measures, such as training of judges; DISS: dissemination of judgments; PUB: publication of judgments/resolutions.

changes expanding the rights of individuals likely to be discriminated against on the grounds of their nationality or sexual orientation. From time to time, adverse judgments by the ECtHR provoked a broader political debate on the issues at stake. The question remains, however, to what extent the resulting reforms have made a noteworthy difference to the overall policy and practice regarding the affected marginalised groups.

Significant amendments with regard to criminal procedures have been achieved as a result of the ECtHR judgments that disclosed major deficiencies in the domestic legal order. The Code of Criminal Procedure was amended several times in order to strengthen the principle of fair trial. These reforms, however, were not geared towards the rights of immigrants or asylum seekers; it was only incidental that some of the applicants in the respective cases were non-nationals. One amendment that was particularly relevant for non-nationals followed from the Court's judgment in *Kamasinski*.[35] It concerned inter alia the obligation to provide for translation assistance and to reimburse translation costs.[36]

The most significant improvements of the Austrian administrative system – the establishment of so-called Independent Administrative Tribunals – can be traced back to the ECtHR's final judgment in *Palaoro*.[37] In this case, a breach of the right to access to a court within the meaning of the Convention was found. Following this judgment, new judicial bodies that were organised as independent and impartial tribunals (as stipulated by Art. 6 ECHR) were put in place in 1991.[38]

A more recent judgment issued by the Strasbourg Court under Article 6 of the Convention, *Jancikova*,[39] triggered a broad debate on the effectiveness and fairness of administrative criminal proceedings. It also resulted in a draft amendment to the Administrative Procedure Act in 2006, which, however, in the end was not approved.[40] It would have introduced the option to reopen administrative penalty proceedings following an adverse judgment by the ECtHR. In most other European countries, the possibility to reopen court cases on the domestic level still only exists within penal law (stipulated in Section 363a of the Austrian Code of Criminal Procedure), but not in matters of administrative penal law, even though there is nothing that would justify this differentiation.

In comparison to the above improvements in mostly procedural matters and matters pertaining to the domestic administrative and justice system, the realisation of reforms in substantive criminal law took much longer than one would have expected. This can be demonstrated, for example, by the struggle to repeal Section 209 of the Austrian Criminal Code. Back in 1989, the Austrian Constitutional Court had explicitly stated that Section 209 was compatible with the principle of equality and did not contravene the prohibition of gender discrimination.[41] In 1995, the Social Democratic Party, the Greens and the Liberal Party brought motions in the Austrian Parliament to annul Section 209, as the different ages of consent were not in line with

European standards.[42] One year later, a parliamentary debate was held on the issue but the provision remained in force. Even the European Parliament had several times expressly called on the Austrian legislator to immediately repeal it.[43] In 1998 it issued a resolution on the rights of gay and lesbian people in the EU, in which it stated that the accession of new member states with provisions in place discriminating against homosexuals would not be approved. Again, Austria was requested to suspend the discriminatory regulation and to release all persons detained on this basis.[44]

It was not until 2002 that the Austrian Constitutional Court – following a second request for review of the provision in question filed by the Innsbruck Regional Court – finally found that Section 209 was contrary to the Constitution. However, its mere repeal was insufficient to rectify the harm inflicted by it.[45] The practice of nationwide storage of data on convictions under this provision as well as its appearance in the criminal records was confirmed by the Constitutional Court in 2006[46] and is still being upheld. It should also not go unnoticed that the repeal of Section 209 went hand in hand with the introduction of a new Section 207b in the Austrian Criminal Code. This new section provides for the protection against sexual abuse of minors (males and females below the age of sixteen) who are not considered to possess the .necessary 'ability to reason' in the context of having sexual contacts with adults. The new provision has often been criticised for being a substitute for the abolished Section 209: it continues to criminalise homosexual contacts in a discriminatory way, which is shown by the disproportionately high percentage of convictions affecting members of this group.[47]

Also with a view to the rights of homosexuals, the lack of a right to enter into a tenancy agreement in the *Karner* judgment did not require legislative action. It did establish a new right domestically, though, as the Austrian Constitutional Court referred to it in the context of another instance of discriminatory treatment of same-sex partners. This concerned the exclusion of same-sex partners from the national system of social co-insurance of stay-at-home partners with their (employed) life partners. In 2006, the Austrian Supreme Court also changed its jurisdiction with regard to tenancy law, explicitly stating that the Rent Act would have to include same-sex partnerships in order to comply with the ECHR and the principle of equality.[48] In view of the wide-ranging impact of the judgment in the *Karner* case, co-health insurance was also opened up to gay and lesbian cohabitants in 2005 by inserting respective provisions in the Social Security Act.[49] This Act did not include the particular social security provisions applying to civil servants, an anomaly that was overcome with an amendment in 2006; however, co-insurance of same-sex partners was allowed only if the respective partner was responsible for childcare or home care with respect to the insured person. This was not a precondition for heterosexual partners. A year later, the law was amended again and the differentiation between homosexual and heterosexual couples was removed. In both cases, partners would only be eligible for social co-insurance if they took care of children or of their life companion living in the same household. Subsequently, the incompatibility of the legal situation with the Convention before the 2007 amendment was also confirmed by the ECtHR in a 2010 judgment (*P.B and J.S.*),[50] which established violations of Article 14 ECHR in conjunction with Article 8.

Other issues concerning the rights of marginalised groups that also became a target of domestic reform as a consequence of ECtHR case law include the expulsion of foreigners. In response to the well-known case of *Ahmed*, the Austrian Parliament in 2003 adopted an amendment to Section 57 of the Austrian Aliens' Act 1997 (based on Article 33 of the 1951 United Nations Convention Relating to the Status of Refugees),[51] which granted individuals much wider protection against expulsion in circumstances similar to those of the applicant. The activities of an individual in a country, however undesirable or dangerous, could not justify an expulsion from that country if it led to a risk of treatment contrary to Article 3 ECHR (irrespective of whether the threat was imputable to the state or resulted from the absence of state authority).[52] This amendment was the only sustainable influence of a judgment from the Strasbourg Court with regard to the Austrian Aliens' Act. Apart from this reform, expulsion cases have often been resolved through friendly settlements, granting rights to specific individuals but not to other persons facing similar situations.

Following the Court's judgment in the case of *Gaygusuz*, the Austrian Parliament amended the Unemployment Insurance Act in 1997, which entered into force in 2000. It provided for general and equal access to emergency assistance by removing the requirement of Austrian nationality as a prerequisite for obtaining it. In the meantime, the Constitutional Court again had to decide on complaints about the unconstitutionality of unequal treatment of foreigners under the (former) Unemployment Insurance Act. In view of the forthcoming amendment, the Constitutional Court changed its earlier jurisprudence and followed the opinion of the ECtHR. It qualified the right to emergency assistance as a pecuniary right under Protocol 1, Article 1 of the Convention and accordingly annulled the provisions in the former Act that were in breach of the Convention with immediate effect.[53]

Regarding the different categories of claim, the ECtHR's judgments have posed decisive challenges both to the Austrian legal order and to the authorities' practices. They have significantly contributed to reshaping domestic laws, as well as to the overall improvement of the system of legal protection. Due to the huge number of reforms concerning procedural law, most deficits in criminal and administrative proceedings could be eliminated.[54] The internal structures that determine the implementation process of the Court's judgments are now well established and the respective competences are clearly defined. But concrete efforts at implementation still vary from case to case, according to the degree of awareness and understanding of human rights of those involved as well as to the willingness of those in charge of implementation to promote human rights in the different issue areas.

Certain amendments following from Strasbourg Court jurisprudence have considerably enhanced the rights of foreigners and homosexuals. However, there is an obvious difference in implementation between judgments that touch upon the substantive rights of members of these marginalised groups in contrast to those dealing with procedural questions. With regard to substantive rights, a certain reluctance to understand the more general consequences resulting from the ECtHR's case law and to apply the inherent principles to similar cases can be observed – even though the pertinent judgments were adequately implemented from a formal perspective. For instance, the ECtHR proved to be a catalyst in prompting the Austrian authorities to repeal Section 209 of the Criminal Code, which discriminated against homosexuals. Yet, no general measures were introduced to rehabilitate and compensate victims of human rights violations in these cases. The individuals concerned still suffer from the stigma of having been convicted under this unlawful provision, since the Section 209 convictions still appear on their criminal records.

The Court's case law did not lead to a reorientation of domestic legal practices towards an increased respect for the rights of foreigners. Matters like immigrants entering and remaining in Austria have been quite resistant to implementation and broader political reform. With regard to politically sensitive areas in migration policy, the need to pass the necessary (substantive) legal amendments appears to have been circumvented by case-by-case solutions, such as the repeal of residence prohibitions on an individual basis. This individualistic approach protects the competent Austrian authorities from attracting public attention, which would be unavoidable if immigration law was to be amended (in the necessary positive manner). Immigration policy is constantly at the centre of public discussions fuelled by parties of the right and centre-right demanding a stop to migration flows for reasons of public and social security. The spirit of the Strasbourg Court's judgments promoting human rights protection of immigrants and asylum seekers is not widely endorsed domestically. It is only the *Ahmed* judgment that brought about significant changes in national law on behalf of asylum seekers regarding the application of Article 3 ECHR, even though it did not result in a positive outcome for the individual concerned.

FACTORS PROMOTING AND PREVENTING SUSTAINABLE CHANGES IN LEGAL PRACTICE AND POLICY DEVELOPMENT

The general awareness of human rights in Austria has been increasing over the past ten to fifteen years. This is supported by a recently conducted survey from the Institute for Empirical Social Research on people's expectations of the judiciary. The research, which was done on behalf of the

Federal Ministry of Justice, revealed that respondents attached predominant importance to equal access to justice, followed by the speeding up of court proceedings, compliance with human rights and victim protection.[55] The ECtHR, however, did not surface as a well-known institution among the public, who expressed difficulty in obtaining information about competent and dedicated lawyers or organisations capable of giving relevant advice and support. Nonetheless, those facing infringements of their human rights have developed a higher level of awareness and an increasing readiness to act against these violations over the past couple of years. The Austrian Institute for Human Rights, located in Salzburg, registers about 100 people each year, who turn to it for information about the protection of their fundamental rights and access to the ECtHR and its jurisdiction.[56]

There are no surveys available that analyse the attitudes of the legislature, the executive or the judiciary (or any other relevant public institution) towards the Convention and the ECtHR. Therefore, it has not been possible to evaluate the overall attitude of these bodies or organisations. Yet a certain lack of knowledge about the general consequences resulting from the Strasbourg Court's judgments can be discerned in some instances. For example, the Federal Ministry of the Interior viewed a judgment by the ECtHR, which found a foreigner's deportation following a conviction for burglary to be in violation of Article 8 ECHR, as being solely declaratory (in other words, not by itself ordering any action by a party or implying damages) with no need to be implemented at the domestic level.[57] Moreover, there is little awareness of the fact that activities undertaken by public authorities acting within the framework of domestic law could infringe human rights guaranteed by the Constitution or the ECHR.

One institution that enjoys a high level of awareness is the Austrian Human Rights Advisory Board, set up within the Federal Ministry of the Interior. It was established following the death of Marcus Omofuma in 1999, a Nigerian citizen, who died on his deportation flight as his mouth had been covered with adhesive tape when he continued an ongoing verbal protest on the plane. The mandate of the board is the monitoring and observation of all activities of the security services, the authorities under the Minister of the Interior and all bodies with power of direct command and compulsion. On the basis of its practical and theoretical work with regard to the protection of human rights, it issues recommendations to the Minister of the Interior.[58] The board has, for example, repeatedly criticised the poor quality of domestic asylum law and procedures.[59]

Since 1968, legal reforms in this area have put in place increasingly complicated, specialised regulations. Amendments to asylum law and related legislation entered into force in 1992, 1997, 2003, 2005, 2007, 2009 and most recently 2011. Unfortunately, although not surprisingly, this excess of regulatory rules has not proved beneficial for individuals seeking rights protection, nor has it enhanced the efficiency of asylum and other residence procedures.

The high number of decisions issued by the Austrian Constitutional Court and Administrative Court show that the domestic authorities are overburdened with implementing the numerous amendments, particularly with regard to human rights issues. Poor reasoning of decisions, among other factors, results in lengthy proceedings and human rights violations (such as the termination of residence rights for long-term Austrian inhabitants after the negative conclusion of asylum procedures, or excessive use of orders for detention pending deportation with regard to minors and/or traumatised people).[60]

One more recent case that demonstrates the domestic authorities' poor practice with respect to aliens' law is *Rusu* v. *Austria*.[61] It concerns a Romanian woman who wanted to return to her home country from Spain in 2002, after her passport had been stolen in France. The Hungarian border police sent her back to the Austrian border police, where she was arrested and arbitrarily detained without any due information of the reasons for her detention. She was provided with standard information forms that referred to outdated legislation and were not related to her specific situation. The ECtHR awarded her just satisfaction (although the applicant had not claimed for it) because of the fundamental importance of the right to liberty. The general measures adopted following the Court's judgment included the translation of information sheets aimed at detainees and the presence of interpreters in order to explain to foreigners the reasons for their detention. Regarding the legal framework, the 1997 Aliens' Act already provided for less stringent measures than detention (such as orders to reside in places defined by the authorities), but no such measures were applied. The entry into force of the Aliens' Police Act in 2005 promised to bring even more lenient measures for avoiding similar violations.[62]

However, members of the Constitutional Court have kept speaking out publicly against the unsatisfactory state of affairs in asylum and migration law, particularly with regard to instances of expulsion of traumatised asylum seekers as well as instances concerning the length of detention prior to deportation. In 2007, the president of the Constitutional Court at the time explained that in certain cases long-term asylum seekers have a right to stay according to the case law of the ECtHR.[63] Consequently, in 2008, eight criteria (including the length of stay, the degree of integration, family ties and integrity, and so on) were developed by the Constitutional Court to guide national authorities in deciding on the residence permit status of asylum seekers and immigrants on humanitarian grounds.[64] These criteria so far have not been subject to a complaint raised with the ECtHR, and it remains to be seen if they have a positive impact in terms of reducing expulsions of third-country nationals.

Generally, the Constitutional Court often reverses political decisions on behalf of marginalised groups. This is for example evidenced in its judgments affecting the equal treatment of homosexuals, in judgments declaring parts of the Asylum Act unconstitutional or in judgments overruling deportation orders. In fulfilling its task to review the constitutionality of administrative decisions and legislative acts, the Constitutional Court has developed juris-prudence closely following the Convention and its interpretations by the ECtHR.

The Austrian Supreme Court, which has the authority to review the deci-sions of judicial bodies, has also started to make references to the Strasbourg Court's case law in recent years. In 2007, it ruled on a complaint requesting the reopening of domestic proceedings concerning a homosexual man's criminal conviction under Section 209 of the Criminal Code without the ECtHR's judgment having been obtained first. The Supreme Court decided that the reopening of domestic proceedings no longer depended on a prior ruling by the Strasbourg Court. Rather, the Supreme Court itself might establish whether or not a violation of the Convention has occurred.[65]

It is evident from the foregoing examples that both Austrian high courts have significantly contributed to implementing the Strasbourg Court's case law on behalf of foreigners and homosexuals. This task has not properly been fulfilled by lower courts and the domestic authorities who are in charge of the respective areas of law and policy, such as the lawmakers and civil servants. Thus, the jurisprudence of the ECtHR appears to have notable effects upon the domestic courts of higher instance than upon those of lower instance. This should not lead to the misperception that human rights only play a role in high court proceedings; quite the contrary, the balanc-ing of conflicting interests is very often and primarily a task of judges in lower courts, where justice can be done at a very early stage of proceedings. Therefore, the role of the judiciary in strengthening the position of margin-alised groups must not be underestimated. Although judges are neutral from the point of view of the law, they cannot totally free themselves of stereo-types and prejudices present in society.[66]

The main actors in the field of migration policies used to be what are known as the social partners. These are Austria's four large representative organisations: – the Austrian Trade Union Federation (ÖGB), the Austrian Economic Chamber (WKÖ), the Federal Chamber of Labour (BAK) and the Chamber of Agriculture (LK). These are not merely interest groups acting as wage and price negotiators and lobbyists who provide services to their members; they are also established institutions anchored in Austria's politi-cal system in many ways.[67] Due to the fact that policy towards foreigners mainly used to contain provisions regulating entry conditions to the labour market, these social partners have been seen as the key actors in this policy field. Yet, public discourse on foreigners has changed, and it is dominated by perceptions of 'asylum abuse' or 'criminalisation of asylum seekers'.[68] Particularly since 9/11, the so-called 'alien problem' has gradually been substituted by the 'Muslim problem', identifying Muslim immigrants as potential threats to European values and public security.[69] Hence, voters have reacted and increasingly called on the government again to recognise its responsibility to take action.

In this context, the right-wing populist Austrian Freedom Party (FPÖ) has been dominating the political agenda in the areas of asylum, immigration and integration policies since 2000. With the rise of the FPÖ, which formed a coalition government with the conservative Austrian People's Party (ÖVP) in that year, and their racist agitations against migrants, successive governments started to tighten the laws and to revert to the slogan 'integration before influx' (*Integration vor Neuzuzug*). The FPÖ generally promotes a distorted concept of human rights, reserving them for 'hard-working' Austrians. As a consequence, the government does not greatly welcome the ECtHR's judgments in support of the rights of immigrants and asylum seekers, and they have been implemented in a rather cautious way in order not to trigger too much attention or reaction from the populist parties.[70] Whenever the respective domestic laws, that is, the Aliens' Act (*Fremdengesetz*), the Aliens' Police Act (*Fremdenpolizeigesetz*), the Security Police Act (*Sicherheitspolizeigesetz*) or the Asylum Act (*Asylgesetz*), are being modified, politicians never get tired of emphasising that the amendments are in compliance with the Austrian Constitution and the ECHR. This clearly shows that the awareness and the implementation of human rights are driven by the political agenda and political discourse, leading to a rather selective perception of human rights.

Besides public discourse, party politics may also hamper the implementation of the ECtHR's judgments and their ability to prompt broader domestic reforms on behalf of marginalised groups. This is particularly the case if the necessary reforms are not in line with core values of the respective parties in power. This can be evidenced in a couple of cases requiring legislative changes. Until 2000, Austria was governed by the Social Democratic Party of Austria (SPÖ) with the ÖVP as junior partner in a so-called 'grand coalition'. The most widely discussed judgments regarding non-nationals were issued during the term of this grand coalition government. However, some amendments could only be pushed through against the will of the coalition partner. For instance, the Austrian Federation of Employees, which is an organisation within the ÖVP, was against amending the Labour Constitution Act and the Chamber of Labour Act in order to give third-country nationals the opportunity to stand as candidates in workers' councils and in the BAK elections. Only after the European Court of Justice (now the Court of Justice of the EU) had issued a ruling on the matter in 2004 (ten years after Mümtaz Karakurt had been deprived of his mandate in the workers' council) was the Austrian government willing to amend the respective Acts in line with the principle of non-discrimination on grounds of nationality.[71]

Concerning the 1997 amendment of the Unemployment Insurance Act to guarantee third-country nationals equal access to emergency assistance, the grand coalition partners attempted to delay the implementation process. It was not known how much this amendment would cost politically, as it had to be implemented alongside a couple of austerity packages in the 1990s. While introducing the amendment that removed Austrian nationality as a prerequisite, the government also decided to link eligibility for emergency assistance to the beneficiary's availability in the labour market and to residence criteria.[72] However, the enactment of this new law was postponed to 2000 – after the parliamentary elections – as party representatives, trade unions and the BAK were concerned that this reform would cost them potential voters or members.

As mentioned, in 2000 this government was replaced by a coalition of centre-right and right-wing parties (ÖVP, FPÖ and later on BZÖ). Policy developments opposing discrimination against homosexuals were influenced by the ECtHR's judgments issued during the term of this government. Interestingly, the FPÖ's most powerful leader, the former Carinthian governor Jörg Haider, who died in a car accident in 2008, was himself said to be homosexual, although he never officially declared it. As a member of Parliament, he even voted against the abolition of Section 209 of the Criminal Code in order to disguise his sexual orientation.[73] But the resistance to abolishing Section 209 must be attributed mainly to the opposition of the conservative People's Party and the diverging views among the Social Democrats. They sought to justify the practical application of different ages of consent in reference to the so-called *Prägungstheorie*, a scientifically and morally questionable theory stating that male adolescents were at a higher risk of being 'recruited' into homosexuality than female teenagers of the same age.[74] The Federal Chancellor at the time and a member of the People's Party, Wolfgang Schüssel, was explicitly opposed to the abrogation of Section 209, emphasising that it was not an issue of discrimination but above all of child protection.[75] The fact that several cases were pending before the ECtHR was most likely the catalyst for annulling the provision. Nonetheless, the government's reaction clearly showed that the right of homosexuals to equal treatment was not a value shared by politicians regardless of their political ideology.

Cases dealing with detention pending deportation were taken to the ECtHR in order to put pressure on the government and to promote the political demands and collective interests of civil society organisations. Although NGOs were not directly involved in the proceedings, civil society bodies that represented immigrants' views kept the issue of their labour market and social security situation on the political agenda. Similarly, organisations fighting for equal treatment of gays and lesbians frequently reminded the government and the legislature of their obligations under the ECHR. Awareness of human rights in specific policy areas is undoubtedly linked to civil society mobilisation. With regard to migration policy, in 1993 the 'sea of lights against xenophobia' organised by the association SOS Mitmensch, opposing the petition for a referendum initiated by the Freedom

Party,[76] offered an incentive for NGOs to become more active in the promotion and protection of human rights on behalf of foreigners. Since then civil society organisations have turned from institutions mainly offering counselling services into political actors defending people whose human rights have been violated.[77]

In nearly all of the cases analysed, lawyers took the initiative in pursuing a legal challenge in the Strasbourg Court. Some of the lawyers are founders or members of quite influential NGOs that aim at raising awareness of human rights and offering legal support to asylum seekers, to members of ethnic minorities or to gay and lesbian people (for instance, Rechtskomitee Lambda, Platform gegen § 209, SOS Mitmensch, Netzwerk Asylanwalt).[78] Their specialist knowledge of ECtHR proceedings enables them to draft expert statements and reports on the human rights situation of specific marginalised groups in Austria. The structures through which applicants are referred to competent lawyers or law firms willing to take cases to the ECtHR are informal rather than formal. Lawyers who get involved in proceedings before the ECtHR usually do so not for economic but for political reasons or due to their personal convictions. In particular, Helmut Graupner, lawyer and president of the Austrian lesbian and gay rights organisation Rechtskomitee Lambda, as well as the founder of Platform gegen § 209, encouraged convicted homosexuals to take their cases to the ECtHR. Similarly, the applicant in the *Gaygusuz* case was represented by a lawyer very active in fighting for the rights of foreigners. Moreover, quasi-autonomous NGOs were keen on pursuing an amendment of the Unemployment Insurance Act and supported the application.

Although a number of NGOs and other associations focus on representing and supporting marginalised groups in Austria, very few seem to be actively involved in cases taken to the ECtHR, at least not without the support of transnational organisations like Amnesty International or the AIRE Centre. NGOs protecting the rights of gays, lesbians and transgender people are evidently much more active in taking cases to Strasbourg than organisations representing the interests of asylum seekers and immigrants. Only in the case of *Karakurt* was an NGO involved, and then only indirectly: a body called Verein zur Betreuung der AusländerInnen,[79] which was the employer of the applicant. These differences may also reflect the fact that the ECtHR seems to be more progressive when it comes to the protection against discrimination on the grounds of sexual orientation rather than on the grounds of race and ethnic origin.

CONCLUSION

Both Austrian law and policy have continuously been influenced by the Convention and the case law of the Strasbourg organs. Clearly, making recourse to the ECtHR has proved catalytic in putting pressure on the domestic authorities to initiate important reforms. Whether they are willing, however, to act and incorporate the real 'spirit' of these judgments into domestic legislation very much depends on how politically sensitive and controversial the issues at stake are. In many cases the legislator has shown to be prepared to follow the opinions of the ECtHR. Our analysis has revealed that those ECtHR judgments which touched upon widely accepted issues like procedural questions were followed by fairly quick and occasionally substantial reforms, entailing a redefinition of policy frameworks in a direction that also supported the rights of foreigners or homosexuals. By contrast, legislative changes strengthening the position of marginalised groups against discrimination in politically sensitive and highly controversial matters (that is, entering and remaining in the country as well as equal treatment of homosexuals) required a lot more effort and have been limited to a few special issues (for example the amendments of the Rent Act or the Social Security Act). Still, the judgments of the Strasbourg Court had a spill-over effect in both of these policy areas. While the positive effects on the protection of homosexuals against discrimination are quite clear, the consequences for the protection of foreigners, immigrants and third-country nationals are more ambivalent.

The variable awareness of human rights in different policy areas is connected to the mobilisation of resources and interests around particular issues. Initiating a litigation strategy before the ECtHR has at times increased the chances for domestic reforms at the national level. This is exemplified in the abrogation of Section 209 of the Austrian Criminal Code, discriminating against male homosexuals, which would not have been achieved by means of national remedies alone. The fight against discrimination of homosexuals was most actively supported by civil society actors, and the affected individuals together with these NGOs fought to improve their general situation. Thus, lobbying activities on behalf of gays and lesbians had a common goal and were therefore stronger than actions on behalf of immigrants and asylum seekers, who mostly sought individual remedies. However, whether or not sufficient or effective (general) implementation measures are being taken seems to be only marginally dependent on the resources and legal support structures of the individual applicants. What seems to be more important is the existence of political will to initiate changes, as well as distinct personal commitment and exertion of influence on the part of persons in high level positions within the administrative machinery.

In principle, the Austrian Constitution already protects all citizens equally. In reality, though, such protection does not apply equally to members of particular groups including for example homosexuals, as the judgments issued by the ECtHR confirm. Protocol 12 to the Convention includes an open list of discrimination grounds and provides for a general prohibition of discrimination that would no longer be limited to the enjoyment of the other Convention rights. Unfortunately, no Austrian government has so far shown any determination to ratify Protocol 12. Reasons might be that governments are afraid the ratification could result in a large number of new applications to the Strasbourg Court, bringing to light even more discriminatory treatment by the public authorities.

In spite of this, this analysis shows that the ECtHR's judgments served as a lever of change in the domestic advancement of the human rights of homosexuals, foreigners and immigrants in Austria. The judgments, often highly critical of state laws and practices, prompted both the domestic courts and the legislature to develop a more profound understanding of what protection against discrimination on grounds of nationality and sexual orientation should include in a liberal democratic society.

Notes

1. Franz Matscher, 'Was 50 Jahre EMRK in Österreich verändert haben', *Die Presse*, 8 September 2008.
2. Kurt Heller, 'Einige Bemerkungen zum Asylverfahren', in A. Bammer et al. (eds), *Rechtsschutz gestern – heute – morgen* (NWV, 2008), p. 193.
3. Rainer Bauböck and Bernhard Perchinig, 'Migrations- und Integrationspolitik', in Herbert Dachs et al. (eds), *Politik in Österreich – Das Handbuch* (Vienna: Manz, 2006), p. 726.
4. While the term 'migrant' is used for people who are moving from one habitat to another on a seasonal basis, the notion 'immigrant' describes a person who leaves one country to settle permanently in another.
5. Statistik Austria, *Volkszählung 2001: Hauptergebnisse I – Österreich* (Vienna: Verlag Österreich, 2002), pp. 15ff.
6. Citizens of the following EU member states also fall within the scope of this Act: Bulgaria, the Czech Republic, Estonia, Hungary, Latvia, Lithuania, Poland, Romania, Slovakia and Slovenia.
7. The term 'alien' constitutes a direct translation from the respective Austrian term for individuals of foreign origin and nationality, and will be used only where the context and meaning requires it.
8. ECtHR, *Jakupovic v. Austria* (no. 36757/97), 6 February 2003; *Yildiz v. Austria* (no. 37295/97), 31 October 2002; *Radovanovic v. Austria* (no. 42703/98), 22 April 2004.
9. ECtHR, *Maslov v. Austria* (no. 1638/03), 23 June 2008.
10. ECtHR, *Moser v. Austria* (no. 12643/02), 21 September 2006.
11. ECtHR, *Ahmed v. Austria*.
12. Katharina Röhl, 'Abschiebung – eine Menschenrechtsfrage', *Forum Recht*, no. 4 (2004), p. 113.
13. ECtHR, *Gaygusuz v. Austria* (no. 17371/90), 16 September 1996.
14. ECtHR, *Karakurt v. Austria* (no. 32441/96), 14 September 1999.

15. Human Rights Committee, 74th Session, *Views: Communication No. 965/2000*, document no. CCPR/C/74/D/965/2000, 4 April 2002.
16. The agreement establishing an association between the European Economic Community and Turkey required that all workers enjoy identical conditions of work and employment, including elections organised by works councils. 'Judgment of the Court (Second Chamber) of 16 September 2004 in Case C-465/01: *Commission of the European Communities* v. *Republic of Austria*', notice no. 2004/C273/02, *Official Journal of the European Union* (2004), vol. 47, no. C273, p. 1.
17. Amendment of the Official Representation of Employees' Act 1992 and of the Labour Constitution Act, *Bundesgesetzblatt für die Republik Österreich* no. 4 (2006), 13 January 2006.
18. ECtHR, *Jancikova* v. *Austria* (no. 56483/00), 7 April 2005; *Jurisic and Collegium Mehrerau* v. *Austria* (no. 62539/00), 27 July 2006.
19. ECtHR, *Oberschlick* v. *Austria* (no. 11662/85), 23 May 1991; *Oberschlick* v. *Austria* (No. 2) (no. 20834/92), 1 July 1997; *Unabhängige Initiative Informationsvielfalt* v. *Austria* (no. 28525/95), 26 February 2002.
20. Anton Pelinka, 'Die FPÖ in der vergleichenden Parteienforschung: Zur typologischen Einordnung der Freiheitlichen Partei Österreichs', *Österreichische Zeitschrift für Politikwissenschaft*, no. 3 (2002), p. 281.
21. The former section read as follows (translation by the authors): 'A male person, who, after attaining the age of 19, fornicates with a person of the same sex who has attained the age of 14 but not the age of 18 shall be sentenced to imprisonment for between six months and five years.' Federal Law No. 134: Criminal Law Amendment Act 2002, *Bundesgesetzblatt für die Republik Österreich* no. 134 (2002), 13 August 2002.
22. ECtHR, *L. and V.* v. *Austria* (nos. 39392/98, 39829/98), 9 January 2003.
23. See the following cases: ECtHR, *S.L.* v. *Austria* (no. 45330/99), 9 January 2003; *Woditschka and Wilfling* v. *Austria* (nos. 69756/01, 6306/02), 21 October 2004; *Ladner* v. *Austria* (no. 18297/03), 3 February 2005; *Wolfmeyer* v. *Austria* (no. 5263/03), 26 May 2005; *H.G. and G.B.* v. *Austria* (nos. 11084/02, 15306/02), 2 June 2005; *R.H.* v. *Austria* (no. 7336/03), 19 January 2006.
24. For example, 'Österreich wegen Paragraph 209 in Straßburg verurteilt', *Der Standard*, 10 January 2003; Wilfried Ludwig Weh, 'Österreich hätte sich das Debakel ersparen können', *Salzburger Nachrichten*, 4 February 2003; '209er: Österreich muss zahlen', *Salzburger Nachrichten*, 27 May 2003.
25. ECtHR, *Karner* v. *Austria* (no. 40016/98), 24 July 2003.
26. Art. 14(3), Federal Law No. 520: Rent Act, *Bundesgesetzblatt für die Republik Österreich* no. 520 (1981), 1 December 1981.
27. ECtHR, *Kobenter and Standard Verlags GmbH* v. *Austria* (no. 60899/00), 2 November 2006.
28. Ibid. para. 9.
29. Ibid.
30. Paul Johnson, '"An Essentially Private Manifestation of Human Personality": Constructions of Homosexuality in the European Court of Human Rights', *Human Rights Law Review*, vol. 10, no. 1 (2010), p. 94.

31. Council of Europe Committee of Ministers, *Supervision of the Execution of Judgments of the European Court of Human Rights: 1st Annual Report 2007* (Strasbourg: Council of Europe, 2008), p. 221.

32. Council of Europe Committee of Ministers, *Supervision of the Execution of Judgments of the European Court of Human Rights: 2nd Annual Report 2008* (Strasbourg: Council of Europe, 2009), p. 53; Council of Europe Committee of Ministers, *Supervision of the Execution of Judgments of the European Court of Human Rights: 3rd Annual Report 2009* (Strasbourg: Council of Europe, 2010), p. 52.

33. Council of Europe Committee of Ministers, *Supervision of the Execution of Judgments of the European Court of Human Rights: 4th Annual Report 2010* (Strasbourg: Council of Europe, 2011), p. 50; Council of Europe Committee of Ministers, *Supervision of the Execution of Judgments and Decisions of the European Court of Human Rights: 5th Annual Report of the Committee of Ministers 2011* (Strasbourg: Council of Europe, 2012), p. 46.

34. ECtHR, *Ahmed v. Austria*.

35. ECtHR, *Kamasinski v. Austria* (no. 9783/82), 19 December 1989.

36. Hannes Tretter, 'Austria', in Robert Blackburn and Jörg Polakiewicz (eds), *Fundamental Rights in Europe: The European Convention on Human Rights and its Member States, 1950–2000* (Oxford: Oxford University Press, 2001), pp. 112.

37. ECtHR, *Palaoro v. Austria* (no. 16718/90), 23 October 1995.

38. Along with their establishment a comprehensive reform of the Code of Administrative Procedure was implemented in 1990, which aimed at organising proceedings before the tribunals in conformity with Articles 5 and 6 of the Convention. Tretter, 'Austria', p. 110.

39. ECtHR, *Jancikova v. Austria*.

40. Bundeskanzleramt Österreich, Draft Federal Law, Call for Opinion, 396/ME XXII. GP, 2 March 2006, available at http://www.parlament.gv.at/PG/DE/XXII/ME/ME_00396/fname_058554.pdf (accessed 12 September 2012), p. 73.

41. Verfassungsgerichthof Österreich, VfGH 3 October 1989, VfSlg 12.182/1989.

42. Council of Europe Parliamentary Assembly, Recommendation No. 924 (1981) on discrimination against homosexuals, 1 October 1981.

43. Committee on Civil Liberties and Internal Affairs, *Annual Report on Respect for Human Rights in the European Union 1995* (A4-0112/97, 20 March 1997); Committee on Civil Liberties and Internal Affairs, *Annual Report on Respect for Human Rights in the European Union 1996* (A4-0034/98, 28 January 1998), Committee on Civil Liberties and Internal Affairs, *Annual Report on Respect for Human Rights in the European Union 1997* (A4-0468/98, 2 December 1998); Committee on Citizens' Freedoms and Rights, Justice and Home Affairs, *Respect for Human Rights in the European Union: Annual Report 1998–1999* (A5-0050/2000, 29 February 2000), Committee on Citizens' Freedoms and Rights, Justice and Home Affairs, *Fundamental Rights in the European Union: Annual Report 2000* (A5-0223/2001, 21 June 2001).

44. Helmut Graupner, *Homosexualität und Strafrecht in Österreich: Eine Übersicht* (Vienna: Rechtskomitee Lambda, 2001), available at http://www.rklambda.at/

dokumente/publikationen/209-9_18082003.pdf (accessed 12 September 2012), p. 23.

45. Manfred Nowak and Alexander Lubich, *Report on the Situation of Fundamental Rights in Austria in 2004* (EU Network of Independent Experts on Fundamental Rights, 2005), p. 61.

46. Verfassungsgerichthof Österreich, VfGH 4 October 2006, VfSlg 17.948/2006.

47. See 'Weiter diskriminierende Vollziehung der § 209-Ersatzbestimmung', Rechtskomitee Lambda, 10 July 2004, available at http://www.rklambda.at/doku mente/news_2004/News-Anfrage-JM-Stat-040710-PA.pdf (accessed 12 September 2012); 'Justiz verfolgt nahezu ausschließlich Homosexuelle', Rechtskomitee Lambda, 16 September 2004, available at http://www.rklambda.at/dokumente/ news_2004/News-PA-Anfrage-JM-Stat-040914.pdf (accessed 12 September 2012).

48. Oberste Gerichtshof, OGH 16 May 2006, 5 Ob 70/06i.

49. Verfassungsgerichtshof Österreich, VfGH 10 October 2005, VfSlg 17.659/2005.

50. ECtHR, *P.B. and J.S. v. Austria* (no. 18984/02), 22 July 2010.

51. Federal Law No. 126: Amendment to the Aliens' Act 1997 (Aliens' Law Reform 2002), the Asylum Act 1997 (Asylum Law Reform 2002) and the Aliens' Employment Act, Official Gazette: BGBl I Nr. 126/2002, 13 August 2002.

52. Committee of Ministers, ResDH(2002)99 concerning the judgements of the European Court of Human Rights of 17 December 1996 in the case of Ahmed against Austria, 7 October 2002.

53. Committee of Ministers, ResDH (98)372 concerning the judgements of the European Court of Human Rights of 16 September 1996 in the case of Gaygusuz against Austria, 12 November 1998; Tretter, 'Austria', p. 116.

54. Matscher, 'Was 50 Jahre EMRK in Österreich verändert haben'.

55. The results of the study are not publicly available, for quotes from the results see 'Bürgerwille: Gleicher Zugang zum Recht', *Salzburger Nachrichten*, 2 February 2008.

56. 'Blickpunkt Menschenrecht', *Salzburger Nachrichten*, 30 January 2004.

57. Friedrich Schwarzinger (legal representative of the applicant in ECtHR, *Jakupovic v. Austria*, no. 36757/97, 6 February 2003), email message to the authors, 30 May 2008.

58. RAXEN Focal Point for Austria, 'Case Study "Omofuma"' (EUMC, 2002).

59. Human Rights Advisory Board, 'Stellungnahme zum Fremden- und Asylrecht', July 2007, available at http://www.menschenrechtsbeirat.at/cms15/index. php?option=com_content&view=article&id=75:2007-stellungnahme-zum-frem den-und-asylrecht-&catid=50:stellungnahmen&Itemid=14 (accessed 12 September 2012).

60. Ibid.

61. ECtHR, *Rusu v. Austria* (no. 34082/02), 2 October 2008.

62. Committee of Ministers, *Supervision of the Execution of Judgments of the European Court of Human Rights: 4th Annual Report 2010*, p. 128.

63. 'Korinek zu Fremdenrecht: "Passt hinten und vorne nicht"', *Die Presse*, 5 November 2007; Austrian Constitutional Court, 'VfGH äußert Bedenken gegen Ausweisungs-Bestimmung im Asylgesetz', press briefing, 11 July 2007,

available at http://www.vfgh.gv.at/cms/vfgh-site/attachments/4/5/9/CH0004/ CMS1192436606150/asyl_u_schubhaft_presseinformation.pdf (accessed 12 September 2012).

64. *Der Standard*, 'Verfassungsgerichtshof legt Kriterien für Bleiberecht fest', 7 July 2008.

65. Supreme Court, OGH 1 August 2007, 13 Os 135/06m.

66. Dieter Schindlauer, 'Die Justiz und das Fremde', *Juridikum*, no. 4 (2002), pp. 179–81.

67. 'The Austrian Social Partnership', available at http://www.sozialpartner.at/sozial-partner/Sozialpartnerschaft_mission_en.pdf (accessed 12 September 2012).

68. Heller, 'Einige Bemerkungen zum Asylverfahren', pp. 184ff.

69. Mathias Rohe, *Perspektiven und Herausforderungen in der Integration muslimis-cher MitbürgerInnen in Österreich*, (Vienna: BM.I/.SIAK, 2006), p. 16. Available at: http://www.fes.de/BerlinerAkademiegespraeche/publikationen/migration/ documents/PerspektivenundHerausforderungen_1.pdf (last accessed 5 July 2012).

70. The Freedom Party split into the FPÖ and the Future Austria Alliance (BZÖ) in 2005, which represents quite similar values.

71. 'Judgment of the Court (Second Chamber) of 16 September 2004 in Case C-465/01: *Commission of the European Communities v. Republic of Austria*', notice no. 2004/C273/02, *Official Journal of the European Union* (2004), vol. 47, no. C273, p. 1.

72. Federal Constitutional Law No. 87: Amendment to the Federal Constitution Act, *Bundesgesetzblatt für die Republik Österreich* no. 87 (1997), 13 August 1997.

73. See the statement issued by the gay rights group HOSI on the occasion of Haider's 'outing' in a German newspaper: 'Homosexuelle Initiative (HOSI) Wien nimmt zum Outing Haiders als Homosexuellen Stellung', No-Racism.net, 22 March 2000, available at http://no-racism.net/article/12/ (accessed 12 September 2012).

74. Verena Murschetz and Stefan Ebensperger, 'Aufhebung des § 209 StGB durch den VfGH', *Juristische Ausbildung und Praxisvorbereitung* (2002/2003), p. 175.

75. 'So viel Bauernschläue', *Salzburger Nachrichten*, 7 June 2002.

76. The referendum 'Österreich zuerst!' ('Austria first!') aimed to implement a con-stitutional provision defining Austria explicitly as a non-immigration country, and to realise several other points discriminating against third-country residents (such as the curtailing of voting rights, the limitation of the number of pupils with non-German mother tongue in school classes, and the immediate expulsion of delinquent foreigners).

77. Katrin Wladasch, 'Stimmen der Zivilgesellschaft – ZARA', in Christiana Weidel (ed.) *Zivilgesellschaft in Europa – Zivilgesellschaft in Österreich* (Vienna: The World of NGOs, 2008), p. 41.

78. For further information see http://www.rklambda.at; http://www.paragraph209. at; http://www.sosmitmensch.at; http://www.asylanwalt.at (all accessed 13 September 2012).

79. The NGO is now called Migrare – Zentrum für MigrantInnen OÖ, and the former ECtHR applicant, Mümtaz Karakurt, has become its CEO: see http://www.migrare.at (accessed 13 September 2012).

Chapter 5

Political opposition and judicial resistance to Strasbourg case law regarding minorities in Bulgaria

Yonko Grozev

Judgments of the European Court of Human Rights (hereafter ECtHR or the Court) against Bulgaria have had a significant influence on introducing human rights principles into the domestic legal system since the late 1990s. A main reason for their strong influence was that these judgments substituted for the lack of a domestic human rights tradition. During the fifty years of communist rule, enforcement of individual rights through the courts was practically non-existent. Another reason for the strong domestic influence of the ECtHR's judgments is the lack of an individual complaints procedure before the Bulgarian Constitutional Court, which significantly limits its role in setting basic rights standards.[1] In this barren domestic landscape, the case law of the ECtHR became quickly the major source of human rights law. Its judgments against Bulgaria brought up major human rights issues as well as structural defects in the domestic legal system, like the habeas corpus procedure, the legality and length of pre-trial detention and guarantees for fair judicial proceedings. They also raised a large variety of other issues,[2] reflecting a fundamental divergence between the domestic legal system and European and international human rights law. Above all, these judgments prompted significant changes in domestic law, demonstrating the importance of the Strasbourg tribunal for the incorporation of human rights law in the domestic legal system.

While most of the Bulgarian cases before the ECtHR brought up procedural issues or substantive legal issues not specific to any minority group, a number of cases pertained to rights of political participation and/or protection of ethnic and religious minorities. These complaints were linked to conditions of social and political exclusion and to the anti-minority bias within society and the domestic justice system. They did not necessarily address the most significant social or economic problems of the respective minority group, but did reflect grave human rights violations. The issues they raised can be grouped into four broad issue areas: (1) the attempts by successive governments to keep under political control the religious activities of Bulgarian Muslims, the country's second largest religious group,[3] (2) the efforts of governments to stop the spread of non-traditional religious groups, like Evangelicals or Jehovah's Witnesses, (3) the efforts to deny a group identifying itself as ethnic Macedonians the right to express its identity and organise itself, and (4) racial violence against the Roma. Claims related to these issues produced about two dozen ECtHR judgments, in which the Court found violations of the European Convention of Human Rights (hereafter ECHR or Convention). These judgments, though, have not produced any tangible progress towards better domestic compliance with international human rights law. Unlike with other systemic, procedural or substantive legal issues addressed by the ECtHR, domestic implementation and changes in legal policy related to minorities have happened slowly, if at all. Evidently, there has also been little change in the basic underlying public attitudes which gave rise to those violations in the first place.

LEGAL SUPPORT FOR MINORITY COMPLAINTS

Human rights litigation before the Strasbourg Court started in Bulgaria in the mid-1990s. This development was intellectually inspired and financially supported by international and Western organisations and donors. With such support, litigation before the ECtHR was initiated by local lawyers. They saw the Court as an attractive venue offering a higher level of protection for human rights than that provided by the domestic courts. A large number of legal issues where domestic law did not meet international legal standards were raised through litigation in Strasbourg. Financial and substantive support from abroad was crucial for human rights litigation for a number of reasons. Lack of legal aid for human rights violations and the sometimes high costs of legal services and litigation were a significant limitation on the protection of basic rights through the national courts in Bulgaria. Lack of domestic human rights law meant that any such litigation had to rely heavily on the case law of the ECtHR, and knowledge of this case law among lawyers and judges was not high. Few lawyers had sufficient knowledge of international human rights law and were capable and willing to undertake human rights litigation pro bono.

Under those circumstances, a crucial role in starting and promoting Strasbourg litigation in Bulgaria was played by a group of human rights organisations created in the early 1990s. They provided both financial support and expertise to victims of human rights violations. These human rights groups were also crucial lobbyists for government policies aimed at improving human rights legislation and protection. Activists and lawyers working for these groups were trained on international human rights law by a network of Western organisations and universities and were receiving logistical and financial support from foreign donors from the very start. The result was that initially, the majority of judgments delivered by the ECtHR were brought and represented by lawyers working with these groups.[4] Particularly indicative was the fact that all the cases that raised issues affecting minority groups were represented by lawyers working for one of three human rights groups.[5] These three groups shared the understanding that the Bulgarian courts were not a reliable forum for human rights litigation and that developing human rights standards would best be achieved through bringing cases internationally. Despite the improvements in the case law of the domestic courts, those organisations still consider the ECtHR a more progressive court in human rights matters.

The approach of the abovementioned groups in supporting and initiating litigation was not always the result of a strategy carefully laid out in advance. Quite often, they have been reacting to human rights issues and problems as they occurred, taking cases on an ad hoc basis. The selection of cases was thus largely affected by these groups' general understanding of what are the most salient human rights issues, as well as by their personal and organisational preferences. Quite often these organisations have been proactive, urging and encouraging victims to litigate and providing the necessary support to make litigation happen. The background and focus of the organisations is not on any specific human rights issue and they do not represent a particular community. Rather their focus is on human rights in general, and they brought a large number of cases before the ECtHR that were not related to minorities.

The litigation pursued by the abovementioned human rights groups concerned the fundamental civil and political rights of religious and ethnic minorities. For the most part, those cases were pursued as a result of cooperation between the human rights groups and the communities affected, with the former having an active role in that relationship. Thus, litigation in individual cases was the result of an established network of cooperation between different actors, which allowed for identifying violations and responding to them in a professional way. This was the pattern with respect to all communities for which minority-related litigation in Strasbourg was undertaken. These included Muslims, other non-Orthodox religious groups, ethnic Macedonians, and Roma victims of violence.

The human rights groups had both a reactive and a proactive approach. They were selecting cases for representation before the courts from among those individuals who had approached them with complaints, according to their own priorities. Working in this way, they represented clients in cases concerning police brutality, religious rights, deportation of foreigners, fair trial, prisoners' rights and defamation against journalists.[6] As already mentioned, the human rights groups often used a proactive approach to litigation: they defined the type of violation in advance and the type of case that would be best suited to bring up the issue, and after that they would take active steps to find a victim and a case with this profile, to bring their cases before the ECtHR.[7]

The deliberate litigation strategy with respect to minority rights was exemplified in regard to racial violence against the Roma. It was the result of a focus on issues affecting the Roma community and racist violence was selected as the most appropriate for international litigation. In the late 1990s, domestic groups and organisations working on Roma rights litigation, often in collaboration with the Budapest-based European Roma Rights Centre (ERRC), have focused on police brutality and racial violence. Their strategy combined fact-finding with litigation, using the reports that were drafted also as evidence in the cases before the ECtHR. Such reports documented that police and racial violence against the Roma are widespread.[8] Eventually these human rights organisations were successful with this strategy, with the judgment in the case of *Nachova*, where the ECtHR found a violation of the right not to be discriminated against under Article 14 of the Convention. Since then, human rights groups have also started working on other issues,[9] like discrimination in access to services and work. Those latter cases, however, were litigated domestically, under the domestic anti-discrimination laws.

JUDGMENTS OF THE ECtHR FINDING VIOLATIONS

While they fell within relatively well-established case law of the ECtHR, judgments concerning religious and ethnic minorities against Bulgaria were breaking new legal ground from the perspective of Bulgarian law, as well as legal and policy implementation. A few minority cases heard by the Strasbourg Court related to governmental decisions to grant, or conversely refuse, official recognition to Muslim religious leaders. This issue is politically highly sensitive, as Islam provides a strong channel of communication with ethnic Turks in Bulgaria, who have overwhelmingly voted for the political party Movement for Rights and Freedoms (DPS) throughout the past twenty years. Both DPS and its political opponents have tried to influence the election of Muslim religious leaders for political benefits. In a couple of other cases heard in the Strasbourg Court, the political issue was control over funding for religious activities coming from Muslim countries in the Middle East. The ECtHR also heard cases related to the refusal of the competent authorities to register non-Orthodox religious groups, and their actions aimed at discouraging the religious activities of those groups.

Another stream of cases related to a small but controversial group of Bulgarian citizens identifying themselves as ethnic Macedonians. The very existence of this group challenges bedrock notions of Bulgarian national identity and history. It is therefore contested by the majority of the population, which has displayed an extremely negative public reaction. This group was systematically denied the right to peaceful assembly and the registration of its organisations and its political party by the Bulgarian courts. These restrictions have led so far to seven judgments of the ECtHR (with a few more pending) that have found violations of the right to peaceful assembly and association. Finally, the Court has considered half a dozen complaints concerning racial violence against the Roma by the police or private individuals, and found violations of Article 14 ECHR in two cases.[10] Altogether, the Strasbourg Court has heard about two dozen cases related to religious and ethnic minorities and has found violations of rights guaranteed under the Convention in practically all of those cases.

In the cases of *Hasan and Chaush* and *Supreme Holy Council of the Muslim Community*,[11] the issue was the refusal by two successive governments to register a certain Chief Mufti and religious leadership. Both the government of the Bulgarian Socialist Party and the one headed by the centre-right Union of Democratic Forces had granted their support to a different individual for the position of the Chief Mufti, while simultaneously refusing to register his rival. In finding a violation of the right to freedom of religion under Article 9 the ECtHR criticised the fact that the Bulgarian governments recognised a religious leader over a rival leader without giving any reasons in support of this decision. In *Hasan and Chaush* the Bulgarian government's decision simply named the Chief Mufti and the members of the council, without taking into account the legitimate election of Fikri Sali Hasan as Chief Mufti. The Supreme Administrative Court, upon appeal, refused to review the decision of the government. It held instead that under the judicial review doctrine endorsed by the Bulgarian courts, it was competent only to review whether the government agency that made the decision had the legal powers to make such a decision. In its judgment, the ECtHR was also critical of the domestic law on registering religious leaderships, as it was unclear and allowed arbitrariness by the authorities in exercising their powers. The Strasbourg Court also held that the refusal of the Bulgarian Supreme Court to review the lawfulness of the government's decision on its merits, and to assess the proportionality of the interference with religious freedom, amounted to a further violation of Article 13 of the Convention, the right to an effective remedy. The case of *Supreme Holy Council of the Muslim Community* was identical to *Hasan and Chaush* from a legal perspective and the ECtHR reached the same conclusions on the basis of identical analysis of both the effective domestic law and the judicial review performed by the Bulgarian courts. The ECtHR again found a violation of Article 9 ECHR on the basis of the same reasoning, namely that the domestic laws did not provide clear standards on which such a dispute should be decided and there was no adequate judicial review of the government's decision.

Several cases before the ECtHR, such as *Christian Association Jehovah's Witnesses*, *Boychev* and *Borisov* related to the refusal by the competent authority to register a non-Orthodox religious group. The legal issue in those cases was the unfettered discretion the government had in deciding whether a religious community is a legitimate religion, and whether it should be granted legal status and registered as a legal entity. Under the effective domestic legislation the government has had such discretionary powers and has used those powers to either explicitly or silently refuse to register certain religious groups. The domestic courts have refused to hear appeals against such explicit or implicit refusals by the government, and to consider the legality of these refusals on their substance. The ECtHR has not yet had the opportunity to scrutinise that legislation, as either a friendly settlement has been reached following the government's consent to register a particular religious community, or the relevant cases are still pending. With a similar legal issue already considered in *Hasan* and in *Muslim Holy Council*, the entire legal framework pertaining to registering religious communities currently in force has also been discussed in the implementation of those judgments.

Control over funding for religious activities coming from Muslim countries in the Middle East was at stake in *Al-Nashif* and *Musa*. The legal issue in those cases was the decision of national authorities to expel Daruish Al-Nashif and Ahmad Musa on grounds of being a 'threat to national security'. The ECtHR examined those cases under Article 8 of the Convention, concerning the right to family life, as the expelled foreigners had family members who were Bulgarian nationals. In its judgments the Court held that the legislation on the basis of which they were deported did not provide sufficient guarantees against arbitrariness, as it did not require the authorities ordering the deportation to give any reasons. This, along with the fact that the deportation was not subject to judicial review, made the relevant legislation incompatible with the Convention. The Court also found a separate violation of the right to an effective remedy under Article 13 of the Convention, as the Bulgarian courts had refused to hear appeals on the basis of domestic legislation explicitly prohibiting judicial review of deportation orders.

The controversy around the group of Bulgarian citizens identifying themselves as ethnic Macedonians gave rise to a number of judgments in which the ECtHR found violations of Article 11 ECHR. The ECtHR ruled that various actions of the Bulgarian authorities, such as refusing to register their organisations, or banning their public rallies, violated Article 11 of the Convention. In *Stankov*, *Ivanov* and *United Macedonian Organization Ilinden* the ECtHR ruled that the decisions of the Bulgarian authorities to ban public rallies and to refuse to register an organisation were all disproportionate. Either the authorities had failed to give any reasons, or the reasons given by them were not relevant and sufficient. As for the ban of the political party by the Constitutional Court in *United Macedonian Organization Ilinden – PIRIN*, the ECtHR ruled that there was no evidence that the party was promoting or supporting any undemocratic policies or activities, and thus its ban was also unlawful.

Besides introducing important legal principles in Bulgarian law, some of the minority-related judgments against Bulgaria also resulted in innovative case law of the ECtHR itself. For example, the Strasbourg Court for the first time established a duty of state parties under Article 14 of the Convention to investigate the racist motives of a crime and prosecute suspects. Having refused to find a violation of Article 14 on claims of racist violence against the Roma by the police,[12] the ECtHR finally found such a violation in *Nachova* in 2005, in which there was evidence that two runaway Roma soldiers might have been shot at and killed by the military police because of racist attitudes. In that judgment the Court held that where there is sufficient evidence that a killing was racially motivated, the domestic authorities are under an obligation to investigate and treat the racist motive as an aggravating circumstance. The failure to conduct such an investigation amounted to a violation of Article 14 of the Convention. In *Angelova and Iliev*, the ECtHR found a violation of Article 14 on the basis of the same reasoning: namely, that the authorities had failed to prosecute a racially motivated assault, allowing the statute of limitations to run out, and that they had failed to charge the suspects with a crime taking into account the racist motives.

IMPLEMENTATION OF THE ECtHR'S JUDGMENTS AND MINORITY-RELATED ISSUES

The large number of ECtHR judgments against Bulgaria have for the most part been widely reported by the media.[13] This has put some pressure on the government to improve the execution of these judgments and more generally, to improve domestic compliance with international human rights law. Still, the country is in the early stages of developing its ability to implement the case law of the ECtHR. Knowledge and understanding of this case law remain limited to a few human rights groups and the government agents representing the country before the ECtHR. Training of judges and prosecutors through the National Institute of Justice has enhanced knowledge of the Strasbourg case law among the Bulgarian judiciary. Overall, though, the level of knowledge among government experts, officials and politicians is still insufficient for informed decision-making and the effective translation of the case law into national legislation. Academic writing on and discussion of those issues is also limited. And with respect to the rulings of the ECtHR on issues affecting religious and ethnic minority groups, there are additional hurdles, as there has been no genuine political will to pursue policy changes.

A major obstacle in the effective implementation of the ECtHR's judgments is the set-up and operation of the key institutions that are assigned responsibility for it. The Office of the Government Agents at the Ministry of Justice (hereafter OGA or the Office) represents the country before the ECtHR and it also provides information on the implementation of the judgments to the Committee of Ministers (CoM) of the Council of Europe. Yet it is rather low in the administrative hierarchy, and it lacks the power to exert any influence. The implementation of the ECtHR's judgments clearly has a secondary role in the responsibilities of the OGA, and its staff dedicates a small amount of time to it. Other government agencies rarely have the in-depth understanding of the issues and would not take the initiative to implement the judgments of the ECtHR.

Implementation of the ECtHR's judgments is not considered a priority of the Committee on Human Rights in Parliament either. The committee may not even get involved at all in reviewing draft legislation introduced in response to a judgment by the ECtHR, if the memorandum accompanying the draft legislation does not explicitly indicate that certain amendments were proposed as a result of such a judgment. The case law of the ECtHR is rarely invoked in discussions of draft legislation in Parliament. Legislation in response to the judgments of the ECtHR is considered as any other piece of legislation submitted by the government. There are practically no examples of legislation adopted by Bulgaria which were triggered by judgments of the ECtHR against other countries, neither are there any signs of influence of the general case law of the ECtHR on the legislative process.

The domestic courts have made efforts to incorporate the ECtHR's case law in their jurisprudence, but the results so far have been mixed. Some of the difficulties are the result of existing tradition and legal doctrine. Basic judicial tools of rights adjudication, like the assessment of 'proportionality' of interference with protected rights, or a distinction between levels of judicial scrutiny, used not to exist and to a large extent still do not exist. The dominant legal doctrine considered such review to be an exercise of discretionary powers, something preserved exclusively for the executive. Judicial review on the other hand was seen to be limited to a 'review of legality', considering whether a specific decision was taken by the competent body within its powers and following the procedure prescribed by law.[14] While both the Supreme Court of Cassation and the Supreme Administrative Court have increasingly relied in their case law on the jurisprudence of the ECtHR, domestic rights protection through the national courts has not sufficiently improved, particularly in cases affecting minority groups.

ECtHR case law has in the first place influenced the interpretation of certain provisions of domestic law as an additional frame of reference, rendering domestic law more compatible with international law. This is evidenced in several rulings of the Supreme Court of Cassation on pre-trial detention and on fair trial guarantees, as well as in judgments of the Supreme Administrative Court on asylum cases, which invoke Articles 5 and 6 of the Convention.[15] A second and more exceptional form of impact occurs when the ECtHR judgments lead to changes in well-established domestic case law, legal provisions and policies. There are far fewer examples of this. The most notable one is the introduction of judicial review on disability benefits and on the deportation of foreigners, with the second still falling short of the standards under the ECtHR case law.[16]

Besides the lack of a tradition of fundamental rights adjudication and a largely formalistic approach to jurisprudence, strong deference to the executive also made it difficult for minorities and disenfranchised groups in Bulgaria to receive protection through national courts. In general, domestic courts are quite self-restrained in exercising their powers, resulting in a position generally more favourable to the government rather than one protective of basic rights. Judgments of the ECtHR finding violations of the rights of individuals from minority groups have not been able to change that balance within the domestic courts.

Implementation and particularly the adoption of general measures is a time-consuming process. As the large majority of judgments against Bulgaria have been delivered since 2002, there has not been sufficient time for the process to be finalised.[17] In the majority of those cases the CoM has noted some positive steps taken by the Bulgarian authorities, such as the dissemination of the judgments, training activities, the adoption of new primary or secondary legislation and the adoption of policy documents. Yet, for a variety of reasons, full implementation has not been accomplished in the vast majority of cases and the CoM continues to monitor the vast majority of judgments that the Strasbourg Court has issued against Bulgaria.[18] While the payment of just compensation awarded by the Court and dissemination of judgments are unproblematic and nearly always granted, the ongoing monitoring of implementation apparently pertains to the failure to adopt general measures of implementation, as well as specific individual measures.

Effective implementation of the ECtHR's judgments, largely through legislative amendments by the government, has involved reforms that were not politically controversial. For instance, domestic implementation has resulted in reforms concerning the right to a fair trial,[19] reforms of the pre-detention procedure with the amendments to the Criminal Procedure Code in 2000,[20] shifts in courts' jurisprudence and legislative amendments to allow for judicial review in cases related to the welfare of persons with disabilities, as well as amendments to domestic legislation regulating the procedure on placing individuals in psychiatric hospitals.[21] Most of those reforms did not touch upon any ideological or politically sensitive issue, or upon any institutional arrangement that was favouring any particular political party. Rather, the reforms in response to Strasbourg Court judgments have led to changes in domestic institutional arrangements, making different government agencies more accountable to the public and limiting their discretionary powers through the introduction of judicial review. The public also had a favourable attitude towards such reforms and since they did not affect the power base of any political party, there was practically no political opposition to them. In addition, concerns about the negative effect on the country's accession to the EU (prior to membership) of losing a large number of cases before the ECtHR, as well as about the reputational and financial consequences of non-implementation, were sufficient to spur the government into action.

By contrast, the implementation of most cases affecting religious and ethnic minorities is still pending before the CoM. In fact, one of the main groups of pending cases against Bulgaria before the CoM, which involve important structural or complex problems, concerns excessive use of firearms by police officers during arrests and the failure to conduct effective investigations. Many of these judgments involve minorities and the Roma in particular.[22] Neither general nor individual measures of implementation have been undertaken. Judgments related to ethnic minority groups have been particularly problematic. They pose major challenges not only for institutional powers, but also for established political interests and widely held public beliefs. The changes and reforms that those judgments require are ideologically largely unacceptable to the majority of voters. Unsurprisingly, there are few political actors with a sufficient interest in the issue to see the implementation measures through. The cases of which the CoM has ceased monitoring implementation have been politically less sensitive, not touching upon the substantive rights and interests of minority groups.

Concerning the rights of religious minorities, the CoM has closed the monitoring of executions only in cases raising complaints on behalf of Jehovah's Witnesses. Some of those cases were related to the convictions of conscientious objectors and to the government's refusal to register Jehovah's Witnesses as a religious group in the country. With regard to the criminal convictions of Jehovah's Witnesses for refusing military service, the CoM decided that Bulgaria had taken all the measures needed to give effect to a friendly settlement that had been reached between the applicants and the government (see below). It introduced an effective alternative non-military service and an amnesty for those convicted for such offences[23] and agreed to register Jehovah's Witnesses as a religious group. Effective general implementation measures were easier in these cases, as they were neutral from a religious minority perspective. The introduction of legislation that allows for alternative national service also found support among broader segments of individuals who sought to make use of it on grounds that were not explicitly religious. Active and well-focused advocacy by Jehovah's Witnesses organisations both at home and abroad was instrumental in promoting domestic implementation in these cases, along with related legal reforms that expanded their rights of religious freedom.

In other cases related to religious minorities, the CoM has reviewed positively certain measures adopted domestically, but due to the lack of individual remedies and broader policy change it has still decided that they are not sufficient. Such measures include amendments to the Religious Denominations Act, which provided for a new procedure for registering religious communities. According to the newly adopted Religious Denominations Act of 2002,[24] a religious organisation was henceforth required to be registered not by the executive but by the courts. The executive could only provide a non-binding opinion to the court in the registration proceedings. Another domestic reform that was positively reviewed by the CoM took place in response to the judgment in *Al Nashif* v. *Bulgaria* in 2002. In that judgment, the ECtHR had held that the lack of judicial review of decisions to deport foreigners on grounds of threat to national security did not provide sufficient guarantees against arbitrariness. In 2002, the Supreme Administrative Court changed its case law to allow for judicial review of those decisions[25] and in 2007, Parliament adopted amendments to the Foreigners Act, explicitly providing for the right to judicial review of those decisions.[26] In spite of the changes to the Religious Denominations Act and the Foreigners Act, however, the lack of individual measures providing a remedy for the disaffected applicants in the cases before the ECtHR have apparently raised concerns about how the amended domestic legislation will be interpreted and applied in practice.

The amendments that introduced judicial review in all cases of deportation of foreigners did not specifically impact on minorities, and they were of a limited character. They did not allow for full judicial review of the decision to deport a foreigner, equivalent to the review performed by the ECtHR. They also did not allow the court to look into the evidence on the basis of which deportation was ordered and therefore to examine whether that decision excessively restricted the individual's right to personal and family life. In fact, the judicial review introduced did not circumscribe the unfettered discretionary powers of the government to deport a foreigner. In the end, despite the advocacy efforts by human rights groups in favour of a fully fledged implementation, the government chose to adopt measures that would allow it to maintain its control and powers over the deportation of foreigners, including those related to religious minorities.

The domestic implementation of the abovementioned measures in minority-related cases has been a rather lengthy and slow process. It took Parliament four years to adopt the amendments to the Religious Denominations Act. The first decision of the ECtHR that exposed this problem was a friendly settlement in March 1998 between the applicants and the government regarding the refusal of the government to register the Jehovah's Witnesses.[27] In 2000, the Court again ruled that the legislation regulating religious organisations created conditions for arbitrary government decisions.[28] The reform of the Religious Denominations Act, which provided for registration of religious organisations by the courts on the basis of clear requirements, was adopted only in December 2002.[29] The adoption of legislation on alternatives to military service took even longer. The delays in adopting such legislative amendments were due to the fact that the issue was politically sensitive. It touched upon the regulation of the two main religious groups present in the country, the Bulgarian Orthodox Church and the Muslims, as well as that of minority religions. Therefore, finding an acceptable legislative solution was a protracted process.

Even though effective legislation on registering religious communities has been adopted, policies of government intervention have in fact continued. The issues raised in the series of cases related to government intervention in the internal affairs of Muslims in Bulgaria have not been adequately resolved. In those cases, the ECtHR ruled that the government did not act in a neutral and unbiased manner in resolving a conflict between rival Muslim leaders.[30] Despite the legislative amendments that formally removed the government's role from the process of registering the leadership of a religious community, Muslims still do not enjoy a free and transparent process for electing their leaders.

The legislative amendments that transferred the registering of religious leaderships to the courts did not bring greater clarity and transparency to this process, nor did they end government interference in it. Government elites, who had a political interest in the issue, were still able to influence the selection of Muslim religious leaders. In 2004, following a court decision declaring a national conference of Muslims in Bulgaria unlawful for procedural failures, Sofia City Court took an unprecedented step that had no legal basis under domestic law. It appointed on its own initiative three individuals to the joint leadership of the Muslims in Bulgaria for an interim period. At the end of 2005 two rival conferences of Muslims were held, each electing a different leader and making a request with the courts to be registered as the overall leader of the Muslim religion. Rather than deciding this dispute on the basis of evidence regarding the legitimacy of the two rival election conferences and on the basis of the applicable procedure, the court simply registered one of the rival leaderships with very limited reasons to justify its decisions. The leadership it registered was the one supported by the DPS political party, representing ethnic Turks and Muslims, which was a coalition partner in two successive governments, between 2001 and 2009.

However, the rival faction appealed against the decision of the city court (the court of first instance), and it was repealed by the appellate court. Sofia City Court still issued an official certificate to the Muslim leadership it registered, declaring it the legitimate leadership, and allowing the person presiding over it to continue to perform the function of Chief Mufti as of June 2008, in effect ignoring the decision of the appellate court. In a judgment of 8 January 2008, the Supreme Court upheld the judgment of the appellate court. It declared the 2005 conference of Muslims unlawful and the Mufti elected at that conference illegitimate.[31] This, however, did not prevent that same Chief Mufti, who had been registered in 2005 by Sofia City Court, from continuing to act as the religious leader of the Muslim community. These developments discredited the legislative reforms concerning the registration of religious groups. They clearly demonstrated that in cases where there is sufficient political interest in maintaining the status quo, as in these Muslim-related cases, amendment of the respective legislative provisions did not in fact change government policy. In these cases DPS has been determined to control and influence the leadership of the Muslim religion.

The legislative amendments in the deportation of foreigners following the *Al-Nashif* judgment and the related changes in the domestic case law clearly did not meet the standards set by the ECtHR. A few months after the 2002 judgment in *Al-Nashif* v. *Bulgaria*, the Supreme Administrative Court changed its case law to allow for judicial review of those decisions.[32] The judicial review allowed by the domestic courts, however, has been very limited: it does not include review of the evidence on the basis of which the person is considered a threat to national security. This is clearly not up to the standards set by the ECtHR. The related legislative amendments suffered from the same deficiency. Later, the ECtHR explicitly ruled so in its judgment in *C.G. and others* v. *Bulgaria*, in which the Bulgarian courts had approved the deportation of a foreigner without collecting and reviewing any evidence in support of the government's claim that the person was a threat to national security.[33]

The Bulgarian government also failed to adopt the necessary individual measures with regard to the applicants in the cases of *Al-Nashif* and *Musa*.[34] In both cases the applicants were deported from the country on the grounds that they had been involved in religious activities aimed at the Muslim community in the country. On the basis of the judgment of the ECtHR finding a violation, the applicant requested the reopening of the domestic judicial proceedings to have his appeal reviewed on merit. As the deportation was the result of three separate administrative decisions – a withdrawal of the residence permit, an expulsion order and a ban on re-entering the country – three separate judicial proceedings were opened. While the withdrawal of the residence permit and the expulsion order were declared unlawful by the domestic courts, for lack of evidence that Daruish Al-Nashif or Ahmad Musa presented a threat to national security, the ban on re-entering the country was confirmed by the courts without any analysis of the circumstances and the proportionality of the measure.[35] An identical development followed the judgment of the ECtHR in the *Musa* case. The domestic courts refused to annul the ban preventing Musa from re-entering the country, without examining the existing evidence and without considering the proportionality of the measure.[36] As a result, despite the judgments of the ECtHR, the applicants were not allowed back in the country.

In other minority cases, the measures that were required as a result of the judgments of the ECtHR did not involve the introduction of new legislation, but rather changes in administrative policies and individual measures, to remedy the individual violations. In cases related to the right to peaceful assembly and association of those Bulgarian citizens who identify themselves as Macedonians, no such change of policy and no effective individual measures were taken. Despite five judgments of the ECtHR in their favour, their efforts to have an organisation or a political party registered are still unsuccessful. Their ability to establish their own organisation or political party has been vehemently opposed by all Bulgarian political parties, without any exception, and their members in the European Parliament have actively lobbied to prevent a formal statement on the matter.[37] In November 2006 the Bulgarian Minister of Foreign Affairs commented on the enforcement of the *United Macedonian Organisation Ilinden – PIRIN and others* v. *Bulgaria* judgment as follows: 'The judgment of the European Court of Human Rights of 20 October 2006 does not require [the] registration of the party. The

Bulgarian government was ordered to pay a fine, which it paid, and there are no more legal consequences of this judgement.'[38]

Following the judgment of the ECtHR in *United Macedonian Organisation Ilinden – PIRIN and others*,[39] which found that the ban of the political party was in violation of Article 11 of the Convention, two further attempts to register their political party have been rejected by the domestic courts. The efforts of the members of the party to have it registered were obstructed by the local police, who summoned individual members to police premises and questioned them about the events related to registration. In response to complaints by party members, the CoM asked the Bulgarian authorities to acknowledge the list of 5,000 party members collected for the first registration attempt. Despite this explicit request, the Supreme Court of Cassation insisted on the refusal to register the party on the sole ground that no fresh list of 5,000 individual party members had been presented, a requirement which had not even existed when the party was first banned in 2000.[40] There has been at least one case where a public rally organised by the group was banned, and efforts to have the association registered have so far been delayed by the domestic courts. A public gathering planned for 22 April 2007 was initially approved by the mayor of the town of Sandanski but later banned by the regional governor, who reasoned that the organisation that submitted the request was not registered according to the Constitution and the laws of Bulgaria.[41] This lack of change in policies is rooted in very strongly held public beliefs about national history and national identity, which find the very assertion that there are ethnic Macedonians in Bulgaria, offensive. Such widespread beliefs among ethnic Bulgarians in the country, which cross party political lines, profoundly influence the decision-making process in every institution and at every level, including the courts.

The lack of domestic implementation has also been evident in the cases of racial violence against Roma. Despite the fact that domestic legislation could well be improved in sanctioning racist violence,[42] no efforts in this direction have been taken. No effective changes have been introduced in investigation and prosecution instructions and manuals, thus leaving criminal law enforcement policies, which brought the violations found by the ECtHR in the first place, intact. No individual measures were taken in those cases of police brutality against Roma and cases of racist violence either. In a number of cases the ECtHR found violations of the right to life and the prohibition of torture and inhuman treatment, on account of the use of force by the police. In some of the cases, it also found that there was insufficient investigation into evidence that the violence was racially motivated.[43] In *Nachova*, the Prosecution Office reopened the criminal investigation, only to close it shortly afterwards, while in *Angelova and Iliev* the proceedings are still pending. The reopened criminal investigations did not proceed speedily and it is still unclear whether criminal charges will be brought and whether the case will proceed to court. In all other cases there have been no steps to investigate and prosecute those guilty of use of illegal force. In March 2011, the Bulgarian Helsinki Committee communicated to the CoM a highly critical assessment pointing to the failure of successive governments to reform the legislation governing police use of force and firearms.[44] As in the ethnic Macedonians' cases, implementation in the Roma-related cases runs up against deeply and widely held prejudices against this minority group. Despite the advocacy by human rights groups, such prejudices inhibit successful implementation measures that do not enjoy any notable political or public support.

FACTORS AFFECTING DOMESTIC IMPLEMENTATION AND POLICY CHANGE

Experience over the past couple of years has demonstrated that general measures in response to judgments of the ECtHR that do not touch upon politically sensitive issues are eventually adopted. There has been a marked tendency, however, to adopt such general measures with delays, which have been significant in certain cases. Where the government has faced a potentially large number of complaints to the ECtHR on a relatively technical issue, it has acted faster, submitting legislative amendments to Parliament, sometimes within a year of the ECtHR's judgment.[45] In other cases, where the threat of multiple complaints and violations has not been so significant, the government has felt under less time pressure to adopt general measures. The amendments of domestic legislation regulating the procedure on placing individuals in psychiatric hospitals took four years, between October 2000, when the ECtHR found a violation of the right to liberty in *Varbanov* v. *Bulgaria*, and August 2004, when Parliament reformed the procedure.[46] The delays in that case did not result from any opposition against reform, but rather from the low priority given by the government to those amendments, which were adopted as part of a more general overhaul of the Health Act.[47]

While eventually adopted, even with delays, implementation measures have been rather restrictive, addressing in a minimalist manner the specific issues raised in the judgments of the ECtHR, and failing to spur a broader policy change. This is for instance evidenced even in non-minority cases, such as those concerning access to judicial review for people with disabilities and individuals on social welfare, in which there was sufficient public sympathy and support for the victims of rights violations and a more general acceptance of the reasons behind the judgments of the ECtHR. Overall, domestic compliance with the ECtHR's case law has been most effective on fair trial and other procedural issues, but much less effective on political and equality rights, particularly those of ethnic and religious minorities.

Domestic implementation of ECtHR judgments is defined by a marked difference between politically non-controversial or less controversial issues, and issues related to basic political rights of minority groups, religious rights and the right not to be discriminated against. Of the second category, the only exception in terms of effective execution were the cases brought by Jehovah's Witnesses, related to the right to freedom of association and the right to conscientious objection. In these cases, what seemed to have made a difference was the relatively small size of this religious minority, which made the change in policy politically less sensitive and consequential, as well as the community's successful organisation and advocacy strategy. The community enjoyed international support and strong transnational networking, and its litigation in the ECtHR was clearly aimed at legal reform that would enable its organisation to be registered, as well as provide for an alternative to military service. For this reason the applicants engaged the government in negotiations already before a final judgment of the ECtHR was issued, and reached a friendly settlement with it. Official registration has allowed the community to develop and apparently has granted it additional legitimacy, thus increasing public tolerance towards the group. While in the late 1990s the media were regularly publishing negative materials on religious minorities, including Jehovah's Witnesses, describing them as a threat to the physical and mental health of its members, some ten years later such publications have subsided, reflecting a change in public attitudes.[48]

In all other cases related to ethnic or religious minority groups, however, domestic implementation has involved either very limited measures or no measures at all. It continues to be monitored by the CoM, despite the fact that in some of those cases judgments were delivered more than six years ago. In these cases, the policies that lead to the violations of rights established by the ECtHR reflect strong negative public attitudes towards minority groups, and they have enjoyed wide political and public support. While the government has occasionally granted ethnic Macedonians permission to hold public rallies under limited circumstances, it has continued to implement a general overall ban. A change in government policy towards this group is unlikely, given strong public attitudes against such change and vocal opposition by virtually all major political parties against allowing ethnic Macedonians to enjoy full rights of association. The media are also passionately supportive of such policies, so any policy change towards ethnic Macedonians would be politically costly. Finally, the group itself is too small to have any political clout or electoral influence.

Similarly, strong negative public attitudes towards the Roma have blocked meaningful implementation measures. While numerically significant, the Roma have not been able to organise politically to pressure for the adoption of policies in their favour. At the same time, strong prejudice against the Roma has triggered the ascent of anti-Roma right-wing political parties. In such a political climate, there is precious little domestic support to change a policy of neglect towards racial violence against the Roma, despite the numerous judgments of the ECtHR.

Policies of governmental interference and control over religious groups also enjoy public support and are not likely to change significantly. Despite the introduction of some changes to the laws on the deportation of foreigners and on the registration of religious groups, domestic law is still not in compliance with the case law of the ECtHR and there is interference in the governance of religious groups. The fact that those cases affected a religious minority group, which was perceived as a national security issue, means that both courts and the media have been more deferential to the police and there has been no public pressure on the Ministry of Interior for effective implementation and policy change. Similarly, no changes have taken place with respect to the governance of the Muslim religion. Muslims in Bulgaria still do not enjoy the freedom to elect their leadership in a transparent and lawful manner, despite legislative changes that removed the role of the government in that process and transferred it to the courts.

In conclusion, factors like government will, judicial deference to the executive and public attitudes decisively affect the domestic implementation of ECtHR judgments and the likelihood that these judgments will result in change of policy. Where the issue raised by a judgment of the ECtHR is more of a technical one, which does not negatively affect any political or institutional interest, or where there is more significant public support, there is a greater likelihood of a change of policy resulting from that judgment of the ECtHR. In such a scenario the prospect of multiple convictions on the same issue and multiple damage awards by the ECtHR could also play a role in prompting a relatively fast overhaul of policy on the part of the government. Where dominant political or institutional interests oppose reform and there is no pronounced public support, domestic implementation is partial or thoroughly resisted, and it is unlikely to lead to rights-expansive reform and policy change that enhances the protection of minorities.

Notes

1. The Constitutional Court only has the powers to interpret the constitutionality of parliamentary legislation in the abstract and thus hears very few cases. In 2005, 2006 and 2007 it heard ten, nine and ten cases respectively, including those not related to basic rights.

2. The complexity and variety of issues reviewed by the ECtHR is evident in the cases concerning two of the rights under the European Convention of Human Rights: the right to liberty and the right to a fair trial. Violations regarding the right to liberty were found, *inter alia*, with respect to adequate procedures for protection against abuse in pre-trial detention, detention for the purpose of deportation, detention for psychiatric treatment, right to appeal of pre-trial detention, and psychiatric detention. Violations of the right to a fair trial were found as a result of lack of access to court in disputes over social welfare and

disability benefits, unfair dismissal of some state employees, and in various criminal proceedings settings.

3. Identical steps were taken by the government also with respect to the biggest religious group in the country, the Bulgarian Orthodox Church, where the government intervened on behalf of one of the groups in an internal dispute and where the Court found a violation of religious freedoms too. See ECtHR, *Holy Synod of the Bulgarian Orthodox Church (Metropolitan Inokentiy) and others* v. *Bulgaria* (nos. 412/03, 35677/04), 16 September 2010.

4. Of a total of 180 judgments delivered by the ECtHR as of May 2008, in 120 cases representation was provided by an NGO or the lawyers representing the victims were affiliated with an NGO.

5. The three human rights groups providing legal representation before the ECtHR are the Bulgarian Helsinki Committee, based in Sofia, a member of the International Helsinki Federation; Bulgarian Lawyers for Human Rights, also based in Sofia; and the European Integration and Human Rights Association, a human rights group based in Plovdiv.

6. Human rights groups have represented the applicants in ECtHR, *Hasan and Chaush* v. *Bulgaria* (no. 30985/96), 26 October 2000; *Supreme Holy Council of the Muslim Community* v. *Bulgaria* (no. 39023/97), 16 December 2004; *Al-Nashif and others* v. *Bulgaria* (no. 50963/99), 20 June 2002; *Musa and others* v. *Bulgaria* (no. 61259/00), 11 January 2007; *Bashir and others* v. *Bulgaria* (no. 65028/01), 14 June 2007; *Hasan* v. *Bulgaria* (no. 54323/00), 14 June 2007; *Angelova and Iliev* v. *Bulgaria* (no. 55523/00), 26 July 2007; ECtHR, *United Macedonian Organisation Ilinden and Ivanov* v. *Bulgaria* (no. 44079/98), 20 October 2005; ECtHR, *Ivanov and others* v. *Bulgaria* (no. 46336/99), 24 November 2005; ECtHR, *United Macedonian Organisation Ilinden – PIRIN and others* v. *Bulgaria* (no. 59489/00), 20 October 2005; *United Macedonian Organisation Ilinden and others* v. *Bulgaria* (no. 59491/00), 19 January 2006.

7. The proactive litigation work of these groups often followed monitoring work, with the factual findings of monitoring work used for an analysis of the existing legal problems. Examples of this approach have been cases brought to the ECtHR on the right of a criminal defendant to a lawyer, prison conditions, psychiatric patients' rights, juvenile justice and deportation of asylum seekers.

8. Roma racial violence cases litigated with the assistance of the ERRC were ECtHR, *Assenov and others* v. *Bulgaria* (no. 24760/94), 28 October 1998; *Angelova and Iliev* v. *Bulgaria*; *Velikova* v. *Bulgaria* (no. 41488/98), 18 May 2000; *Anguelova* v. *Bulgaria* (no. 38361/97), 13 June 2002; *Ognyanova and Choban* v. *Bulgaria* (no. 46317/99), 23 February 2006; *Tzekov* v. *Bulgaria* (no. 45500/99), 23 February 2006; *Nachova and others* v. *Bulgaria* (nos. 43577/98, 43579/98), 6 July 2005.

9. Elsewhere in the region the ERRC initiated cases before the ECtHR on other issues as well, such as school segregation. For instance, see ECtHR, *D.H.* v. *Czech Republic* (no. 57325/00), 13 November 2007.

10. Violation of Art. 14 was found in the cases of *Nachova* v. *Bulgaria* and *Angelova and Iliev* v. *Bulgaria*.

11. ECtHR, *Hasan and Chaush* v. *Bulgaria*; *Supreme Holy Council of the Muslim Community* v. *Bulgaria*.

12. The ECtHR refused to find such a violation in the following cases: ECtHR, *Assenov and others* v. *Bulgaria*; *Velikova* v. *Bulgaria*; *Anguelova* v. *Bulgaria*; *Ognyanova and Choban* v. *Bulgaria*.

13. Since Bulgaria acceded to the ECHR in the 1990s, the ECtHR has issued 395 judgments against it (out of a total of 437 concerning Bulgaria). See *Overview 1959–2011* (Strasbourg: European Court of Human Rights, 2012).

14. This legal formalism and tradition of deference to government action is still very dominant. As a result, the ECtHR on many occasions found violations of the right to an effective remedy under Article 13 of the Convention, in addition to the basic rights violations, precisely because of the refusal of the domestic court to assess the proportionality of government interference with basic rights.

15. For a sample of such decisions, see Ruling No. 24, Case No. 210/2003, Criminal Chamber Supreme Court; Ruling No. 76, Case No. 507/1997, Criminal Chamber Supreme Court; Ruling No. 593, Case No. 203/2004, Criminal Chamber Supreme Court of Cassation; Judgment No. 99, Case No. 1033/2004, Criminal Chamber Supreme Court; Judgment No. 204, Case No. 18/1999, Criminal Chamber Supreme Court; Judgment No. 209, Case No. 103/2000, Criminal Chamber Supreme Court; Judgment No. 231, Case No. 111/2002, Criminal Chamber Supreme Court.

16. On disability benefits see Ruling No. 1580, Case No. 4869/1998, First Chamber Supreme Administrative Court, and on deportation of foreigners see Ruling No. 8910, Case No. 7722/2004, Fifth Chamber Supreme Administrative Court.

17. The dynamic of judgments against Bulgaria delivered by the Court is quite telling. In 1997, 1998 and 1999 there was one judgment delivered against Bulgaria per year; in 2000, 2001 and 2002 there were three judgments per year. From then onwards, however, there was a dramatic outbreak: in 2003 eleven judgments were delivered, in 2004 twenty-seven, in 2005 twenty-three, in 2006 forty-five and in 2007 fifty-three. In 2008 there were thirty-two judgments delivered as of June.

18. By the end of 2011, 344 judgments against Bulgaria were still pending execution before the CoM. At the end of the same year, judgments against Bulgaria accounted for 9 per cent of all leading cases pending execution before the CoM. See Council of Europe Committee of Ministers, *Supervision of the Execution of Judgments and Decisions of the European Court of Human Rights: Annual Report 2011* (Strasbourg: Council of Europe, 2012), pp. 37, 49.

19. See CoM, ResDH(2007)69 in the cases of ECtHR, *Pramov* v. *Bulgaria*, (no. 42986/98), 30 September 2004 and *Neshev* v. *Bulgaria* (no. 40897/98), 28 October 2004.

20. See CoM, ResDH(2000)109, 2 October 2000, in the case of *Assenov and others* v. *Bulgaria*; ResDH(2000)110, 2 October 2000, in the case of *Nikolova* v. *Bulgaria*.

21. See amendments to the Health Act, *Darzhaven Vestnik*, no. 70, 10 August 2004.

22. This is the *Nachova/Velikova* group of cases, as it is described in the latest report of the CoM. Committee of Ministers, *Supervision of the Execution of Judgments of the European Court of Human Rights*, p. 41.

23. CoM, ResDH(2004)32 of 15 June 2004 in the case of *Stefanov* v. *Bulgaria*.
24. See Religious Denominations Act, *Darzhaven Vestnik*, no. 120, 29 December 2002.
25. See Ruling No. 117, Supreme Administrative Court, 2002.
26. See Section 42, Foreigners in the Republic of Bulgaria Act, *Darzhaven Vestnik*, no 65, July 2007.
27. See ECommHR, *Khristiansko Sdruzhenie 'Svideteli na Iehova'* v. *Bulgaria* (no. 28626/95), 3 July 1997.
28. ECtHR, *Hasan and Chaush* v. *Bulgaria*.
29. See Religious Denominations Act, *Darzhaven Vestnik*, no. 120, 29 December 2002.
30. See ECtHR, *Hasan and Chaush* v. *Bulgaria*; *Supreme Holy Council of the Muslim Community* v. *Bulgaria*.
31. See Supreme Court of Cassation, Judgment No. 982 of 8 January 2008, case file 572/2007.
32. See Supreme Administrative Court, Ruling No. 117 of 2002.
33. See ECtHR, *C.G. and others* v. *Bulgaria* (no. 1365/07), 24 April 2008.
34. See ECtHR, *Al-Nashif and others* v. *Bulgaria*; *Musa and others* v. *Bulgaria*.
35. In its final judgment the Supreme Administrative Court refused to consider whether there was evidence supporting the claim that the applicant was a threat to national security and reasoned that the ban on entering the country was not raised as an issue in the proceedings before the ECtHR. See Supreme Administrative Court, Judgment No. 3976 of 3 April 2008, case file 12452/2007.
36. See judgment of the Supreme Administrative Court of 3 April 2008 in *Ahmad Musa* v. *National Security Agency*.
37. See 'Polititsite edinni sreshtu popravkata v EP za "makedonsko maltsinstvo"', Mediapool website, 14 November 2006, available at http://www.mediapool.bg/show/?storyid=123382 (accessed 14 September 2012).
38. See 'Prisadata na Strasburg sreshtu Balgaria e izpalnena . . .' (The Strasbourg sentence against Bulgaria is implemented . . .), 4 November 2006. The article was published in the electronic news portal 'Focus' (www.focus-news.net).
39. ECtHR, *United Macedonian Organisation Ilinden – PIRIN and others* v. *Bulgaria*.
40. See Supreme Court of Cassation, Judgment No. 762 of 11 October 2007, case file 753/2007.
41. Order No. OA-158/18.04.2007 of the Blagoevgrad Regional Governor.
42. The only explicit provision of domestic law against racist violence is Article 162 para. 2 of the Criminal Code, defining 'racist violence' as a crime that carries a punishment of up to four years' imprisonment. The crimes of assault, bodily injury and murder do not carry a heavier punishment. See Articles 116, 124 and 131 of the Criminal Code, *Darzhaven Vestnik*, no. 26, 2 April 1968, last amended in *Darzhaven Vestnik*, no. 102, 22 December 2009.
43. See ECtHR, *Angelova and Iliev* v. *Bulgaria*; *Velikova* v. *Bulgaria*; *Anguelova* v. *Bulgaria*; *Ognyanova and Choban* v. *Bulgaria*; *Tzekov* v. *Bulgaria*; *Nachova and others* v. *Bulgaria*.
44. CoM, DH-DD(2011)298, 'Communication from an NGO and reply of the

government in the cases of *Velikova* v. *Bulgaria* (41488/98) and *Nachova and others* v. *Bulgaria* (43577/98)', 26 April 2011.

45. General measures that were adopted relatively fast were the introduction of a new habeas corpus procedure and other basic rights guarantees in the Criminal Procedure Code in 1999, effective as of January 2000 (Criminal Procedure Code Amendment and Supplement Act), *Darzhaven Vestnik*, no. 70, 6 August 1999) and court fees in the State Liability for Damages Act, effective from 30 May 2008 (see *Darzhaven Vestnik*, no. 43, 29 April 2008).

46. See ECtHR, *Varbanov* v. *Bulgaria*, (no. 31365/96), 5 October 2000; Health Act, *Darzhaven Vestnik*, no. 70, 10 August 2004, effective as of 1 January 2005.

47. Health Act, *Darzhaven Vestnik*, no. 70, 10 August 2004, effective as of 1 January 2005.

48. A good example of that change is provided by a big public event held in Sofia in June 2007 by Jehovah's Witnesses where attempts by a nationalist group to boycott it, as they had successfully done in the past, manifestly failed because of lack of public or media support for such actions. See 'Ot VMRO protestirakha sreshtu kongres na "Svideteli na Iekhova"', Darik News website, 26 July 2008, available at http://dariknews.bg/view_article.php?article_id=275952&audio_id=23767 (accessed 14 September 2012).

Chapter 6

Under what conditions do national authorities implement the European Court of Human Rights' rulings? Religious and ethnic minorities in Greece

Dia Anagnostou and Evangelia Psychogiopoulou

Courts have often served as an alternative arena for minorities to claim their rights when other avenues of political participation are closed or ineffective. While not specifically intended to protect minorities, the European Court of Human Rights (hereafter ECtHR) has pre-eminently provided such an arena. Over time, it has developed a substantial case law related to minority rights by creatively, and at times expansively, interpreting the fundamental rights contained in the European Convention of Human Rights (hereafter ECHR or Convention).[1] However, the ability of courts to uphold the rights of minorities and to influence how governments treat them has been a highly controversial issue.[2] Such influence is contingent and varies across different issue areas and perhaps time periods. While judicial bodies lack the power to enforce their decisions, their authoritative interpretations of minority rights claims can have important legal and policy-related effects. This chapter examines the conditions under which the judgments of the ECtHR can promote rights-expansive legal reforms and domestic policy change pertaining to minorities by focusing on the case of Greece.

Small but salient historical minorities, religious and ethnic ones, remained excluded for most of the post-World War II period from Greece's political system and society. The preservation of emergency legislation which had been enacted during the civil war of the 1940s into the Cold War period undermined the enforcement of constitutional rights guarantees against state abuses, particularly for political or ethnic groups that were considered actually or potentially disloyal to the Greek nation.[3] The existence of non-Orthodox religious communities, as well as Turkish and Muslim minorities, presented a particular challenge for the dominant conceptions of nationhood while at the same time being viewed as a severe national security threat. The advent of a military regime in 1967 prompted Greece to withdraw from the Council of Europe (CoE) in the face of the country's imminent expulsion from it. A few years later, the transition to democracy in 1974 paved the way for the restitution of constitutional rights, as well as for the country's re-entry into the CoE and the ECHR system. Nonetheless, while constitutionalism and basic rights were restored for citizens in general, ethnic and religious minorities continued to have their rights, whether de jure or de facto, curtailed.

Following Greece's acceptance of the right to individual petition in 1985, individuals from religious and ethnic minorities were among the first to resort to and seek redress in the Strasbourg-based Court.[4] Domestic courts had not been sympathetic to their claims concerning restrictions to the freedom to practise their religion or to set up associations. The first individual petition against Greece to be lodged with the Court concerned the right to religious freedom (Art. 9 ECHR) and originated from Minos Kokkinakis, a Jehovah's Witness (JW). The *Kokkinakis* case along with others, such as *Manoussakis*, would prove instrumental in defining the basic parameters of the ECtHR's religious freedom jurisprudence as a whole. Over the next fifteen years, JWs lodged a total of ten applications in the ECtHR on the basis of various Convention provisions, and succeeded in persuading the Court that their rights had been violated nearly on all cases. Similar to JW litigation in the US Supreme Court,[5] the relevant case law can be seen as a precursor to the ECtHR's growing involvement with minority claims. From the 1990s onwards, an increasing number of petitions were also brought by individuals from the Turkish Muslim and Slav-speaking communities inhabiting the north of Greece. These have led to several condemnations of the Greek state for breach of the Convention, mainly with regard to the freedoms of expression and association.[6]

Since the early 1990s, the Strasbourg Court has issued about a dozen judgments in which it condemned Greece for violating the rights of non-Orthodox individuals. In the process of their implementation by Greek authorities, these judgments have had a major impact on promoting the liberalisation of religious rights. This is evidenced in the dramatic decline of relevant petitions after 2000 both in domestic courts and in the ECtHR. By contrast, a series of adverse judgments originating in claims from Slav Macedonians and Turkish Muslims have on the whole been met with resistance, essentially remaining 'dead letters'. How influential have the ECtHR's judgments been (if at all) in altering Greek law and policy pertaining to minorities in a more Convention-friendly and rights-expansive direction? Why have national authorities in Greece been responsive in implementing the ECtHR's judgments concerning non-Orthodox religious communities in a rights-expansive direction, while they have firmly resisted this in the judgments pertaining to ethnic minorities? What accounts for such different implementation responses concerning the two kinds of minority groups, towards which public attitudes have been equally prejudicial, if not hostile?

This chapter compares the implementation of judgments originating in petitions by members of non-Orthodox communities (mainly JWs) with the refusal of national authorities to give effect to the ECtHR's judgments concerning the rights of individuals that assert an ethnic minority identity.

The first part of this chapter examines the patterns of litigation in the ECtHR on the part of the minorities under study, as well as the relevant judgments issued by the Court. The second part explores how national authorities implemented (or failed to do so) the relevant case law. Finally, the third part identifies and discusses the factors which conditioned the Greek authorities' implementation performance for both sets of cases.

This chapter argues that ECtHR judgments do not prompt in themselves legal and policy change, but can act as important catalysts in a process of change. This is decisively conditioned by the socio-political circumstances surrounding the dispute which forms the object of the Court's review. The analysis of the Greek case shows that the ECtHR's potential to contribute to domestic policy change is more convincingly depicted by the so-called 'constrained court' model, identified in Gerald Rosenberg's classic study.[7] Judiciaries are on the whole extremely limited in their ability to bring about policy and social change, unless their decisions are already supported by dominant political, government or other elites. At the same time, the Greek case also reveals that the ECtHR's judgments and the legal mobilisation that surrounds them can have, and have had, important constitutive effects. They influence the views and perceptions of minority actors themselves in ways that may have important ramifications for political and social change.

LITIGATION BY RELIGIOUS AND ETHNIC MINORITIES IN THE ECtHR

The fact that the first instances of Greek litigation in the Strasbourg Court concerned religious freedom was not accidental. The constitutional recognition of the Eastern Orthodox Church of Greece (OCG) as the prevailing religion in Greece sets the overarching frame defining relations between the church and the state.[8] Article 13 of the Greek Constitution, in particular, establishes that freedom of worship is only protected for 'known religions', that is, religions whose worship is not against the public order or morals. Such kinds of assessment have routinely been made by Greek state officials, who examine applications for establishing a place of worship, and in practice have resulted in discrimination against non-Orthodox faiths.

The restrictions of non-Orthodox religious rights, though, would not have come under the purview of the ECtHR without the activism of JWs. Less than a handful of committed lawyers were willing to defend them at a time (the late 1980s) when, with few exceptions, Greek lawyers in general were still unaware of the Convention and its judicial arm. From 1988 onwards, JWs lodged ten cases with the ECtHR, which found Greece in violation of ECHR provisions in nearly all of them.[9] Lawyers from the association of JWs, which was in close contact with the broader religious community, selected cases that reflected the full gamut of problems and the institutional, legal and political constraints facing JWs. Nine of the ten JW cases in the ECtHR were defended by three lawyers who were also law professors. The leading one was Phaedon Vegleris, a professor with a scholarly record and activist involvement in the protection of constitutional rights. After the transition to democracy in 1974, Vegleris became president of the Hellenic League of Human Rights, the oldest Greek NGO in the field of human rights. In 1985, he provided legal defence to the first individual to file a case against Greece, Minos Kokkinakis, whose persecution on grounds of proselytism was found to violate religious freedom under the ECHR. The experience and the commitment of Vegleris, combined with the activism of the JWs' association, led to the first wave of Strasbourg-based litigation. Subsequently, a larger number of petitions raising religious freedom claims were filed by members of other non-Orthodox Christian communities, such as Catholics, Old Calendarists and Pentecostalists.

Recourse of Turkish Muslims to the Strasbourg tribunal had an early start too but it took several years to become more concerted and widespread, as well as succeeding in getting a favourable response from the Court. Despite the restitution of constitutional rights after 1974, members of this community remained subject to a series of informal but widespread restrictive measures, including the arbitrary deprivation of Greek citizenship, which thoroughly curtailed their rights. Cross-party consensus that such measures were necessary in the name of national interests and in order to combat the 'Turkish threat' demoted the Muslim minority within the Greek political system, which turned to its kin-state (Turkey) for political support and advocacy.[10]

Litigation in the Strasbourg Court started to be employed as an alternative minority strategy alongside political mobilisation. A number of factors account for the hesitant, limited and largely unsuccessful use of litigation in the ECtHR in the earlier period (the late 1980s and first half of the 1990s) after the individual right to petition was accepted by Greece: the ambivalent role of Turkey, which exercises far-reaching influence in minority politics in Thrace; the survival of an inter-war minority treaty (the 1923 Lausanne Treaty), which predominantly defines the legal frame of protection and provides for the role of the kin-state; the absence of an independent civil society among the minority; and the lack of adequate and/or competent legal advice and support.[11] In the late 1990s, Turkey's attitude towards minority litigation in the ECtHR began to change and become more accepting. The quality of legal support also improved with assistance from Turkey and with the growing knowledge and experience of lawyers who had handled cases in Strasbourg.[12]

For the most part, Strasbourg litigation by Turkish Muslims, as well as by Slav-Macedonians, has proved a form of political action and protest against the Greek authorities. Taking recourse to Strasbourg has not simply been intended to gain legal correction of an alleged violation of the Convention; it has also aimed to express diffused grievances about the circumscribed level of protection afforded to minority identities in Greece by employing a rights-based discourse and arguments. The process of selection of muftis in Thrace and the right to establish associations are the two main issues that Turkish Muslims have pursued systematically through litigation in the ECtHR. Violations of Articles 9 and 11 of the ECHR have indeed been found in several instances. For Slav-Macedonians, their ability to establish associations and political parties defending their rights has been the subject of ECtHR litigation, which led to two condemnations on grounds of Article 11 ECHR.

DO NATIONAL AUTHORITIES IMPLEMENT THE ECtHR'S RULINGS CONCERNING MINORITIES?

By reviewing the resolutions issued by the Committee of Ministers (CoM) together with material obtained through interviews and from the press, this section examines the measures that Greek authorities have so far taken in order to redress the human rights violations identified by the ECtHR. The implementation of the ECtHR's rulings pronounced in response to applications by individuals from non-Orthodox communities has displayed significant variation. It has ranged from mere dissemination of the judgments to substantial legislative and constitutional modifications. Six cases brought by JWs, Pentecostalists and Old Calendarists challenged the restrictions in establishing non-Orthodox places of worship and the Greek legal provisions prohibiting proselytism.[13] Two of these cases ended with a friendly settlement.[14] General measures in the remaining four judgments involved notable changes in administrative practice, but not any legislative reform. In all cases, implementation was accompanied by the dissemination of judgments to competent judicial authorities, along with their publication on the website of the State Legal Council and in widely read legal journals.

Both in the landmark first case of *Kokkinakis* and later in *Larissis and others*, the dissemination of the judgments to raise awareness of the Court's case law among Greek judges was the main general measure accepted by the CoM as apposite to align judicial practice with the ECHR requirements. It took three and a half years for the CoM to close *Kokkinakis*, but nearly six years to close the case in *Larissis and others*. In *Kokkinakis*, the Court came close to finding the domestic legal ban on proselytism to be at odds with the Convention, while in *Larissis and others* the ECtHR found fault with improper interpretation of the relevant legislation on proselytism by the national courts. Besides payment of just satisfaction, the applicants in *Larissis and others* were also able to seek annulment of their criminal convictions on the basis of Law No. 2865/2000, which allowed for the reopening of domestic proceedings in criminal cases. Perhaps one reason for the lengthier process of implementation in this case was the anticipated introduction of this law, on the basis of which proselytism convictions could be reversed.

In *Manoussakis and others*, where the Court condemned existing legal and administrative restrictions in establishing non-Orthodox places of worship, the applicants were promptly granted such a permit in the next few months following the judgment. When the condemnation in *Manoussakis* came in 1996, two more cases involving the persecution of JWs for operating a place of worship without permit were pending before the Court (*Pentidis and others* and *Tsavachidis*). The Greek government pursued friendly settlements accommodating the claims of the applicants, evidently aware that with the precedent of *Manoussakis*, they would result in further condemnations.

Although the applicants in *Manoussakis* quickly received a permit to establish a place of worship, it was nine years before the CoM considered the case to be implemented with regard to general measures. Based on the content of the resolution issued by the CoM, it can be conjectured that it took some years for the Greek government to provide proof that Greek judicial interpretations had actually aligned with the ECtHR's judgment.

The condemnations in two further cases, *Valsamis* and *Efstratiou*, on grounds of failure to provide a domestic remedy (Article 13 ECHR),[15] even though they were about the right to be exempted from school parades on the basis of religious beliefs, added to pressure for change in Greek judicial attitudes towards JWs. The CoM relied on the Greek government's conviction that no similar violations would occur in the future in order to close these cases in 2001 but waited for some proof in the earlier case of *Manoussakis*. Such proof came with a 2001 decision of the Greek Court of Cassation that relied on *Manoussakis* to judge against the sole discretion of administrative authorities in the granting of permits for non-Orthodox places of worship, which it now considered to be a limitation to freedom of religious worship.[16]

On the whole, the absence of convictions for proselytism over the past ten years demonstrates that Greek judicial practice has been brought into conformity with Convention standards.[17] The same could be said with regard to the granting of authorisations for the establishment of non-Orthodox places of worship, notwithstanding occasional bureaucratic delays.[18] Administrative control has been loosened to a great extent. It has concentrated on the formal conditions laid down in national legislation for the grant of permission, while abstaining from any kind of 'preventive control', namely, from assessing whether the applicant non-Orthodox group poses a threat to public morals.[19] At the same time, however, the outdated legal framework from the 1930s, which criminalises proselytism and lays down restrictive conditions for the establishment of non-Orthodox places of worship, has remained in place. In implementing the relevant ECtHR judgments, the Greek authorities confined themselves to undertaking administrative adjustments and to encouraging a shift in judicial stance. Yet they did not amend the legislative provisions and statutes that favour the Orthodox religion while disadvantaging the non-Orthodox minorities. This reflects a restrictive kind of compliance and a compromised acceptance of the ECtHR's jurisprudence.

Notably, the ECtHR's rulings led to a substantial increase in the protection afforded to individuals exercising their right to conscientious objection. Even though the specific circumstances differed, the cases in question – *Tsirlis and Kouloumpas*, *Georgiadis* and *Thlimmenos* – were all about prejudiced attitudes that JWs faced when seeking exemption from compulsory military service as conscientious objectors or because they were religious ministers. *Thlimmenos* reinforced the reform momentum that began with the first two cases. Adopted largely in response to these cases, Law No. 2510/1997 gave conscientious objectors the right to perform civilian or other unarmed service in the army, and this right to alternative service was recognised with the 2001 revision of the Greek Constitution. It must be noted that the adopted measures allowing for an alternative non-military service were long overdue, given that this was a practice followed by most European countries. Pressures from domestic organisations defending minority rights, the Greek Ombudsman, international human rights organisations, academic scholars and the media had been mounting, creating a fertile ground for the adoption of relevant legislation.[20] In fact, it could be argued that Strasbourg case law confirmed and added to a reform momentum already under way by bolstering domestic demands for respect and protection of religious pluralism.

Tsirlis and Kouloumpas, *Georgiadis* and *Thlimmenos* also added to broader reform pressures in two other areas that were not related to religious pluralism, but to broader issues pertaining to the administering of justice and the justice system. Domestic legislation made clear that ministers of a 'known religion' could be exempted from military service. The evident disregard that the military courts showed towards established case law of the Supreme Administrative Court, which recognised JWs' ministers as ministers of a 'known religion', led to the conviction and imprisonment of the applicants in *Tsirlis and Kouloumpas*, and subsequently to a condemnation of the Greek state for violating the right to liberty and security (Art. 5 ECHR). Such neglect of Greek courts towards the settled jurisprudence of higher domestic courts had only a year before been the basis of the country's conviction in *Canea*.[21] The ECtHR judgments reviewed so far also added to broader and intensive pressures on Greek courts to provide detailed reasoning in support of their decisions in general. A number of legislative measures taken to comply with the rulings of the Court further led to changes in the entitlement of compensation in cases of detention, which enhanced the position of the individual, as well as his/her right to a fair hearing.[22] Finally, *Thlimmenos* became an opportunity for Greek authorities to present to the CoM a series of changes aimed at reducing the length of administrative judicial proceedings.[23]

What becomes evident from the above is that the procedural issues and problems with the justice system that often additionally emerge from the ECtHR's judgments involving substantive rights are more likely to become a target of reform measures by the Greek government.[24] Not only are the procedural issues and problems less controversial, but they also reveal pervasive structural problems, well known and addressed by a large number of the ECtHR's rulings. For such kinds of problems, there is often a consensus about the need to undertake reforms, which, however, may be of such scale that they are difficult to accomplish in practice and/or require a long time to complete.

Unlike the judgments regarding the religious rights of non-Orthodox communities, the national implementation of the ECtHR's judgments brought by members from Turkish Muslim and Slav-Macedonian communities has been strongly resisted. Execution has been limited to disseminating information about the Court's jurisprudence, without any evidence that it has exerted any influence on Greek judicial practice. The Court's rulings have mainly dealt with erroneous judicial interpretation of domestic legislation criminalising the usurping of the functions of a minister of a 'known religion' in cases regarding the appointment of muftis in Thrace. They also criticised national court decisions for refusing applications to register minority associations. None of these judgments, however, have led to a comprehensive reorientation of judicial reasoning in the light of the ECHR.[25] Indeed, in subsequent cases, dealing, for instance, with the establishment and operation of minority associations or Muslims' religious representation, domestic judicial reasoning still has not gravitated in the direction of the ECtHR case law.[26]

The applicants in the cases of *Serif* and *Agga* (Nos. 1, 2, 3 and 4) were individuals who claimed status as religious leaders (muftis) following their election by congregations of Turkish Muslims in Thrace.[27] Since the muftis in Thrace are appointed by Greek state authorities, those who were elected by congregations from within the community were convicted by the Greek courts on the grounds of usurping the function of a religious minister of a 'known religion'. With the exception of *Agga* (No. 1), where the issue on appeal that was considered by the Court concerned the excessive length of domestic proceedings, the ECtHR found the applicants' conviction to constitute an interference with their right to religious freedom. Following changes in domestic case law in decisions of first-instance and appeal courts in 2001 and 2002 in line with the ECtHR's case law, the CoM closed the *Serif* and the *Agga* (Nos. 1, 2 and 3) judgments. The information that we obtain from the CoM reports, however, is contradictory and shows that actual implementation of these has not taken place. While in 2010, the CoM closed in principle its examination of *Agga* (No. 3) on the basis of the abovementioned 2002 shifts in national courts' approach, it said nothing of the fact that the Strasbourg Court again identified similar violations in *Agga* (Nos. 3 and 4) in 2006.[28]

In a number of minority-related cases, the legal issue that was on appeal in the ECtHR was a procedural matter and did not address the substantive right that was being contested. For instance, in cases like *Nurioglu, Tsingour, Raif Oglu* or *Sadik Ahmet and others*,[29] the ECtHR identified a violation of Article

6 ECHR on the grounds of excessive length of proceedings. However, the underlying dispute that dragged on for several years in the Greek justice system originated from a contested minority right, which was not raised by the applicant and/or was not addressed by the Court. The case of *Raif Oglu*, which closed with a friendly settlement, built on the dismissal of a teacher in the minority primary school of Xanthi. In his capacity as a member of the Union of Muslim Teachers of Western Thrace, Atnan Raif Oglu had published and distributed documents containing assertions of 'Turkish' ethnic origin. The decision of the prefect to dismiss the applicant had already been quashed by the Administrative Court of Appeal, but the prefecture authorities were refusing to comply with it. Evidently and rightly anticipating a condemnation on grounds of Article 6 ECHR, the Greek government pursued a friendly settlement to close the case by reappointing the applicant, who also received compensation for salaries and benefits due for the period of dismissal.

Dissemination of information about *Nurioglu*, a case concerning the refusal of Greek authorities to grant a Turkish Muslim a licence to establish a pharmacy, met with the CoM's accord in 1999.[30] *Tsingour*, in turn, concerned the refusal of the Pharmaceutical Association of Xanthi to receive a Turkish Muslim as member. Both were formally implemented; however, the adopted measures dwelled on the procedural issue and were completely extraneous to the minority-related dispute that gave rise to the violations identified by the ECtHR. They were grouped together with fifteen cases concerning the excessive length of proceedings. In 2005, the CoM closed its proceedings of these cases, acknowledging that constitutional, legislative and administrative measures designed to prevent unreasonably lengthy proceedings before the Council of State and Greek administrative courts had been taken. Domestic implementation was similarly formalistic and unrelated to the minority dispute at stake in *Sadik Ahmet and others*, which was also treated by the CoM together with eighty-five other cases regarding excessively lengthy proceedings in administrative courts and the lack of an effective domestic remedy.[31]

By contrast, in the judgments that raised solely substantive issues related to minority rights, implementation of individual and general measures has been thoroughly obstructed and never in practice realised. These concerned the refusal of Greek authorities to recognise the associations of Slav-Macedonians and Turkish Muslims, resulting in breaches of Article 11 ECHR. In the case of *Sidiropoulos*, where the refusal of Greek courts to register an association known as the Home of Macedonian Culture was condemned,[32] the CoM took it in good faith that the judgment's transmission to local judicial authorities in the northern town of Florina and its dissemination to Greek judges in general would pre-empt further violations, and closed the case.[33] In reality, however, this association has to this day not managed to gain registration due to the fact that no one among the local lawyers was willing to represent it in court, where it would seek registration.

In a related case, *Ouranio Toxo and others*,[34] the applicant political party was established with the aim of defending the minority rights of Slav-Macedonians in Greece. Two of its members complained about the wave of violent protests against them, triggered by a sign affixed to the party's headquarters that contained its name in both Macedonian and Greek. On account of the acts of violence directed against them and the inability of local police to take action to ensure public peace, the Court found breach of freedom of association. In 2011, the CoM finally closed its supervision of the implementation of this case on the basis of administrative measures aimed at strengthening the policing and protection of sensitive targets (such as political party offices) and at providing assistance in case of riots against such targets.[35] While potentially effective, such an administrative order does little to redress the underlying dispute of the minority with the state.

The established Greek state policy, which refuses to recognise the existence of a Slav-Macedonian minority and a Turkish minority in Thrace (which the 1923 Lausanne Treaty refers to as a Muslim minority), has completely blocked any kind of substantive implementation of the abovementioned judgments regarding the violation of Article 11 ECHR. Guaranteeing the associational rights of minorities that define themselves (at least, certain segments among them do) along ethnic lines, according to Greek authorities, would be tantamount to granting recognition to groups which allegedly pose a threat to state security and national integrity. Over the past couple of years, the ECtHR has found new violations of Article 11 on the grounds of dissolving or refusing registration to minority associations in the cases of *Bekir Ousta, Emin and others* and *Tourkiki Enosi Xanthis and others*.[36] While individual remedies in these cases have not been provided, at least on the surface due to procedural reasons, the Greek authorities in 2010 reported to the secretariat of the CoM that between 2008 and 2010, thirty-two out of thirty-three applications to register associations having the word 'minority' in their title or indicating a minority origin were accepted. These cases remain under the supervision of the CoM.[37]

UNDER WHAT CONDITIONS DO NATIONAL AUTHORITIES IMPLEMENT THE ECtHR'S JUDGMENTS?

It becomes evident from the preceding section that the domestic implementation of the ECtHR's judgments regarding non-Orthodox religious communities has been characterised by limited legislative change, for instance with regard to alternative non-military service for conscientious objectors. It has also involved encompassing shifts in administrative practice, as well as in government and judicial approach, without, however, any concomitant legal amendments of the antiquated law which bans proselytism and determines the restrictive conditions for the establishment of non-Orthodox places of worship. By contrast, judgments related to claims raised by individuals from ethnically defined communities have been characterised for most part by non-implementation. While some individual measures have been adopted, there has been a nearly total absence of general measures, apart from the dissemination of the relevant judgments to Greek judges. Besides the diverging patterns of legal mobilisation among the actors involved in the two sets of cases, this section argues that the differences in patterns of political support and national judicial response are central in explaining the variable degree of domestic influence of the ECtHR's judgments.

The willingness and the ability of individual and collective actors to bring a compelling claim to the attention of the Court is a crucial precondition for the ECtHR and its case law to be in a position to have any kind of domestic impact. One cannot understand why the Court's religious freedom-related condemnations have been so influential without understanding the nature and dynamics of the legal mobilisation instigated by Greece's JWs from the 1980s onwards. JWs were pioneers and repeat players in the use of legal action to raise human rights claims before the Strasbourg tribunal. Their legal mobilisation was organised and concerted, relying on the selection of test cases. From the start, it had a clear and specific aim: to change the restrictive state policy towards adherents of non-Orthodox creeds.

Immediately after the right to individual petition was accepted by Greece, JWs made a strategic choice to pursue litigation in the Strasbourg Court in light of the fact that other domestic channels of influence and pressure were limited, if not entirely non-existent. Greek laws and state practices banning proselytism, allowing the Greek administration to exercise preventive control of non-Orthodox communities seeking to establish places of worship, or criminalising conscientious objection to bear arms reflected the institutional privileges enjoyed by the OCG over non-Orthodox communities. Any move to challenge such laws and practices was viewed as undermining the church's centrality in Greek society by seeking to equalise it with that of other religious faiths. Even though a cross-section of political elites after 1974 were increasingly dissatisfied with the privileges enjoyed by the OCG and the abovementioned restrictions for non-Orthodox communities, political parties were hesitant to take up their cause, particularly on behalf of JWs.

In order to overcome such domestic constraints in their efforts for legal and policy change, in the 1980s and the 1990s JWs engaged in systematic litigation in the ECtHR as a form of political action. As their leading and veteran activist described in an interview, each of the applications lodged with the Court was carefully and strategically chosen from the many complaints and personal stories reaching the association of JWs, so as to expose and document how particular legal provisions and administrative practices restricted JWs' freedom to express and practise their faith.[38] The mobilisation of the ECHR by JWs reflects an exemplary instance of strategic litigation, employing legal action in pursuit of collective goals and policy change. An initial screening of potential cases was undertaken by lawyers in the association of JWs. In the first ever individual case taken against Greece, *Kokkinakis*, the applicant personified the whole history of systematic persecutions of the JWs' community throughout the twentieth century.[39] The lawyers and activists who supported his cause in Strasbourg had discerned that his case was unmistakeably compelling, besides being well founded in legal terms.

Litigation by JWs in the ECtHR was undertaken in tandem with political campaigning towards national policy makers but also towards European and other institutions abroad. Such campaigning aimed at publicising their issues, raising awareness and harnessing broader support for these among human rights organisations and important institutional actors, such as the Parliamentary Assembly of the Council of Europe and the European Parliament. With assistance from NGOs, such as Human Rights without Frontiers, and from their co-religionists' associations in other countries, JWs' campaigning and lobbying activities were organised in advance of the judicial review by the Strasbourg Court. They also followed the announcement of each of the Court's judgments that vindicated the claims raised, with the goal of pressuring domestic and European officials to pursue reforms in compliance with the Court's judgments.

Domestically, JW leaders and activists were highly successful in linking up and working together with individuals from the academic and political elite, as well as from the legal profession. Many of these individuals saw in the JWs' cause and in the challenge it posed to the privileges of the OCG an extension of the struggle to strengthen post-1974 democracy in Greece. Supporters from the communist left in particular were able to relate to the kind of politically motivated persecutions by the state that JWs had suffered in the course of the twentieth century. Such an affinity is exemplified by the fact that the term 'proselytism', which epitomised the plight of JWs, was also contained in legislation from the 1930s which aimed at suppressing the propagation of communist convictions.[40] After the first couple of adverse judgments, the Greek government started to get concerned about the convictions won against it by JWs in Strasbourg and to search for ways to prevent them.

Similarly to JWs, after 1974 the Muslims of Thrace were for most part unable to exercise any influence among Greek political parties and institutions. Yet, unlike JWs, Thrace's minority did not systematically pursue legal tactics in the ECtHR, at least in the first ten years after Greece accepted the right to individual petition, nor did it wage a broader campaign to influence European institutions. Instead, its political strategy from the mid-1980s, when its politicisation on the basis of Turkish ethnic identity began to gain momentum, capitalised upon the close ties and extensive dependencies with 'motherland' Turkey, which provided its support and advocacy.[41]

A number of petitions lodged by Turkish Muslims in the first half of the

1990s, which were linked to Turkish diplomatic efforts, were considered inadmissible by the ECtHR either for non-exhaustion of domestic remedies or because the claims that they raised were manifestly ill founded.[42] In part, their failure to convince the ECtHR had to do with the Court's highly restrained approach in the early 1990s, which was unwilling to substantively address minority claims.[43] It may have also stemmed from the poor quality of applications that were lodged with the Court, reflective of the low priority that the minority placed on them. In turn, the failure to obtain any favourable ruling acted as a disincentive for further legal action in Strasbourg. As a former minority member of the Greek Parliament explained in an interview, diplomatic authorities from Turkey involved with the minority issue in Thrace did not favour a litigation strategy in Strasbourg. They were not convinced that this would have any positive results for their main issue and demand, namely the collective self-determination of the minority as 'Turkish'.[44]

Interestingly, though, over the past ten to fifteen years, minority members have increasingly began to take recourse to the Strasbourg Court. A series of petitions by the Turkish Muslims of Thrace have led to judgments in which the Court established breach of the Convention. The legal victories obtained in the *Serif* and the four *Agga* cases in the late 1990s made the ECtHR an attractive forum for the minority to engage in as part of its rights campaign at the European level. Following the path earlier taken by JWs, the minority's leaders and associations have increasingly engaged in strategic litigation in the ECtHR, looking for and selecting appropriate cases to take to it. The quality of their petitions has also improved, as the lawyers preparing them take a careful approach aimed at a legal victory rather than at making a resounding political statement about the rights of the 'Turkish ethnic minority'. In the 5th International Assembly of Western Thrace Turks in Istanbul in 2006, recourse to the ECtHR was repeatedly highlighted in the ten-page final declaration and for the first time featured as a central component of the community's international and domestic political strategy.[45]

Systematic litigation in Strasbourg combined with a mobilisation campaign is an essential precondition for a minority to win favourable rulings from the Court, yet far from sufficient as an effective lever of pressure on government to implement them. More decisive for achieving the latter is the ability of a group to find influential allies domestically (but also abroad) to support and advocate its cause. The nature and extent of political support that JWs were able to elicit, as well as shifts in national judicial approach, were instrumental in promoting the domestic implementation of the Court's case law. In the Greek context, such a judicial shift must be seen, at least in part, as a corollary to a change in the government's position, even if the latter was not explicitly announced and even if it did not involve legislative amendments.

In respect of the states' margin of appreciation, the ECtHR does not generally dictate what national authorities must do to comply with its judgments but leaves it up to them to decide how to restore individual rights and to pre-empt future infringements. In this light, the Court did not explicitly pronounce the existing legal frame as problematic in cases of proselytism and the issuing of permits for establishing places of worship. Yet its judgments criticised the restrictive ways in which domestic legislation was interpreted by national courts and implemented by administrative authorities, so as to curtail the rights of non-Orthodox faiths. Any policy shift that would restore the rights of non-Orthodox communities and consequently challenge the privileges of the OCG was for most part opposed by the church.

For cultural and historical reasons, the OCG has been in a position to exert far-reaching influence among Greek society at large, including on political matters. This explains the lukewarm and ambivalent manner in which governments after 1974 have engaged in reforms that question the church's privileges despite the presence of substantial segments of political and academic elites opposed to these privileges. The acquiescence (or collaboration) of the leadership of the OCG with the military regime in 1967–74 had instilled a lasting perception that the church was on the side of the powers, even when these are presided over by an authoritarian government.[46] Such perception, marked by diffused resentment, was particularly pronounced among the left but also among the democratic forces in general that had openly fought or silently resisted the junta. For the post-1974 democratic forces, the struggle for democracy became closely associated with an anti-clerical stance, impatient with the privileges enjoyed by the OCG. Although this sentiment was widespread, the socialist party PASOK, which came to power in the 1980s, backed down on its promise to reform church–state relations in the constitutional revision of 1986.[47]

Determined efforts to reform church–state relations were only evidenced in the second half of the 1990s, when PASOK won back power under the premiership of Costas Simitis in 1996. Simitis represented the Europeanised segment of the socialist party and made convergence with the EU and entry into the monetary union the main goals of his government. Individuals who had a broad-minded perspective on issues of rights were appointed in key positions, such as in the leadership of the Ministry of Foreign Affairs, the Ministry of Justice and the Greek Court of Cassation. During the same period, the Greek Ombudsman was also established as a constitutionally recognised, independent authority, and included a department aimed at promoting human rights in the public administration. Yet, the government's will and the determination to bolster rights protection did not have a broad base of support among political officials and elected representatives, or among the Greek society at large.

The narrow political support for reforms challenging the supremacy of the OCG became evident in the sharp conflict between the government and the church over the so-called 'identity crisis' in 2000. The 'identity crisis' concerned the government's decision to remove the declaration of religious affiliation from citizens' identity cards. In an unprecedented wave of counter-mobilisation which it spearheaded, the OCG went so far as to call for a referendum on the issue, for which it collected nearly one and a half million signatures. During this conflict, few among high party officials (whether from the governing or the opposition party) took a public stance on the issue, and on the rare occasions that they did, it was half hearted. At the same time, it must be noted that equally few parliamentary representatives (at least from the governing party) disagreed strongly enough with the removal of religious identification to take a stance to oppose it in public. In this regard, the latent but widespread anti-clericalism that had lingered among the political class (at least of the left and centre-left) after 1974 resulted in a kind of passive consent that in the end made reform possible.

The implementation of the ECtHR's judgments concerning the freedom and rights of non-Orthodox creeds must be understood within the political context of the second half of the 1990s depicted above. These judgments became both a cause and a pretext for the Simitis government to initiate a shift in government policy, which, however, left the existing legal frame largely intact.[48] It adopted legislation providing for an alternative to military service, which did not in and of itself pose any challenge to the privileges of the OCG. At the same time, it did not abolish the legal provisions that banned proselytism or required the approval of Orthodox religious leadership for the granting of permits for non-Orthodox places of worship, which would have challenged established prerogatives of the OCG and therefore come up against strong resistance from it. Within these limits, the ECtHR's judgments prompted a new, albeit publicly undeclared, governmental policy that manifested itself in a more permissive administrative review of applications for the establishment of non-Orthodox places of worship. It was accompanied by training courses for law enforcement officials, as well as actions aimed at familiarising Greek judges with the ECtHR's case law. These reforms and measures to promote religious freedom were also supported by segments of the Greek academic community, local NGOs, the Greek Ombudsman and the National Commission for Human Rights.

The shift in government policy was also reflected in the appointment of a new president of Greece's Court of Cassation, who was liberal minded and an avid advocate of Convention-compliant judicial review and institutions. This gave Greek judges (and the Court of Cassation in particular) the green light to adjust their interpretations accordingly, leading, together with a change in police practices on the issue, to a dramatic decline of persecutions on religion-related grounds. The Greek judiciary, though, has occasionally continued to display a wavering attitude. In a 2001 judgment, the Court of Cassation condemned an applicant who was operating a Buddhist temple without prior permit from the administration, against two dissenting judges who considered domestic legislation on the issue as contrary to Article 9

ECHR and the ECtHR's case law.[49] While the majority opinion of judges referred to the jurisprudence of the ECtHR, they approached it in a formalist way that failed to reappraise Greek law and practice afresh in accordance with the spirit of the Convention. Still, such judicial conservatism is arguably waning with the progressive replacement of a whole generation of judges who were trained at a time when scant attention was afforded to the ECHR and the Court's rulings.

On the other hand, the implementation of ethnic minority-related ECtHR judgments, some of which had already come out in the second half of the 1990s, has been confined to some individual measures or has been non-existent. The rights-based reform initiatives quietly pursued under the Simitis government did not extend to or touch upon the rights of ethnic minorities. The claims of minorities seeking recognition along ethnic lines (i.e. Turkish or Slav-Macedonian) became closely associated with vital national security issues. Seen as a disguise for the territorial claims of neighbouring countries, most importantly Turkey, they made even liberal-minded political officials and academics shy away from taking a clear and public stance. Given the sensitive, strongly controversial and unpopular nature of minority issues, considerations of electoral cost proved paramount among parliamentary and party representatives, as well as among government officials.

The lack of political will to accept the registration of minority associations bearing the name 'Turkish' or 'Macedonian' has gone hand in hand with the refusal of domestic courts, including the Court of Cassation, to change their approach. In the 1990s, the decisions of the Court of Cassation exhibited a reluctance to uphold rights against state prerogatives, as well as a distinct nationalist ethos. The reasoning that the domestic court provided to legitimate the banning of the Home of Macedonian Culture (an association established by the Slav speakers of the north of Greece) in the *Sidiropoulos* case is indeed striking. In the lengthy text that is quoted in the relevant judgment of the Strasbourg Court, Greece's Court of Cassation made extensive references to national history textbooks, classified secret service documents and extreme nationalists to ground its decision to restrict what is at the heart of liberal democracy's political pluralism, namely the right to association. As a recent article published in Greece's major centre-left daily aptly notes, 'such lengthy reasoning resembles more a politician's article from Greek Macedonia in the [politically tumultuous period] of the early 1990s than a court decision'.[50] At the end of 2003, a local court in the northern town of Florina again denied registration to the Home of Macedonian Culture on the grounds that its name created 'confusion about its associational activities'.[51]

Despite Greece's indictment in the *Sidiropoulos* case, the Court of Cassation in the early 2000s continued to defy constitutional or Convention guarantees regarding freedom of association in the case of minorities, leading to three more adverse judgments by the ECtHR.[52] In those cases, the Court of Cassation had upheld the non-registration or dissolution of

Turkish Muslims' associations, on the grounds that they openly and falsely sought to claim the presence of an ethnic Turkish minority in Greece. This contravenes the 1923 Lausanne Treaty, which recognises not a Turkish but a Muslim minority, a position that is the cornerstone of the policy of the Ministry of Foreign Affairs. In one of these cases the Court of Cassation accepted the banning of a minority association that did not even bear the word 'Turkish' in its title, but which was considered suspect because it did not bear the characterisation 'Muslim' either. While the Court of Cassation was reviewing these cases, an alleged leak to the press that the court rapporteur was going to vindicate the litigants triggered a great deal of protest in the press, with another major Greek daily talking about a 'bomb for the minority in Thrace'.[53] In the end, the rapporteur was not the one who was originally claimed to have been favourably predisposed to the litigants, and the final court decisions refused to register or allow the operation of the minority associations.

Greek courts and the Court of Cassation in particular could play an ultimately decisive role in implementing the ECtHR's judgments regarding minority associations without any concomitant change in government policy. Indeed, the weight of implementation falls on to national courts, because the existence of the banned minority associations is only denied de jure, while de facto they continue to exist and operate. The denial of de jure recognition despite the acceptance of their de facto existence can only be understood from the viewpoint of the authorities' concern to avoid any official statement that there is any kind of entity that is 'Turkish', which would arguably be tantamount to recognising an ethnic Turkish minority. However, the registration of an association concerns the fundamental individual right to association and should not be conflated with the collective self-determination of a minority.[54] In light of this, Greek judicial and government authorities are hard pressed to redefine their position.

CAN A TRANSNATIONAL COURT INFLUENCE DOMESTIC POLITICAL CHANGE AND EXPAND RIGHTS FOR MINORITIES?

The implementation of the ECtHR's judgments concerning religious freedom for minorities has prompted more permissive administrative practices, albeit with limited legislative change, and a shift to Convention-compliant judicial interpretations (with the exception of the rights of the historical Muslim minority living in Greece). By contrast, judgments concerning the rights of members of historical minorities identifying themselves along ethnic lines have not been implemented. This chapter has sought to explore and analyse the factors that account for these differences. Explaining these differences in domestic implementation and the variable ability of Strasbourg judgments to prompt rights-expansive reform above all requires an understanding of legal

mobilisation, as well as the underlying patterns of support for and opposition to the necessary reforms domestically. In the first place, the systematic
litigation of JWs in the ECtHR, along with their well-coordinated political
mobilisation, resulted in bringing specific issues to European supervision,
and created pressures upon the Greek government to implement rights-
related change. Such action was a necessary, but not sufficient, condition to
explain the willingness of national authorities to implement, albeit restrictively, the resulting judgments.

The analysis of the Greek case confirms, albeit with some modifications,
the 'constrained court' model: judicial decisions can elicit compliance when
sufficient political support is already there and public opposition is low or
can be diffused.[55] This should not be surprising with regard to the ECtHR,
given that national authorities are afforded a considerable degree of discretion in the institutional make-up of the Convention system as to how they
implement the Court's judgments. The Greek case shows that such domestic
political support for the protection of the rights of non-Orthodox faiths had
a narrow base, while public opposition was potentially substantial. In this
context, the ECtHR's judgments provided a shield or cover for administrators and elected officials fearful of political reaction, by allowing them to
support legal and policy change without openly declaring it. Significantly,
the implementation of the Court's case law proceeded via the highest ech-
elons of the Greek government rather than through national courts; the
latter followed, rather than led, policy change, as perhaps might have been
expected.

By contrast, the lack of political will combined with judicial conservatism
has thwarted the implementation of judgments pertaining to the establishment and the registration of minority associations and political parties. Their
limited impact has been due to the lack of political and/or sufficient public
support at the national level to give effect to these judgments, except for an
occasional prima facie compliance. This is particularly evidenced in judgments that have challenged fundamental state prerogatives regarding national
security. The lack of a liberal tradition among domestic judiciaries, which
have tended to be highly deferential to the government and to consider rights
claims from the angle of national interests, has also resulted in the almost
non-implementation of the Court's case law.

To be sure, the implementation of the ECtHR's religious freedom judgments has left much to be desired. To this day, no government has been
daring enough to reform the obsolete legal frame from the 1930s that bans
proselytism and requires an administrative review of non-Orthodox religions applying for permits to establish places of worship. This has emerged
as a major problem in contemporary Greece where hundreds of thousands of
Muslim immigrants have established a large number of makeshift mosques
that fail to meet even rudimentary safety standards. In spite of the latter,
their operation is overlooked and silently tolerated by national authorities

due to the lack of an appropriate legal framework. Such a framework would do away with administrative discretion (with the opinion of the local archbishop) about how 'known' a religious dogma is and the extent to which a place of worship is necessary. It would instead provide for permits to establish places of worship that meet general urban planning and safety criteria.

At the same time, the Greek case also reveals that implementation and policy change is only one dimension of the kind of impact that judicial decisions can bear upon political and social reform. Besides the individual and general measures that governments may undertake, the ECtHR's judgments constitute highly authoritative pronouncements and a powerful lever in the hands of elites and constituencies seeking rights-expansive reform in church–state relations and other areas more broadly. For instance, the ECtHR's case law has become a point of reference in initiatives to accommodate the religious needs of the large number of immigrants currently residing in the country. In the discussions that took place in the Greek Parliament in reference to a law that provides for the construction of a central mosque in Athens, national representatives advanced their support for a pluralist and less centralised approach to such a project through repeated even if abstract references to Strasbourg Court rulings.[56]

Besides policy-related consequences, court decisions and legal norms in general are seen to have significant constitutive effects through their potential, albeit highly variable and indeterminate, to reconstruct the perceptions and interests of social actors.[57] The Greek case shows that the ECtHR's judgments have over time influenced the perceptions of minority actors themselves and the way in which they frame their demands, with potentially important consequences for their politics. In this respect, notable is the Turkish Muslims' reappraisal of their political strategy and their reorientation from an exclusive reliance on Turkey's political and diplomatic weight to a European legal strategy. Such a reorientation seems to have stemmed from the increasing influence that European human rights have within the young and educated members of the minority as a normative and judicial arena in which to pursue their demands. In addition, the attitude of the kin-state seems to have partly given way to taking legal action in the ECtHR, encouraged by the legal victories obtained until now, or prompted perhaps by Turkey's own extensive experience and encounters with the Strasbourg Court over the past ten years. The latter has probably contributed to the accumulation of a great deal of familiarity and legal expertise with the Convention system, along with the presence of Turkish lawyers willing and capable of petitioning in the ECtHR on behalf of their co-ethnics across the border in Thrace, Greece.

Whether stemming from within the minority or from Turkey proper, this new interest in and engagement with European human rights law suggests a reformulation of traditional minority demands for collective self-determination and official recognition. Making a convincing appeal to the ECtHR

requires a formulation congruent with the Convention's normative frame
and the Court's jurisprudential approach, which do not protect minorities as
collective entities. Therefore, in the recent cases that were vindicated, what
was claimed was not the right to collective, ethnic self-determination, but the
individual right of some members of the minority to association. This is an
important departure from traditional minority politics, as well as an important compromise that minority litigants have had to make in order to engage
European human rights law in support of their interests. To the extent that
such strategic reorientation is sustainable and manages to dissociate minority politics from Turkey proper, it may eventually lead to an improvement
in the domestic implementation of the ECtHR's case law.[58] In this regard,
Convention norms and the ECtHR's jurisprudence can be seen to have had a
notable impact beyond implementation in influencing the conceptualisation
and framing of minority demands.

Notes

1. Patrick Thornberry and María Amor Martín Estébanez, *Minority Rights in Europe* (Strasbourg: Council of Europe, 2004), especially chapter 1.
2. Gerald Rosenberg, *The Hollow Hope: Can Courts Bring About Social Change?* (Chicago: University of Chicago Press, 1991).
3. See Yiannis Tasopoulos, 'O Kanonas kai oi Eksereseis tou: To Syntagma tou 1952 kai I (A)sinechia tis Syntagmatikis Mas Paradosis', in Mihalis Tsapogas and Dimitris Christopoulos (eds), *Ta Dikaiomata stin Ellada 1953–2003* (Athens: Kastaniotis, 2004), pp. 37–9.
4. See in this respect Evangelia Psychogiopoulou, 'The European Court of Human Rights in Greece: Litigation, Rights Protection and Vulnerable Groups', in Dia Anagnostou and Evangelia Psychogiopoulou (eds), *The European Court of Human Rights and the Rights of Marginalised Individuals and Minorities in National Context* (Leiden: Martinus Nijhoff Publishers, 2010), p. 215.
5. See Iddo Porat, 'On the Jehovah's Witnesses Cases, Balancing Tests, and Three Kinds of Multicultural Claims', *Law and Ethics of Human Rights*, vol. 1, no. 1 (2007), p. 429.
6. For a detailed account, see Konstantinos Tsitselikis, 'Minority Mobilisation in Greece and Litigation in Strasbourg', *International Journal on Minority and Group Rights*, vol. 15, no. 1 (2008), pp. 35–8.
7. Rosenberg, *The Hollow Hope*.
8. See Article 3 of the Greek Constitution.
9. ECtHR, *Kokkinakis v. Greece* (no. 14308/88), 25 May 1993; *Manoussakis and others v. Greece* (no. 18748/91), 26 September 1996; *Tsilis and Kouloumpas v. Greece* (nos. 19233/91, 19234/91), 29 May 1997; *Valsamis v. Greece* (no. 21787/93), 18 December 1996; *Efstratiou v. Greece* (no. 24095/94), 18 December 1996; *Georgiadis v. Greece* (no. 21522/93), 29 May 1997; *Pentidis and others v. Greece* (no. 23238/94), 9 June 1997; *Tsavachidis v. Greece* (no. 28802/95), 21 January

1999; *Thlimmenos v. Greece* (no. 34369/97), 6 April 2000; *Galanis* v. *Greece* (no. 69333/01), 6 February 2003.

10. Dia Anagnostou, 'Breaking the Cycle of Nationalism: The EU, Regional Policy and the Minority of Western Thrace, Greece', *South European Societies and Politics*, vol. 6, no. 1 (2001), p. 99.

11. See Tsitselikis, 'Minority Mobilisation in Greece and Litigation in Strasbourg', p. 39.

12. Minority political leader, interview by Evangelia Psychogiopoulou, Athens, 23 May 2008.

13. ECtHR, *Kokkinakis v. Greece*; *Manoussakis and others v. Greece*; *Pentidis and others v. Greece*; *Larissis and others v. Greece* (nos. 23372/94, 26377/94, 26378/94), 24 February 1998; *Tsavachidis v. Greece*; *Vergos v. Greece* (no. 65501/01), 24 June 2004.

14. See ECtHR, *Pentidis and others v. Greece*; *Tsavachidis v. Greece*.

15. ECtHR, *Valsamis v. Greece*; *Efstratiou v. Greece*.

16. Court of Cassation, Judgment No. 20/2001, 6 December 2001.

17. See Stephanos Stavros, 'Human Rights in Greece: Twelve Years of Supervision in Strasbourg', *Journal of Modern Greek Studies*, vol. 17, no. 1 (1999), p. 14; European Commission against Racism and Intolerance, *Third Report on Greece* (Strasbourg: Council of Europe, 2004), CRI(2004)24, p. 21.

18. Policy officer at the Ministry of Education and Religious Affairs, interview by Dia Anagnostou, Athens, 28 March 2008.

19. It is reported that in all similar cases (except in one concerning Scientologists where the application was rejected on procedural grounds), the applicants were provided with the desired permits. See in this respect CoM, ResDH(2005)87 concerning *Manoussakis and Others against Greece* (judgment of 26 September 1996), 26 October 2005. The Ministry of Education and Religious Affairs also raised objections regarding the establishment of places of worship by believers in the Twelve Gods of Olympus (*Dodekatheistes*). See Yiorgos Kaminis and Michalis Tsapogas, 'Porisma 11155.02.2.3 (20.11.2002)', *To Syntagma*, no. 6 (2002), available at http://tosyntagma.ant-sakkoulas.gr/praxeis/item.php?id=795 (accessed 14 September 2012).

20. Activist from the association of JWs in Greece, interview by Dia Anagnostou, Athens, 3 March 2008.

21. ECtHR, *Canea Catholic Church v. Greece* (no. 25528/94), 16 December 1997.

22. For instance, Law No. 2915/2001 provided for the removal from criminal records of sentences on grounds of insubordination for religious or ideological reasons.

23. See CoM, ResDH(2005)89, adopted on 26 October 2005.

24. See also Dia Anagnostou and Yonko Grozev, 'Human Rights Litigation and Restrictive State Implementation of Strasbourg Court Judgments: The Case of Ethnic Minorities from Southeast Europe,' *European Public Law*, vol. 16, no. 3 (2010), pp. 401–18.

25. Director of the Directorate General of Human Rights and Legal Affairs of the Council of Europe and lawyer at the Department for the Execution of Judgments

of the ECtHR, interview by Evangelia Psychogiopoulou, Strasbourg, 7 June 2007.

26. See Court of Cassation, Judgments Nos. 304/2002, 708/2002, 4/2005, 58/2006.
27. ECtHR, *Serif* v. *Greece* (no. 38178/97), 14 December 1999; *Agga* v. *Greece* (No. 1) (no. 37439/97), 25 January 2000; *Agga* v. *Greece* (No. 2) (nos. 50776/99, 52912/99), 17 October 2002; *Agga* v. *Greece* (No. 3) (no. 32186/02), 13 July 2006; *Agga* v. *Greece* (No. 4) (no. 33331/02), 13 July 2006.
28. This was Court of Cassation Decision No. 1045/2002, reported in Council of Europe Committee of Ministers, *Supervision of the Execution of Judgments of the European Court of Human Rights: 4th Annual Report 2010* (Strasbourg: Council of Europe, 2011), p. 169.
29. ECtHR, *Nurioglu* v. *Greece* (no. 18545/91), 17 May 1995; *Tsingour* v. *Greece* (no. 40437/98), 6 July 2000; *Raif Oglu* v. *Greece* (33738/96), 27 June 2000; *Sadik Ahmet and others* v. *Greece* (no. 64756/01), 3 February 2005.
30. See CoM, ResDH(99)11, adopted on 18 January 1999.
31. CoM, Interim Resolution CM/ResDH(2007)74 on excessively lengthy proceedings in Greek administrative courts and the lack of an effective domestic remedy, adopted on 18 July 2007.
32. ECtHR, *Sidiropoulos and others* v. *Greece* (no. 26695/95), 10 July 1998.
33. CoM, ResDH(2000)99, adopted on 24 July 2000.
34. ECtHR, *Ouranio Toxo and others* v. *Greece* (no. 74989/01), 20 October 2005.
35. CoM, ResDH(2011)218 on execution of the judgment of the ECtHR *Ouranio Toxo and others against Greece*. Adopted in the 1,128th meeting (DH), 29 November–2 December 2011.
36. ECtHR, *Bekir-Ousta and others* v. *Greece* (no. 35151/05), 11 October 2007; *Emin and others* v. *Greece* (no. 34144/05), 27 March 2008; *Tourkiki Enosi Xanthis and others* v. *Greece* (no. 26698/05), 27 March 2008.
37. See Council of Europe Committee of Ministers, *Supervision of the Execution of Judgments of the European Court of Human Rights*, p. 178.
38. Activist from the association of JWs in Greece, interview by Dia Anagnostou, Athens, 3 March 2008.
39. For details on Minos Kokkinakis's life history, see Michael D. Goldhaber, *A People's History of the European Court of Human Rights* (New Brunswick, NJ: Rutgers University Press, 2007), chapter 7.
40. Yannis Ktistakis, *Thriskeftiki Eleftheria kai Evropaiki Symvasi Dikaiomaton tou Anthropou* (Athens: Sakkoulas, 2004), p. 103.
41. On this, see Anagnostou, 'Breaking the Cycle of Nationalism', p. 107.
42. See for instance ECtHR, *Ahmet Sadik* v. *Greece* (no. 18877/91), 15 November 1996; *Agko* v. *Greece* (no. 31117/96); ECtHR, *Imam and others* v. *Greece* (no. 29764/96).
43. Ktistakis, *Thriskeftiki Eleftheria kai Evropaiki Symvasi Dikaiomaton tou Anthropou*, p. 256.
44. Interview by Evangelia Psychogiopoulou, Athens, 23 May 2008.
45. Final Declaration, 5th International Assembly of Western Thrace Turks, Istanbul, 15–17 September 2006.

46. Effie Fokas, 'A New Role for the Church? Reassessing the Place of Religion in the Greek Public Sphere', GreeSE Paper No. 17 (London: Hellenic Observatory, 2008), available at http://www.lse.ac.uk/collections/hellenicObservatory/pdf/GreeSE/GreeSE17.pdf (accessed 17 September 2012).
47. Ibid., pp. 19–20.
48. Scientific officer at the Greek Ombudsman, interview by Evangelia Psychogiopoulou, Athens, 31 July 2007; former president of the Greek Court of Cassation, interview by Evangelia Psychogiopoulou, Athens, 19 March 2008.
49. Court of Cassation, Judgment No. 20/2001.
50. 'Ta dikaiomata sto edolio – meionotites ypo dikastiki apagorefsi', *Eleftherotypia*, 4 March 2007, pp. 53–5.
51. 'Ena akomi "dikastiko lathos"', press release, Elliniki Enosi gia ta Dikaiomata tou Anthropou, 13 February 2004, available at http://www.hlhr.gr/details.php?id=20 (accessed 17 September 2012).
52. These were: ECtHR, *Bekir-Ousta* v. *Greece*; *Emin and others* v. *Greece*; *Tourkiki Enosi Xanthis and others* v. *Greece*.
53. 'Bomba gia ti meionotita sti Thraki', *To Vima*, 2 October 2003.
54. See Nikos Alivizatos, 'Dikaiomata choris ekptoseis', *Ta Nea*, 23 September 2006.
55. Rosenberg, *The Hollow Hope*.
56. Greek Parliament, *Parliamentary Proceedings*, 7 November 2006. See also Dia Anagnostou and Ruby Gropas, 'Domesticating Islam and Muslim Immigrants: Political and Church Responses to Constructing a Central Mosque in Athens', in Victor Roudometof and Vasilios N. Makrides (eds), *Orthodox Christianity in 21st Century Greece: The Role of Religion in Culture, Ethnicity and Politics* (Farnham: Ashgate, 2010), pp. 89–110.
57. Michael McCann, 'Causal versus Constitutive Explanations (or, On the Difficulty of Being so Positive. . .)', *Law and Social Inquiry*, vol. 21, no. 2 (1996), p. 457.
58. Greek lawyer specialising in the field of human rights, interview by Dia Anagnostou, Athens, 17 March 2008.

Chapter 7

A complicated affair: Turkey's Kurds and the European Court of Human Rights

Dilek Kurban and Haldun Gülalp[1]

INTRODUCTION

The conflict between the Kurdish movement and the state remains the deepest faultline in Turkish politics. Obsessed with the preservation of national unity and homogeneity, the Turkish state has had little tolerance for Kurdish demands for greater legal recognition and a measure of autonomy. In a strategic move in its application for membership to what was then the European Community, Turkey decided in 1987 to give its citizens the right to petition the European Court of Human Rights (ECtHR/ the Court/Strasbourg). It was subsequently faced with the Kurds' effective use of this mechanism to raise international awareness to their plight. Since the early 1990s, the Kurdish question has been the greatest source of problems for Turkey before the ECtHR, and the cases taken to the Court by Turkey's Kurds provide a repository of information on the nature of the conflict.

Kurdish uprisings against the state's forced assimilation policies have led to repeated and often violent confrontations since the early years of the Republic. The most recent uprising has lasted the longest. The Kurdistan Workers' Party (PKK), founded in the late 1970s and strengthened in reaction to the oppression of the military regime of 1980–3, launched its first serious offensive against the Turkish army in 1984, starting an endless cycle of mutual violence. A state of emergency regime was declared in 1987, in eastern and south-eastern Turkey, that is, the Kurdish-populated territory where the armed conflict was taking place. This regime formally remained in force until 2002. During this period the security forces engaged in widespread violations of the human rights of Kurdish civilians, leading in turn to a flood of petitions to the ECtHR. Most of these thousands of applications concerned the routine actions of security forces. Cloaked in the language of 'war on terrorism', such actions included the forced displacement of civilians from villages and district centres, the destruction of homes and other property, and the burning of forests, as well as extra-judicial killings, disappearances and torture. ECtHR case law has played a significant role in bringing these violations to light.

Turkey gained candidate status for EU membership in December 1999, soon after the PKK leader, Abdullah Öcalan, was abducted in Kenya and brought to Turkey for prosecution. Turkey's candidacy necessitated reforms and increased the existing international pressure on the government to revise its mode of dealing with the insurgency and with Kurdish political and cultural demands more generally. After the electoral victory of the Justice and Development Party (AKP) in 2002 on a pro-EU platform, democratisation gained further, albeit temporary, momentum. The EU demanded that Turkey first and foremost execute the ECtHR's judgments on Kurdish issues, but also grant the Kurds limited linguistic rights in order to fulfil minority rights protection as part of the membership accession criteria. Yet, as we argue in this chapter, although there has been some improvement, the problem has not been eradicated nor has there been any substantive change in government policy on the Kurdish question.

THE ECtHR'S APPROACH TO KURDS

The Court's judgments and decisions in cases filed by the Kurds have addressed such issues as the actions of security forces in the state of emergency region, violations of the right to fair trial, deprivation of liberty without due process, and violations of freedoms of expression and association. In its judgments, the Court has ruled that Turkey has violated Articles 2, 3, 5, 6, 8, 10, 11 of the European Convention on Human Rights (ECHR/Convention) and Article 1 of Protocol 1.

During the state of emergency, the actions of the military and law enforcement officials resulted in disappearances, unlawful killings and the destruction of property, prolonged detention without judicial review, lack of access to a lawyer, and torture and ill treatment inflicted during custody. Victims were unable to claim compensation for these violations or even to effectively demand investigations into them. Local courts in the region were unwilling to exercise jurisdiction over allegations of human rights abuses committed by security forces during the fighting with the PKK.[2] Because domestic remedies were de facto unavailable at the time, Kurdish groups took direct recourse to Strasbourg.

In an unprecedented ruling in the case of *Akdıvar*, the ECtHR practically acknowledged this situation and made an exception to the principle of the exhaustion of domestic remedies.[3] Considering the 'insecurity and vulnerability of the applicants', following their eviction from their homes and the destruction of their property, and the absence of any official inquiry into the incidents, the Court assessed the prospects of a decision against security forces by the national courts as 'negligible'. It also emphasised that the said exemption was confined to the particular circumstances of *Akdıvar* and did not absolve future applicants from the obligation to exhaust domestic remedies. Still, the ECtHR was subsequently inundated by thousands of petitions that demonstrated the existence of similar exceptional circumstances and thus merited direct review.

The ECtHR ruled that Turkey had violated Article 8 ECHR (right to respect for private and family life) and Article 1 of Protocol 1 (protection of private property), but it did not address the petitioners' claims regarding the systematic nature of human rights abuses by security forces. Although the applicants alleged that the state pursued a discriminatory policy of forced displacement targeting the Kurdish population, the ECtHR either held that Article 14, which prohibits discrimination, was not violated[4] or it declined review altogether.[5] Somewhat changing its position in *Doğan and others*,[6] the Court identified for the first time a structural problem of internal displacement in Turkey and called upon the government to develop a durable solution.[7] The Court held that Turkey's recent policy to facilitate the return of internally displaced persons (IDPs) had failed and that the measures adopted to improve the conditions of the victims were inadequate. As in previous judgments in similar cases,[8] the Court stressed that 'effective legal remedy' in the meaning of the ECHR required not only the payment of compensation for the pecuniary and non-pecuniary damages of victims, but also the identification and punishment of perpetrators who committed human rights violations. Still, as in previous judgments, the Court did not rule that Turkey discriminated against its Kurdish citizens.

One month after the *Doğan* judgment, in July 2004, Turkey passed a new law to compensate the IDPs and began to enforce it later in the same year.[9] But only fifteen months into the implementation of the law, whose implementation was very slow and non-uniform across the country, the ECtHR prematurely ruled in its *İçyer* decision that this new law constituted an effective domestic remedy and rejected the 1,500 pending applications.[10] The IDPs were now required to pursue this path of domestic redress before they could petition Strasbourg. The Court's decision, endorsing a law that did not compensate emotional pain and suffering, conflicted with its previous rulings in similar cases, where the applicants' non-pecuniary damages were also awarded compensation.[11] The Court also ignored the fact that Turkey had not introduced a legal mechanism to identify and prosecute those who had committed human rights violations, although, again, it had previously stressed that this was a precondition for an effective legal remedy.

Kurdish litigants also raised the issue of incompatibility between Article 6 ECHR (right to a fair trial) and the trials at state security courts, which included a military judge among a bench of three. Since its seminal judgments in *Incal* and *Çıraklar* in 1998, the ECtHR has held that the presence of a military judge implies the lack of independence and impartiality of these courts, and violates the right to a fair trial.[12] It ruled that a retrial, upon request, was in principle an appropriate remedy. In *Öcalan*, originating from the sentencing to death of Abdullah Öcalan by a state security court, the

ECtHR did not accept the replacement of the military judge by a civilian one during the proceedings as an adequate measure and still held that Turkey had violated Article 6.[13]

Some cases concerned Article 5 of the ECHR (right to liberty and security), because the state of emergency allowed lengthy detentions before appearing in court. At the time, the State of Emergency Law allowed *incommunicado* detention without access to a judge for up to thirty days, if a person was suspected of having committed terrorism-related offences. In *Aksoy*, the ECtHR found these practices in violation of ECHR Article 5(3), because accusations of terrorism did not justify *incommunicado* detention for such a long period.[14]

There were also other Article 5 cases, brought by Kurds in western parts of Turkey. In *Sakık and others*, applicants were former members of Parliament from the pro-Kurdish Democracy Party (DEP). Their immunities had been lifted by Parliament in 1994 so that they could be prosecuted on charges of terrorism and put on trial in a state security court. The applicants were detained for 12–14 days before being brought before a judge. The ECtHR judgment stated that this charge did not give investigating authorities *carte blanche* to hold suspects in detention without judicial review.[15] The Court also found that the inability of individuals to claim compensation in domestic courts, due to lack of a remedy for unlawful detentions, violated Article 5(5) ECHR.[16]

Another set of cases concerned the dissolution of eight pro-Kurdish political parties between 1991 and 1997.[17] The Turkish Constitutional Court had held that these parties undermined 'the territorial integrity and the unity of the nation' by advocating Kurdish self-determination, promoting a federal system or merely criticising Turkey's policies and advocating the rights of the Kurdish people. The legal grounds for the closure of these parties were in the Turkish Constitution and the Law on Political Parties (LPP). Most of these parties were dissolved solely on the basis of their party programmes and/or the statements of their leaders, often shortly after their establishment.[18] The ECtHR found the dissolution of all eight parties to be in violation of Article 11 ECHR (freedom of assembly and association).

Finally, there were a number of ECtHR judgments related to Article 10 ECHR (freedom of expression), in which journalists, politicians, authors and intellectuals were convicted by the state security courts. In nearly all cases, the applicants had publicly expressed dissenting views on the Kurdish question in publications or speeches and thus violated former Articles 159 and 312 of the Criminal Code and former Articles 6, 7 and 8 of the Anti-Terrorism Law. In the '*Incal* group' of cases, the Court found violations of Article 10 ECHR on account of the applicants' conviction by the state security courts.[19] The Court emphasised the essential role that media plays in a democracy and hence the indispensability of freedom of expression even where the ideas voiced may offend, shock or disturb others.[20]

TURKEY'S COMPLIANCE: THE ASSESSMENT OF THE COMMITTEE OF MINISTERS

The ECtHR's case law played an indispensable role in bringing to light Turkey's egregious human rights record in the late 1980s and early 1990s.[21] The Court's fact finding in cases concerning disappearances, unlawful killings, arbitrary detentions, torture and the destruction of property revealed a pattern of systematic violations by security forces against Kurdish civilians, the impunity of perpetrators, and the unavailability of domestic legal remedies for victims. Moreover, the ECtHR's case law demonstrated not only the dismissive attitude of the legislative and executive authorities towards human rights in Turkey, but also the absence of an impartial judiciary upholding the principles of the rule of law and human rights.

Regardless, the real improvement in human rights only came with the emergence of the EU as an actor in Turkish politics. The EU's declaration of Turkey as a candidate for membership in 1999 initiated a reform process, which gained further momentum with the election of the AKP into office on a pro-EU platform in November 2002. A number of reforms had already been carried out by the previous coalition governments. The Code of Criminal Procedure was amended to prohibit the use of torture or ill treatment as a method of interrogation (1 December 1992), pre-trial *incommunicado* detention was shortened and detainees were granted the right to bring habeas corpus proceedings (6 March 1997). Also, the constitution was amended to remove military judges and prosecutors from the state security courts (18 June 1999), to limit pre-trial detention to a maximum of four days (17 October 2001) and to abolish the death penalty in peacetime (9 August 2002). Constitutional amendments in October 2001 also removed from Articles 26 and 28 the restriction on the use of 'languages prohibited by law' in the expression and dissemination of thought and in broadcasting. Yet the concept of the endangerment of 'the indivisible integrity of the State with its territory and nation' remained in place. Finally, the geographical area under the state of emergency was narrowed between 1999 and 2002.

Soon after the AKP came into office, the state of emergency was completely abolished (30 November 2002) and Protocol No. 13 on the abolition of the death penalty in all circumstances was ratified (9 January 2004). The constitution was amended to give the ECHR and the ECtHR case law supremacy over national law (7 May 2004).[22] Finally, the government abolished the state security courts (22 May 2004) and enacted a compensation law for the displaced (17 July 2004).

There were also amendments to the Anti-Terrorism Law and the Law on Associations. Article 8 of the Anti-Terrorism Law, which prohibited statements and demonstrations aimed at 'undermining territorial integrity', was repealed in May 2003, resulting in the annulment of convictions under this provision and their removal from the criminal records of individuals. Also in

2003, the Law on Associations was amended, removing some of the restrictions in the use of languages other than Turkish (primarily meaning Kurdish) in associational activities: only when engaging in official correspondence with government authorities were associations required to use Turkish.[23] With regard to freedom of expression, the CoM noted that Turkey's legal framework still fell below the ECHR standards. It stated:

> The provisions which triggered the violations of the ECHR in these cases are no longer in force. However, it seems that the new provisions, which replaced the old ones, while phrased differently, are of the same substance as the previous ones. The mere change of wording introduced by the recent reforms cannot ensure compliance with the ECHR requirements as set out in the ECtHR's judgments. In this context, special responsibility to apply domestic law in conformity with the ECHR and thus preventing new, similar violations lies with Turkish judges and prosecutors.[24]

Successive Turkish governments also adopted executive measures to facilitate the implementation of ECtHR judgments. In the mid-1990s, the Military Chief of Staff organised human rights training for the security forces.[25] In later years, the Ministry of Interior (MoI) and the Prime Minister's office issued executive circulars to provincial governors and law enforcement officials instructing them to observe Turkey's obligations arising from international human rights law. The Ministry of Justice (MoJ) disseminated Strasbourg case law in Turkish translation, provided training to judges, prosecutors and lawyers on ECHR standards, and instructed prosecutors and judges to follow ECtHR case law in their decisions. The MoI provided training to the police and gendarmerie on human rights.[26]

Nonetheless, a vast majority of cases still await execution and are being monitored by the CoM.[27] The CoM has acknowledged the progress that Turkey has made in recent years in executing the ECtHR judgments, but has closed its review in only a very small number of cases in order to wait and see the actual impact of the reforms. On the violations of Articles 2, 3, 8 ECHR and Article 1 of Protocol 1, for example, the CoM noted that they resulted from structural problems, such as the general attitude and practices of the security forces and their inadequate training, the legal framework that regulates their activities, the lack of criminal liability of the perpetrators, and the lack of adequate reparations for the victims.[28] The individual measures required to execute the ECtHR judgments would involve criminal investigations against the security forces, but this in turn depended on the adoption of general measures such as comprehensive constitutional, legislative and regulative amendments as well as changes in practice.[29] The CoM also encouraged Turkey to improve the safeguards governing police custody, to reorganise the training of security forces, to promptly and efficiently implement the Compensation Law, to ensure that law enforcement officers accused of committing serious crimes be prosecuted without prior administrative authorisation, and to pursue the training of judges and prosecutors on ECtHR case law.[30]

Principal issues in the ECtHR's Article 5 judgments such as the '*Demirel* group' of cases[31] had concerned

> the excessive length of the applicants' detention on remand and the absence of sufficient reasons given by domestic courts in their decisions to extend such detention . . . the absence of a domestic remedy whereby the applicants could challenge the lawfulness of their detention on remand . . . the absence of a right to compensation for the applicants' unlawful detention on remand.

The Turkish government legislated a new Code of Criminal Procedure in 2005, which still did not fully meet the Council of Europe's expectations. The Parliamentary Assembly observed that in some cases applicants were 'still detained on remand' and the information provided by the government on domestic court decisions did not lead to a 'conclusive assessment' as to the implementation of the new law.[32]

The CoM has also repeatedly demanded the retrial of those applicants who continued to serve in prison in disregard of ECtHR judgments that found Article 6 violations in their trials. Particularly important for the CoM was the judgment in the high-profile case of *Sadak and others*.[33] The applicants were former members of Parliament from DEP, convicted to fifteen years' imprisonment. The ECtHR found a violation of Article 6 due to the presence of a military judge on the bench of the state security court. The CoM urged Turkey to reopen the proceedings in this case.[34] Turkey passed reform laws, in August 2002 and January 2003, which granted individuals whose Article 6 rights were violated the right to seek retrial within one year of the ECtHR's final judgment.

Following these measures, *Sadak and others* was reopened. The state security court accepted the applicants' demand for retrial on 28 February 2003, but upheld their conviction on 21 April 2004. Under pressure from the CoM[35] and the European Commission, the Turkish authorities took one of the most radical individual measures in executing the ECtHR's judgments. On 9 June 2004, the High Court of Appeals quashed the judgment of the state security court (which had by then been abolished), suspending the execution of the sentence and ordering the release of the applicants. The CoM subsequently declared that Turkey had abided by Article 46 ECHR (execution of judgments).[36] However, upon retrial, the heavy penal court in Ankara reached the same verdict as the state security court that it had replaced, except that it lowered the sentence by half, taking note of the new Criminal Code adopted in June 2005. The defendants' appeal to the High Court of Appeals was unsuccessful.[37]

Although it ceased to monitor the case of *Sadak and others*, the CoM closely followed the implementation of the abovementioned 2003 law on the right of retrial because it had repercussions for a number of ECtHR judgments pending execution. The law only provided for the reopening of proceedings in respect of the ECtHR's judgments which became final *before* 4 February 2003 or judgments given in applications filed with the Court *after* this date.[38] This temporal scope excluded those cases which were filed – but not concluded – before that date and hence introduced an element of inequality before the law. Although other applicants were affected as well, the temporal limitation was specifically aimed to preclude the retrial of the PKK leader, Abdullah Öcalan, as his application to the ECtHR had been lodged before 4 February 2003 and the case had not yet been concluded. Regardless, Öcalan filed for retrial. The domestic court ruled that, while it would refuse to apply the temporal limitation, an examination of the applicant's submission did not justify a retrial, given the nature of the crime and the evidence in the case file, including the applicant's confessions. A retrial would have to lead to the same outcome, that is, life imprisonment. Based on this judgment, the CoM closed its examination of the *Öcalan* case. Specifically, it noted that a Turkish court had heard the applicant's request for a retrial, albeit unsuccessfully for the applicant, and that the death sentence was commuted to life imprisonment due to the abolition of the death penalty. The CoM also pointed out that Turkey had adopted general measures to prevent similar violations.[39]

But with regard to the continued imprisonment of other individuals whose Article 6 rights were found to have been violated, the CoM adopted three interim resolutions[40] and two decisions,[41] and sent two letters to the Turkish government.[42] The CoM's tone was exceptionally critical, 'deeply deplor[ing]' the Turkish authorities' failure to respond to the interim resolutions and to provide a firm commitment for legislative reform that would allow a retrial in similar cases. The CoM reiterated that a continuation of the situation would amount to a manifest breach of Turkey's obligations under Article 46 ECHR.

The government also took a number of measures, both individual and general, to comply with the eight judgments in which the ECtHR had found violations of Article 11 in the dissolution of political parties. A constitutional amendment in 1995 had already turned the permanent ban on the political activities of all members of dissolved parties into a five-year ban only on those party leaders who were responsible for the actions leading to the dissolution. A further constitutional amendment on 17 October 2001 stipulated that the Constitutional Court had to demonstrate the persistence of constitutionally prohibited actions by members of a political party before the party could be dissolved. The Constitutional Court would also have to consider other sanctions short of dissolution, such as partial or total withdrawal of public financial support.

An amendment to the LPP in January 2003 made dissolution contingent on a qualified, rather than a simple, majority vote of the Constitutional Court. However, the law continues to stipulate that political parties are prohibited to claim the existence of national minorities distinguished by religion, ethnicity, race or language, and may not engage in activities that would protect, advance or spread languages and cultures other than Turkish. Also, they may not use any non-Turkish language in their party programmes, meetings, conventions and campaigns. Notwithstanding these significant restrictions on freedom of association, the CoM was satisfied with Turkey's progress in executing the ECtHR's judgments concerning party dissolutions. Based on the general measures of constitutional and legislative reform and the individual measures that enabled applicants to resume their political activities, the CoM closed its examination of all eight judgments.[43]

POLITICAL AND IDEOLOGICAL CONSTRAINTS

The ECtHR's judgments and CoM resolutions were initially ignored by the Turkish government. Despite the profusion of judgments of violation, particularly relating to Kurds under the state of emergency, Turkey did no more than introduce some cosmetic changes in legislation and policy. Violations continued even as Turkey reported to the CoM that measures were being taken to execute ECtHR case law. For example, at a time when the Gendarmerie General Command's Human Rights Section reportedly provided human rights training for troops in the mid- to late 1990s (see above), it continued to be the principal perpetrator of violations in eastern and southeastern Turkey. According to a government-commissioned academic study on the IDPs, from 1987 until 1999, between 950,000 and 1,200,000 civilians in the region were displaced, often as a result of their forcible eviction by the gendarmerie.[44]

Real improvement only began after 1999, when Turkey was declared a candidate for EU membership. The EU treated the ECtHR's judgments and CoM resolutions as benchmarks to measure Turkey's progress in fulfilling the Copenhagen political criteria. This mode of monitoring forced successive Turkish governments to adopt substantial general measures and pursue their implementation. The reform process gained further momentum when the AKP came to power in 2002 with a pro-EU agenda, so that in its December 2004 summit the EU resolved to begin accession negotiations with Turkey. The EU, with its leverage on the accession process, has been much more effective than the CoM in both monitoring and pressuring Turkey. Also, while the CoM's resolutions and decisions have been low profile, the EU's annual progress reports, including an assessment of Turkey's execution of the ECtHR's judgments, receives greater public attention and media scrutiny at the national level.

Furthermore, the EU went beyond the CoM in its demands for reform on the Kurdish question. The Turkish government introduced relatively significant, albeit still limited, language rights to the Kurds and other select ethnic minorities in order to fulfil the EU's requirement of providing protection to minorities. Starting in 2002, Kurds were granted the right to study their mother tongue in private courses, and to have public and private TV and radio broadcasting, albeit subject to stringent content and time restrictions.[45] On 1 January 2009, the state-owned Turkish Radio and Television (TRT) established a new channel, TRT 6, to broadcast exclusively in Kurdish, and more recently it has also become possible to study Kurdish language and culture at a few select universities.[46] The EU accession process, then, has been the most important factor in promoting the implementation of the ECtHR's judgments.

On the other hand, a political culture of conservatism persists that dominates all levels of the state, including the military, the judiciary and the civilian political elite and bureaucracy. The authoritarian mentality prevalent in these institutions has often been a bigger obstacle than the legislative framework against the execution of ECtHR judgments. The state's founding ideology, sanctifying 'territorial integrity and national unity', is strongly embedded in the nation's legal and political culture. This ideology retains a critical role in the formal education and professional training of the members of the state bureaucracy and judiciary. For many, the preservation of state interests is more important than the protection of individual rights.

The judiciary, although formally entrusted with the execution of ECtHR judgments, has in effect been a principal obstacle to human rights reforms. The judicial authorities have only in recent years begun, slowly and in limited ways, to incorporate the Convention and ECtHR case law in their decisions. Although there is no systematic study that compares the low and high courts in terms of their tendency to implement Strasbourg jurisprudence, the high courts seem to put up greater resistance.[47] Judges and prosecutors in Turkey lack professional tenure and are subject to interference along political and ideological lines by the executive and judicial branches of government. A recent study on their mindset describes the near-uniform domination of nationalist and statist ideology. Typical statements include the following: 'The state comes first'; 'I am a statist jurist'; 'When my country is in question, I do not care about the law'; 'As a prosecutor of the republic, I must protect the state and the regime. I am the prosecutor of the regime . . . I can disregard democracy'; 'Human rights are a bit exaggerated.'[48] These statements are a reflection of the promotion mechanism that rewards judges and prosecutors who adhere to the statist mentality and the disciplinary mechanism that sanctions those that diverge from it.

The mentality may be observed, for example, in the judicial tendency to accentuate the limitations on free speech already available in domestic laws. Prosecutors are inclined to expansively interpret the restrictive provisions when they bring charges against those advocating minority rights in general and Kurdish rights in particular. While much national and international attention has focused on prosecutions based on Article 301 of the Penal Code,[49] prosecutors also resort to other less noticed restrictive articles of the same code to curtail the peaceful advocacy of minority rights. For example, Article 220(8), which prohibits 'the propaganda of an [illegal] organisation or its goals', poses a particular threat to the expression of dissenting views on the Kurdish question, because it may criminalise any opinion that is perceived to parallel PKK demands.

Prosecutors and judges tend to interpret the concept of undermining the 'indivisible unity of the state with its territory and nation' as a catch-all phrase to include all kinds of dissent.[50] In the words of Human Rights Watch, 'Turkish courts are notoriously lenient towards members of the security forces who are charged with abuse or misconduct, contributing to impunity and the persistence of torture and the resort to lethal force.'[51] Security forces, including the military and the police, continue to benefit from a culture of impunity that neither the ECtHR nor the EU has been able or willing to penetrate.[52] Moreover, although there are laws that allow in a limited way for the prosecution of security personnel who have committed torture, prosecutors and judges remain reluctant in implementing these laws and continue to shield public officials with impunity.[53]

In addition to all this, an overwhelming majority of judges and prosecutors do not speak a foreign language, have not lived or even travelled abroad, and have both a low socio-economic status and a heavy workload. They are therefore unable to follow the developments in international human rights law or to attend international conferences and interact with colleagues from other countries. Judges and prosecutors in Turkey generally tend to retain their conservative tendencies, even though many of them may have received training on ECtHR judgments from the MoI and MoJ.

During its first years in power, the AKP was keen on portraying itself as the embodiment of progress and reform against the opposition of a conservative civilian and military bureaucratic establishment. When its Islamist predecessor, the Welfare Party, was driven out of power under military pressure in 1997, and subsequently dissolved by the Constitutional Court in 1998, the founders of the AKP came to realise that EU membership was perhaps the only remedy against the Turkish military's frequent interference with civilian politics. During its first term in power, particularly between 2002 and 2004, the AKP followed a pro-EU programme and undertook radical legal reform. However, it soon became clear that the AKP leadership did not have a principled commitment, but only a pragmatic approach to human rights reform. It appeared that their primary goal was to take the absolutely minimal necessary steps to meet the EU criteria and to avoid high amounts of compensation for Strasbourg judgments. Under constant threat from the military and civilian bureaucracy, and in an effort to preserve its position of power, the AKP government was also torn between the EU's stringent accession criteria and a political establishment determined to maintain the status quo. In its struggle with the establishment, the AKP initially followed a policy of negotiating for power, only to join the resistance front later on, when it felt firmly established. Many progressive legal measures were subsequently either weakened or practically reversed.

A prime example of the AKP government's cosmetic reforms is the abolition of state security courts in 2004 and their replacement by 'heavy penal courts with special powers'. It was clear to Kurdish human rights lawyers that the new courts were state security courts by another name, bearing continuity in mandate, rules of procedure, judges, personnel, archives and case files.[54] This continuity was evident, for example, in Sadak and others, discussed above, where the ECtHR had found a violation of Article 6 ECHR, but the heavy penal court upon retrial reached the same verdict as the state security court that it replaced. The institution of special courts furnished with special powers for prosecuting certain crimes, including terrorism offences, reveals the persistent duality of the Turkish legal system. It also discloses the real motivation of the government in creating the illusion of abolishing state security courts so as to 'prevent potential criticisms from the EU and compensation penalties by the ECtHR'.[55]

Similarly, in the area of freedom of expression, the repealed draconian provisions of the Penal Code were in effect reintroduced under new names. A large number of the ECtHR's judgments concerned journalists, politicians, authors and other intellectuals convicted by the state security courts for violations of Articles 159 and 312 of the former Penal Code and former Articles 6, 7 and 8 of the Anti-Terrorism Law. Those two articles of the Penal Code were effectively replaced by Article 301, discussed above, and Article 216, on 'inciting enmity or hatred on the basis of class, race, religion or sect', of the new Penal Code, introduced by the AKP government in June 2005. Under persistent domestic and international pressure, the government eventually amended Article 301 of the new code in May 2008, but only cosmetically. The maximum penalty was lowered from three to two years of imprisonment, the commission of the crime abroad was abolished as an aggravating factor, the phrase 'insulting Turkishness' was replaced with 'insulting the Turkish nation', and prosecutorial investigation was made subject to authorisation from the MoJ. The human rights community in Turkey is highly sceptical that these changes will make a significant difference and it is actually more concerned about other outstanding articles, such as Article 220(8) discussed above, than this particular one.

While the AKP pursued a reformist agenda during its first years in power, it effectively changed course in the second half of its first term, after securing a date from the EU for the beginning of accession negotiations. After 2005, a number of new laws increased the powers of law enforcement and effectively rolled back the previous advancement. For example, in June 2006, amendments to the Anti-Terrorism Law introduced an overinclusive definition of terrorism, based on intention rather than action. The law carries a long list of 'terrorism offences': it brings new restrictions to free speech, and treats speech and action deemed to be 'in accordance with the aims of a terrorist organisation' as tantamount to membership of a terrorist organisation. It also imposes severe sanctions on the media, including prison sentences, and reintroduces temporary suspension of periodicals without a formal hearing, indeed with no more than a simple order by a prosecutor.[56] A provision in the new law allowed the treatment of minors over the age of fifteen as adults, leading to their prosecution in heavy penal courts. As a result of effective international and national campaigning, legislation was passed in July 2010 to delimit the Anti-Terrorism Law as it applied to child demonstrators. It then became possible to prosecute all minors at juvenile courts, limit the nature of charges brought against them, and reduce or postpone their sentences.[57] Before this improvement, several thousand minors, some as young as nine, had been arrested and charged with membership of a terrorist organisation, simply for participating in mass demonstrations and allegedly throwing rocks at the police.[58]

Amendments to the Law on the Duties and Authority of the Police were hastily adopted in June 2007, despite protests from human rights organisations. According to the government's report to the CoM, the new law allows the police to use force only when confronted with resistance and to use it in a non-diffuse and proportionate manner. NGOs, however, argue that the new law has 'institutionalised the police state already in force' and 'introduced a state of emergency across the country'.[59] It has 'provisions reminiscent of totalitarian and authoritarian regimes' that grant the police wide new powers to arbitrarily stop and search without court order, fingerprint citizens and use disproportionate force.[60] Human rights defenders hold this law responsible for the rapid increase in incidents of ill treatment and torture by the police.[61]

The AKP has also effectively halted its previously declared 'Zero Tolerance to Torture' policy. Recent reports indicate that security forces circumvent the new laws that protect the detainees by holding them in ways other than formal detention and committing ill treatment or torture outside detention centres, such as in police cars or outdoor areas.[62] Security forces now seem to have reverted to their previous modes of operation.[63] They have put down lawful demonstrations by resorting to disproportionate use of force, particularly in the predominantly Kurdish provinces, in some cases resulting in the deaths of demonstrators. These kinds of incident reveal that the ECtHR's rulings have had only a minimal impact after all.[64]

Finally, the state of emergency was formally lifted by Parliament soon after the AKP came to power, but in reality it has continued in a legally dubious form. Particularly since the middle of 2007, when the AKP began its second term in office, the government has authorised the military to announce repeatedly, through the Chief of Staff's website, the coordinates of what are euphemistically called 'temporary security zones'. With the declaration of such a zone, the military effectively occupies the area and limits the entry, exit and movement of civilians within it, so that military units may freely conduct operations in pursuit of 'terrorists'. The legal basis of this authorisation has been questioned by members of Parliament, particularly those belonging to the pro-Kurdish parties. Although the government has never offered a satisfactory answer to this question, the legal basis appears to be a law that was passed by the military regime in 1981 and still remains in effect.[65]

KURDISH DISCONTENT WITH THE ECtHR

There is no doubt that the ECtHR's judgments and the CoM's recommendations have been instrumental in pressuring Turkey to introduce human rights reforms. But, paradoxically, in recent years Kurdish litigants and their advocates have begun to lose faith in the Court and to see it as a partial and biased institution that makes politically motivated decisions.[66] A number of judgments by the ECtHR have been critical in creating this sentiment. Kurdish lawyers have objected, first and foremost, to the *İçyer* decision that found the domestic compensation mechanism satisfactory. They complain that the Court should have observed the implementation of the Compensation Law and assessed its effectiveness before issuing a pilot decision.[67] Despite dissatisfaction with this judgment, however, Kurdish lawyers continued to litigate against problems originating from the implementation of the Compensation Law. These efforts also failed when the ECtHR released four inadmissibility decisions on 8 July 2011 and rejected a total of 200 such applications.[68]

Another ECtHR judgment that generated discontent was in the case of *Yumak and Sadak*.[69] Turkey implements a 10 per cent threshold in national elections for a political party to send deputies to Parliament. This threshold, the highest in Europe, has served to prevent a series of pro-Kurdish parties from gaining any parliamentary seats, even though they receive the majority of votes in the predominantly Kurdish-populated provinces of eastern and south-eastern Turkey. In *Yumak and Sadak*, the Court ruled that the threshold did not violate Article 3 of Protocol 1 ECHR (right to free elections).

Kurdish lawyers also criticise the Court for having stopped fact-finding missions and trials. They feel that the Court now tends to issue hastily written and poor-quality opinions and takes too long in bringing its evaluations to a conclusion. Moreover, they argue, the Court rules many applications inadmissible without justification, awards lower compensation amounts, rigidly applies the rule of exhaustion of domestic remedies, and no longer tolerates the procedural mistakes of inexperienced lawyers. In their opinion, the Court will become even more inaccessible with the entry into force of Protocol 14, which requires that petitions are filed in French or English, because many of the lawyers in the Kurdish region do not speak these languages.

Friendly settlements are another source of complaint. A Kurdish lawyer stated that recently the ECtHR has begun to pressure litigants to accept friendly settlement offers by awarding them compensation amounts that are lower than in the settlement offers. She also criticised the friendly settlement procedure for allowing the government to simply express regret for human rights violations without having to prosecute their perpetrators.[70]

Explanations vary as to the deterioration in the quality of the Court's decisions, the increase in the number of inadmissibility decisions and the negative outcome in several critical cases. Some lawyers attribute them to the Court's interest in easing its workload, which has grown with the expansion of the Council of Europe. They argue that this factor was critical in the ECtHR's inadmissibility decision in the İçyer case, when thousands of similar cases were waiting in the pipeline. Many lawyers also point to the EU accession process as a factor. They believe that the Court started to issue inadmissibility decisions or to rule in favour of the government as a 'nice gesture for its EU membership process', 'to give Turkey a chance' and 'to facilitate political relations between Turkey and the EU'.[71] A Kurdish lawyer also remarked that 'in the 1990s Turkey was a laboratory for the ECtHR, which built most of its jurisprudence through the judgments it issued against Turkey', whereas now the Court has lost interest owing to repeat cases and can no longer generate new case law.[72]

One Kurdish lawyer distinguished between 'sensitive and not-so-sensitive issues' and suggested that the ECtHR tends not to touch upon sensitive issues, such as the electoral threshold, discrimination, administrative practices leading to systematic violations in the state of emergency region and the wearing of the headscarf, all of which somehow directly relate to the core identity issues of the Turkish state. He argued that this distinction is evident in the government's implementation. While measures requested by the CoM in 'non-sensitive cases' are dutifully adopted, such as those relating to university entrance exams, social security or public works, there is resistance to implementation in areas that relate to the 'most vital issues', such as the impunity of security personnel in their 'war against terrorism'. As an example, he cited the case of *Tanış and others*,[73] where the government failed to launch an investigation into the disappearance of two local Kurdish politicians despite the ECtHR's finding that they disappeared after having been detained by the Gendarmerie Command.[74]

CONCLUSION

There is no question that the ECtHR's judgments, combined with pressure from the EU, have significantly contributed to reforms in Turkey. But while the CoM may have found many of these reforms and their implementation satisfactory, we argue in this chapter that a closer look into both their substance and their mode of implementation reveals significant weaknesses. Practices such as torture and lack of fair trial still prevail; there are still significant restrictions on freedom of speech; the LPP still allows the dissolution of parties for merely using Kurdish in their activities; and the Penal Code and Anti-Terrorism Law still generate convictions for advocating Kurdish rights or participating in demonstrations. The reforms have not introduced a substantial change in Turkey's minority policies or granted the Kurds the right to education in their mother tongue. The Prime Minister included Kurdish phrases in his public address when he launched the state-run Kurdish channel, TRT 6, but hundreds of Kurdish politicians, activists and even elected officials still get prosecuted for simply using their own language in political campaigns.

Heavy penal courts, furnished with extraordinary powers and with exclusive jurisdiction over terrorism offences, have replaced the state security courts, which were abolished in response to pressure for reform. Hundreds of adults and children have been convicted of terrorism and sentenced to prison simply for participating in demonstrations. Yet another pro-Kurdish political party, the Democratic Society Party, was dissolved by the Constitutional Court in December 2009. There are thousands of political prisoners, including current and former elected Kurdish politicians, academics, journalists, publishers and civil society activists, put in jail for their alleged association with the PKK. Meanwhile, the executive commissions in charge of implementing the Compensation Law have been arbitrarily rejecting as inadmissible thousands of applications filed by Kurdish IDPs.[75]

This paper has attempted to explain this situation in terms of the AKP government's ambivalent and inconsistent attitude towards human rights, the authoritarian mindset of the judiciary, the persistence of the civilian and military political establishment to preserve the status quo, and the pervasive culture of impunity for public officials who commit human rights violations. The CoM also seems to bear some responsibility in so far as it has prematurely finalised its review of a number of issues on the basis of cosmetic legal changes, such as in the case of party dissolutions, and relieved the pressure on Turkey to continue with the reform process. But the Kurdish question is first and foremost a political issue and piecemeal legal reforms will fail to address the root causes of the violations that led to the ECtHR cases in the first place.

The growing Kurdish discontent against the ECtHR and the CoM also merits serious attention. Whether justified or not, the Kurdish sentiment that these institutions tend to side with the Turkish government reveals the sensitivity of the issue all around. Nonetheless, despite their criticisms, the Kurds continue to litigate before Strasbourg. This shows that they still regard the ECtHR as the only available avenue to seek justice and accountability, and will probably do so until Turkey develops a durable political solution.

Notes

1. This chapter is based on a report prepared by a research team that included Ozan Erözden, of Yıldız Technical University, in addition to the two authors of this chapter.

2. Yaşar Aydın and Ruhşen Doğan of TOHAV, interviewed by Dilek Kurban, Istanbul, 15 October 2007; Kurdish lawyers Mesut Beştaş, Sedat Çınar, Tahir Elçi, Serhat Eren and Reyhan Yalçındağ, group interview, conducted by Haldun Gülalp and Ozan Erözden, Diyarbakır, 16 February 2008.

3. ECtHR, *Akdıvar and others* v. *Turkey* (no. 21893/93), 16 September 1996.

4. See e.g. ECtHR, *Akdıvar and others* v. *Turkey*; *Selçuk and Asker* v. *Turkey* (nos. 23184/94, 23185/94), 24 April 1998.

5. See e.g. ECtHR, *Orhan* v. *Turkey* (no. 25656/94), 18 June 2002.

6. ECtHR, *Doğan and others* v. *Turkey* (nos. 8803/02–8811/02, 8813/02, 8815/02–8819/02), 29 June 2004.

7. This new approach by the Court was a result of the mandate granted by the Committee of Ministers (CoM) of the Council of Europe (CoE), whereby the ECtHR was authorised to issue pilot judgments if it found structural problems in a member state. See CoM, Rec(2004)6 concerning the improvement of domestic remedies, adopted on 12 May 2004.

8. See e.g. ECtHR, *Menteş and others* v. *Turkey* (no. 23186/94), 28 November 1997; *Selçuk and Asker* v. *Turkey*.

9. Law No. 5233 (Law on Compensation for Losses Resulting from Terrorism and the Fight against Terrorism), 17 July 2004.

10. ECtHR, *İçyer* v. *Turkey* (no. 18888/02), 12 January 2006.

11. See, for example, ECtHR, *Menteşe and others* v. *Turkey* (no. 36217/97), 18 January 2005; *İpek* v. *Turkey* (no. 25760/94), 17 February 2004.

12. ECtHR, *Incal* v. *Turkey* (Grand Chamber) (no. 22678/93), 9 June 1998; *Çıraklar* v. *Turkey* (no. 19601/92), 28 October 1998.

13. ECtHR, *Öcalan* v. *Turkey* (no. 46221/99), 12 May 2005.

14. ECtHR, *Aksoy* v. *Turkey* (no. 21987/93), 18 December 1996. The ECtHR reiterated this principle in subsequent cases that raised similar issues. See e.g. ECtHR, *Demir and others* v. *Turkey* (nos. 21380/93, 21381/93, 21383/93), 23 September 1998.

15. ECtHR, *Sakık and others* v. *Turkey* (nos. 23878/94–23883/94), 26 November 1997.

16. For similar rulings, see also ECtHR, *İkincisoy* v. *Turkey* (no. 26144/95), 27 July 2004; *Sevgin and İnce* v. *Turkey* (no. 46262/99), 20 September 2005.

17. ECtHR, *United Communist Party of Turkey and others* v. *Turkey* (no. 19392/92), 30 January 1998; *Socialist Party and others* v. *Turkey* (no. 21237/93), 25 May 1998; *Freedom and Democracy Party (ÖZDEP)* v. *Turkey* (no. 23885/94), 8 December 1999; *Yazar and others* v. *Turkey* (nos. 22723/93–22725/93), 9 April 2002; *Dicle for the Democracy Party (DEP)* v. *Turkey* (no. 25141/94), 10 December 2002; *Socialist Party of Turkey (STP) and others* v. *Turkey* (no. 26482/95), 12 November 2003; *Democracy and Change Party and others* v. *Turkey* (nos. 39210/98, 39974/98), 26 April 2005; *Emek Partisi and şenol* v. *Turkey* (no. 39434/98), 31 May 2005.

18. CoM, ResDH(2007)100 concerning execution of the judgments of the European Court of Human Rights in the case of United Communist Party of Turkey (judgment of Grand Chamber of 30/01/1998) and seven other cases against Turkey concerning the dissolution of political parties between 1991 and 1997, adopted on 20 June 2007.

19. See 'Implementation of judgments of the European Court of Human Rights: Addendum to the Report, Committee on Legal Affairs and Human Rights', Doc. 12455 (Parliamentary Assembly of the Council of Europe, 25 January 2011). Available at http://assembly.coe.int/Documents/WorkingDocs/doc10/edoc12455Add.htm (accessed 9 October 2012).

20. One exceptional case is *Zana* v. *Turkey*, where the ECtHR did not find a violation of Article 10. In drawing the boundaries of freedom of expression, the Grand Chamber pointed out that the applicant was a highly influential Kurdish politician, who made statements in support of 'the PKK national liberation movement', which killed women and children 'by mistake,' and the interview appeared in a major national daily paper while PKK attacks were going on. ECtHR, *Zana* v. *Turkey* (no. 18954/91), 25 November 1997.

21. The reports and statements of various international organisations, such as the European Parliament, and UN treaty bodies, such as the Committee against Torture, have also played a critical role.

22. The following clause was added to Article 90 of the Constitution: 'In case of a conflict between international agreements in the area of fundamental rights and freedoms duly put into effect and the domestic laws due to differences in provisions on the same matter, the provisions of international agreements shall prevail.'

23. CoM, Interim Resolution, ResDH2004(38), Freedom of expression cases concerning Turkey: General Measures, 2 June 2004.

24. See 'Freedom of Expression in Turkey: Progress Achieved – Outstanding Issues, Ministers' Deputies Information Documents, CM/Inf/DH(2008)26, (Council of Europe Committee of Ministers, 23 May 2008). Available at https://wcd.coe.int/ViewDoc.jsp?id=1294549&Site=CM (accessed 9 October 2012).

25. For example, in 1995–6, a human rights education programme was delivered to the security forces of Diyarbakır, Van and Elazığ provinces; in 1996–7, the Gendarmerie General Command introduced human rights education programmes; and in 1998 the command headquarters published a brochure on human rights to raise awareness among personnel. 'General Measures Adopted to Prevent New Violations of the European Convention on Human Rights: Stock-taking of Measures Reported to the Committee of Ministers in Its Control of Execution of the Judgments and Decisions under the Convention (Application of Former Articles 32 and 54 and of Article 46)', H/Exec (2006)1 (Council of Europe, May 2006), p. 245.

26. The EU and the CoE have been actively involved in the training programmes through individual and joint efforts. Within the framework of CoE–European Commission Joint Initiative, practice-based human rights training was given to prosecutors, judges and lawyers on the ECHR and the application of the

ECtHR's case law. See CoM, ResDH2005(43) concerning general measures to ensure compliance with the judgments of the European Court of Human Rights in the cases against Turkey concerning actions of members of the security forces, adopted on 7 June 2005. The MoJ also provided regular in-service training for judges and prosecutors as part of the Human Rights Education in Turkey Programme 1998–2007 for training. See CoM, ResDH2008(69) concerning general measures to ensure compliance with the judgments of the European Court of Human Rights in the cases against Turkey concerning actions of members of the security forces, adopted on 18 September 2008. Some of this training was given in the newly opened Turkish Academy of Justice. The Turkish government also participated in the CoE programme called 'Police and Human Rights – Beyond 2000,' which aimed to ensure that the training programmes for police officers and gendarmerie complied with CoE standards. See CoM, Interim Resolution 2005(43), 7 June 2005.

27. Statistical data on execution of judgments are available in Council of Europe Committee of Ministers, *Supervision of the Execution of Judgments and Decisions of the European Court of Human Rights: Annual Report 2011* (Strasbourg: Council of Europe, 2012), available at http://www.coe.int/t/DGHL/MONITORING/EXECUTION/Source/Publications/CM_annreport2011_en.pdf (accessed 17 September 2012).

28. See generally the CoM's interim resolutions on Turkey.

29. Council of Europe Committee of Ministers, *Supervision of the Execution of Judgments of the European Court of Human Rights: 1ˢᵗ Annual Report 2007* (Strasbourg: Council of Europe, 2008), p. 38, available at http://www.coe.int/t/DGHL/MONITORING/EXECUTION/Source/Publications/CM_annreport2007_en.pdf (accessed 17 September 2012).

30. CoM, Interim Resolution 2005(43), 7 June 2005.

31. ECtHR, *Demirel* v. *Turkey* (no. 39324/98), 28 January 2003.

32. See 'Implementation of Judgments of the European Court of Human Rights', Doc. 12455 Addendum (Parliamentary Assembly of the Council of Europe, Committee on Legal Affairs and Human Rights), 25 January 2011.

33. ECtHR, *Sadak and others* v. *Turkey* (nos. 29900/96–29903/96), 17 July 2001.

34. CoM, ResDH2002(59) concerning the judgment of the European Court of Human Rights of 17 July 2001 in the case of *Sadak, Zana, Dicle and Dogan* against *Turkey*, adopted on 30 April 2002.

35. CoM, ResDH2004(31) concerning the judgment of the European Court of Human Rights of 17 July 2001 in the case of *Sadak, Zana, Dicle and Dogan* against *Turkey*, adopted on 6 April 2004. The resolution deplores the fact that 'notwithstanding the re-opening of the impugned proceedings, the applicants continue to serve their original sentences and thus remain in detention almost three years after the Court's finding of a violation of the Convention.'

36. *Committee of Ministers*, ResDH2004(86) concerning the judgment of the European Court of Human Rights of 17 July 2001 in the case of *Sadak, Zana, Dicle* and *Dogan* against Turkey, adopted on 9 December 2004.

37. Tahir Elçi, a Kurdish lawyer who represented numerous Kurdish litigants in

Strasbourg, points out that, after all, the ECtHR's judgment was not executed and that any impact the Court and the CoM might have had was limited to securing the retrial of the applicants.

38. CoM, ResDH(2004)86 concerning the judgments of the European Court of Human Rights of 17 July 2001 in the case of *Sadak and others* against *Turkey*, adopted on 9 December 2004.

39. CoM, ResDH2007(1) concerning the execution of the judgment of the ECtHR in the case of *Öcalan* against *Turkey*, adopted on 14 February 2007.

40. CoM, ResDH2005(113) concerning the judgment of the ECtHR of 19 June 2003 in the case of *Hulki Güneş* against *Turkey*, adopted on 30 November 2005; ResDH2007(26) concerning the execution of the judgment of the ECtHR of 19 June 2003 in the case of *Hulki Güneş* against *Turkey*, adopted on 4 April 2007; ResDH2007(150) on the execution of the judgment of the ECtHR of 19 June 2003 in the case of *Hulki Güneş* against *Turkey*, adopted on 5 December 2007.

41. CoM, CM/Del/Dec(2007)987, adopted on 15 February 2007; CM/Del/Dec(2007)1007, adopted on 19 October 2007.

42. The letters were dated 21 February 2005 and 12 April 2006.

43. CoM, ResDH2007(100), 20 June 2007.

44. Hacettepe Üniversitesi Nüfus Etütleri Enstitüsü, *Türkiye Göç ve Yerinden Olmuş Nüfus Araştırması* (Ankara: Hacettepe Üniversitesi Nüfus Etütleri Enstitüsü, 2006).

45. For further details and critical analysis, *see* Dilek Kurban, 'Unraveling a Trade-off: Reconciling Minority Rights and Full Citizenship in Turkey', *European Yearbook of Minority Issues*, vol.4 (2004/5), pp. 341–72.

46. The permission to open a department of Kurdish language and culture, or to offer Kurdish as an elective course, is still subject to the discretion of the central government and has been denied to some universities in the region.

47. Sedat Çınar, group interview, Diyarbakır, 16 February 2008; Salim Özdemir, interviewed by Haldun Gülalp and Ozan Erözden, Ankara, 7 March 2008.

48. Mithat Sancar and Eylem Ümit Atılgan, '*Adalet Biraz Es Geçiliyor . . .*': *Demokratikleşme Sürecinde Hâkimler ve Savcılar* (Istanbul: TESEV, May 2009). Only a minority expresses the opposing view: 'The state should not be deemed sacred'; 'One must protect the citizen before the state'; 'I am against the violation of democracy in the name of the state.'

49. Legislated on 12 October 2004 by the AKP government, Article 301 penalised denigrating 'Turkishness, the Republic or the Grand National Assembly of Turkey' and the government, the judiciary, the military or security organisations, with imprisonment ranging between six months and three years. If the offence were committed abroad, the punishment would increase by one third. Under much pressure, the government slightly amended this article on 8 May 2008. See below.

50. In a letter sent to the Turkish Parliament on 21 May 2006, the UN special rapporteur on the Promotion and Protection of Human Rights and Fundamental Freedoms While Countering Terrorism warned that the vague and broad definition of terrorism had the danger of criminalising non-violent advocacy

of minority rights. 'Disregard of UN Warnings on Anti-Terror Act', Bianet website, 5 July 2006, available at http://www.bianet.org/english/politics/81682-disregard-of-un-warnings-on-anti-terror-act (accessed 17 September 2012).

51. 'Turkey: Events of 2007', Human Rights Watch website, 31 January 2008, available at http://hrw.org/englishwr2k8/docs/2008/01/31/turkey17727.htm (accessed 17 September 2012).

52. Tahir Elçi, group interview, Diyarbakır, 16 February 2008. Reyhan Yalçındağ stated in the same interview that she had never come across a police officer or a gendarme found guilty of torture in Turkey during the previous ten years, in which she had been involved in human rights litigation in the region.

53. Yaşar Aydın, interview, cited above, Istanbul, 15 October 2007.

54. Tahir Elçi, group interview, Diyarbakır, 16 February 2008.

55. Muhsin Keskin, 'Özel Yetkili Ağır Ceza Mahkemelerinin Anayasal İlkeler ile Temel Hak ve Özgürlükler Işığında İncelenmesi', İdeal Hukuk website, available at http://www.idealhukuk.com/hukuk/hukuk.asp?mct=duyurudetay&x=mak ale&y=Makaleler&id=60&tit=Ozel-Yetkili-Agir-Ceza-Mahkemelerinin-Ana yasal-ilkeler-ile-Temel-Hak-Ve-Ozgurlukler-Isiginda-incelenmesi-/-Muhsin-KES KiN (accessed 17 September 2012). These courts gained further notoriety in recent years when they seemed to target nearly all political opposition to the government as members of often imaginary 'terrorist organisations'.

56. Law No. 5532 (Law on the Amendment of the Law on the Fight against Terrorism), 29 June 2006.

57. Human Rights Watch, *Protesting as a Terrorist Offense: The Arbitrary Use of Terrorism Laws to Prosecute and Incarcerate Demonstrators in Turkey*, November 2010, available at http://www.hrw.org/reports/2010/11/01/protesting-terrorist-offense (accessed 17 September 2012).

58. UNICEF-Turkey, *Field Visit Report on Children Deemed to Be Terrorist Offenders for Participating in Demonstrations*, April 2010, available at http://www.bianet.org/files/doc_files/000/000/105/original/kitap_tamamı.pdf (accessed 17 September 2012).

59. Petition to the former President Ahmet Necdet Sezer filed on 11 June 2007 by the Contemporary Lawyers Association, who requested the President to veto the new law. Ufuk Yaşar, 'Çağdaş Hukukçular polis yasasını protesto etti', *Birgün*, 12 June 2007.

60. 'İHGD: PVSK Değerlendirmesi', Savas Karsitlari website, 18 June 2007, available at http://www.savaskarsitlari.org/arsiv.asp?ArsivTipID=9&ArsivAnaID=39652 (accessed 17 September 2012). See also 'Turkey: Events of 2007'.

61. The Turkish Human Rights Foundation reported that in the first three months after this law came into force, from 14 June 2007 to September 2007, sixteen individuals applied to the Izmir branch alone for allegations of torture and ill treatment. 'TİHV "Polis Yasasını Değiştirin" Diyor: AKP Hak Örgütlerini Dinlemedi İşkence Arttı,' Bianet website, 28 September 2007, available at http://www.bianet.org/bianet/siyaset/102050-akp-hak-orgutlerini-dinlemedi-iskence-art ti (accessed 17 September 2012).

62. In 2007, 34.9 per cent of cases of ill treatment and torture took place in cars and

outdoor areas, in contrast to 30.6 per cent in police headquarters, 19 per cent in police stations and 5.3 per cent in gendarmerie premises. S. Erdem Türközü, Evren Özer and Marko Perels, *Türkiye İnsan Hakları Raporu 2007* (Ankara: Türkiye İnsan Hakları Vakfı, 2008), p. 61, available at http://www.tihv.org. tr/dosya_arsiv/96023654eab8fffa756ba2a764b64c8b.pdf (accessed 17 September 2012).

63. On the disproportionate use of force, ill treatment and torture by law enforcement officers and the regime of impunity, see Kerem Altıparmak, 'İşkenceyi nasıl bilirsiniz? Türkiye'de orantisiz güç kullanma sorunu', *Toplum ve Bilim*, no. 115 (2009), pp. 138–76.

64. Reyhan Yalçındağ, group interview, Diyarbakır, 16 February 2008.

65. Law No. 2565 (Law on Prohibited Military Zones and Security Zones), 18 December 1981.

66. The information in this section was gathered in the TOHAV interview, Istanbul, 17 October 2007, and the group interview, Diyarbakır, 16 February 2008.

67. For an overview of the implementation of the Compensation Law based on a field study in three provinces of south-eastern Turkey, see Dilek Kurban et al., *Coming to Terms with Forced Migration: Post-displacement Restitution of Citizenship Rights in Turkey* (Istanbul: TESEV, 2007).

68. ECtHR, *Akbayır and others v. Turkey* (no. 30415/08 and 108 others), 28 June 2011; *Fidanten and others v. Turkey* (no. 27501/06 and 104 others), 28 June 2011; *Bingölbalı and others v. Turkey* (no. 18443/08 and 54 others); *Boğuş and others v. Turkey* (no. 54788/09 and 91 others), 28 June 2011.

69. ECtHR, *Yumak and Sadak v. Turkey* (no. 10226/03), 8 July 2008.

70. Reyhan Yalçındağ, group interview, Diyarbakır, 16 February 2008.

71. TOHAV interview, Istanbul, 17 October 2007; group interview, Diyarbakır, 16 February 2008.

72. Ruhşen Doğan, TOHAV interview, Istanbul, 17October 2007.

73. ECtHR, *Tanış and others v. Turkey* (no. 65899/01), 2 August 2005.

74. Tahir Elçi, group interview, Diyarbakır, 16 February 2008.

75. Dilek Kurban and Mesut Yeğen, *Adaletin Kıyısında: 'Zorunlu' Göç Sonrasında Devlet ve Kürtler/ 5233 Sayılı Tazminat Yasası'nın bir Değerlendirmesi – Van Örneği* (Istanbul: TESEV, 2012).

Chapter 8

The European Court of Human Rights and minorities in the United Kingdom: catalyst for change or hollow rhetoric?

Kimberley Brayson and Gabriel Swain

> Human rights are not an ideology or a thought system: they are more a matter of *praxis* than of *logos*. To have any meaning in the lives of individuals and communities, they must be embedded in practice. A judgment of the European Court of Human Rights is not an end in itself, but a promise of future change, the starting point of a process which should enable the rights and freedoms to be made effective.[1]

The United Kingdom can generally be seen as a dependable defender of human rights and civil liberties. A particularly vibrant legal activist community is dedicated to protecting individual rights, and efforts to protect those rights are routinely made by both state and non-state actors. There are instances, though, in which the UK is found to violate the European Convention on Human Rights (ECHR) and is faced with the decision of how best to implement the corresponding judgments of the European Court of Human Rights (hereafter ECtHR or the Court). The implementation of the ECtHR's judgments can be a quick and easy process or it can be long and laborious, depending on the circumstances surrounding the individual case and the general and individual measures required to compensate the violation. Data from the UK and the other eight countries analysed in the present volume provide a glimpse into the rates of implementation and the time taken by respective governments to do so. Figure 8.1 compares the percentage of finalised judgments that have been successfully implemented (as opposed to those still pending implementation) and the average time taken to implement a judgment. The UK's record is comparatively quite good: it has implemented 60 per cent of its judgments and has the lowest average implementation time at thirty-two months.

Notwithstanding the overall good implementation record of the UK, significant internal variation can be observed across different categories of the ECtHR's judgments and the respective rights that they address. To gain a better understanding of the conditions that dictate the UK's implementation of the ECtHR's judgments, the present study analyses three sets of cases that have produced markedly different implementation outcomes. The

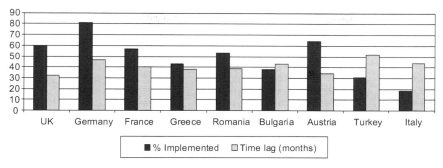

Figure 8.1 *Implementation of Articles 8–11 and 14*
Source: Dia Anagnostou and Alina Mungiu-Pippidi, *Why Do States Implement Differently the European Court of Human Rights Judgments? The Case Law on Civil Liberties and the Rights of Minorities* (JURISTRAS Project, 2009), available at http://www.juristras.eliamep.gr/wp-content/uploads/2009/05/why-do-states-implement-differently-the-european-court-of-human.pdf (accessed 18 September 2012).

analysis begins by looking at cases brought by homosexual and transgender applicants. Cases brought by these two groups represent a set of judgments whose implementation has led to the introduction of policy instruments that enhance the protection of their individual rights. The legal norms emanating from the Strasbourg Court's case law and the related civil society mobilisation in the UK have contributed to the legislative institutional changes in respect of the rights of the homosexual and transgender communities.

On the other hand, judgments condemning the UK for violations of the Convention in connection with police violence and wrongful imprisonment in Northern Ireland have encountered substantial implementation difficulties. While the applicants in those cases were vindicated in Strasbourg, they have not seen the respective judgments implemented in the same way — in some cases the victims or their families have been waiting for full implementation of the ECtHR's judgments for over a decade. The experience of homosexual and transgender applicants seeking justice in the ECtHR is further contrasted by that of Gypsies in the UK. In the few cases in which they received a favourable judgment, the implementation by national authorities has been sluggish at best. Indeed Gypsies have a weak success rate before the Court and have experienced a relative absence of meaningful policy reform as a result of Strasbourg rulings.

Comparing judgments that are characterised by successful implementation with those that have been met with non-implementation makes it possible to explore the conditions that promote or conversely restrict the ability of European human rights norms to influence legal and policy change in the UK. The analysis of this chapter shows that such variation depends in large part on the social and political stakes surrounding each individual case. Cases brought by members of a minority group with considerable support from civil society, such as homosexuals, seem more likely to result in concrete policy change. Conversely, groups with less support from civil society, Gypsies for example, have been less successful in convincing the ECtHR about their claims and in pressuring the UK government to implement those judgments in which they were vindicated.

Another trend that emerges is the degree to which political sensitivity of an issue area affects a group's chances to convince the Court, as well as the extent to which the ECtHR's judgments are domestically enforced. Cases won by victims of abuse by Northern Ireland security forces epitomise slow or non-existent implementation because they involve sensitive national security issues that render the implementation of the Committee of Ministers' (CoM) requirements a tedious, conflict-ridden and protracted process. Even though they do not involve national security issues, cases brought by Gypsies involve public order and land use regulations that apply to the population as a whole. This translates to a lack of public support and a lack of motivation on the part of legislators and politicians to risk losing popularity by ardently supporting the right of Gypsies to a traditional way of life. Conversely, cases brought by homosexual and transgender applicants do not affect the rest of the population in the same way and this may go a long way to explaining those groups' success in using the ECtHR to affect policy change. It is to these two groups that the focus of this paper now turns.

SUCCESSFUL IMPLEMENTATION: THE RIGHTS OF HOMOSEXUALS AND TRANSGENDER PERSONS

In front of the Strasbourg Court, homosexual and transgender applicants often raise claims that seek to assert their own personal freedoms based on 'autonomy, identity and integrity'[2] by invoking Article 8 ECHR, the right to private and family life. In asserting their personal liberties, homosexual and transgender individuals are claiming rights which do not have a far-reaching impact upon society or bear any security implications for the state. This stands in contrast to judgments against the UK concerning Northern Ireland and Gypsies, which carry with them considerations of national security and public order. With the introduction of the Human Rights Act 1998 the constitutional fabric of the UK changed and a new era of rights ideology was ushered in by the Labour government.[3] Homosexual and transgender rights are two areas where rights can confidently be said to have been brought home.[4] The ECtHR case law in the area of homosexual rights is an example of the assertion of individual rights in a liberal state and in a society that had, to all extents and purposes, accepted the rights of gay individuals, albeit on an informal, non-institutionalised basis. The ECtHR's case law undoubtedly paved the way for other marginalised groups in the UK such as transgendered people and women to assert their rights. On an institutional level, this case law can also be considered the catalyst which resulted in the promulgation of the Human Rights Act 1998 in the UK.[5]

The right to privacy of homosexual men was first recognised under Article 8 ECHR in *Dudgeon* v. *United Kingdom*[6], which resulted in the amendment of the Homosexual Offences Order. This judgment was reaffirmed in *Norris* v. *Ireland*.[7] Both of these cases targeted national laws criminalising the homosexual activity of adult men. However, even though the right to practise homosexual acts without being considered a criminal had been recognised by the Strasbourg Court, the fact remained that across the Council of Europe (CoE) signatory states there existed significant variation in the age of consent for homosexuals. More often than not this meant that domestic legislation set the age of consent for homosexual men at a higher age than that for heterosexuals or lesbians.[8] Despite the fact that the differential in age of consent was a common factor in many CoE states, the age of consent for homosexuals varied across states thus the Strasbourg Court had difficulty in discerning any 'European consensus' on the matter.[9] This is undoubtedly attributable to the varying philosophical and religious ideologies which prevail in CoE countries.

Whether due to a certain degree of social openness on issues related to homosexuality or to a strong history of political lobbying in the UK, there has been a proliferation of relevant case law that has come out of the Strasbourg Court against the UK. Another reason for this may be that in the UK, the age of consent for male homosexuals (21) was significantly higher than in other CoE countries such as Italy (14) or France, Greece and Turkey (15).[10] In addition, the UK had highly restrictive legislation in place regulating homosexuals in the Armed Forces. Official policy allowed for discharging employees who revealed themselves to be homosexual, regardless of their conduct and by virtue of their homosexuality alone. In the cases of *Lustig-Prean and Beckett* v. *United Kingdom*,[11] *Smith and Grady* v. *United Kingdom*,[12] *Perkins and R.* v. *United Kingdom*[13] and *Beck, Copp and Bazeley* v. *United Kingdom*,[14] the ECtHR found UK policy to be in breach of Article 8 (right to private life) of the Convention.

Until the 2000s, powerful opposition to lifting the ban on homosexuals in the army[15] was further reinforced by the policy of the Ministry of Defence.[16] Policy guidelines produced in 1994 reaffirmed that individuals could be discharged for taking part in homosexual acts as such acts were 'considered incompatible with service in the armed forces'.[17] In *Lustig-Prean and Beckett*, the government argued that the legitimate aim of the restriction of gays in the military was the operational effectiveness of the armed forces, a vital issue of national security. It asserted that to allow homosexuals in the military would have an adverse effect on the latter. The government's stance most likely manifested a reluctance to engage in issues which belong to what has traditionally been termed the 'private' sphere,[18] rather than expressing a belief that the homosexuality of servicemen could *actually* affect national security.

In response to the ECtHR judgments described above, the ban on homosexuals in the military was lifted following the adoption of the Armed Forces Code of Social Conduct Policy Statement. In the subsequent judgment of *Smith and Grady* the ECtHR found a breach in relation to Article 8 and also Article 13 (right to an effective remedy) in favour of gays in the military. These judgments were implemented through relevant policy change and legislation that expanded the rights of homosexuals. Their implementation involved the adoption of the Armed Forces Code of Social Conduct along with the Armed Forces Disciplinary Act 2000. These measures represented a 'dramatic policy change'[19] in that they enabled homosexuals to be legally employed by the armed forces and allowed those who had been dismissed from the military because of their sexual orientation to take legal action.[20]

In *B.B. v. United Kingdom*[21] the Strasbourg Court found the comparatively higher age of consent for homosexual men as opposed to heterosexuals and lesbians in the UK to be in breach of Article 8 in conjunction with Article 14 ECHR. The UK had in fact legislated pre-emptively in this area by amending the Sexual Offences (Amendment) Act in 2000 and reducing the age of consent for male homosexuals to the same as for heterosexuals and lesbians.[22] As is indicated in other case studies included in this volume, imminent pressure from Strasbourg can lead national governments to act more fastidiously and in the interests of minority and marginalised groups, in instances where such action was previously tardy or non-existent. In sum, the cases dealing with homosexual rights provide relatively clear examples of how Strasbourg case law can directly result in change of legislation on a domestic level. They have been cited as being extremely influential in prompting the Labour government in the UK to draft and adopt the Human Rights Act in 1998.[23]

The legislative changes that expanded the rights of homosexuals represented a formalisation of existing social mores within the UK. Formalising these rights did not affect wider public interest issues, thus the government had no real grounds on which to refuse or stall implementation. However, it must be noted that although civil society in general was receptive to the cementing of homosexual rights, there was resistance from within the military to the change of policy on discharge of homosexuals. Some went as far as to term the shift in policy 'ridiculous' and suggested that it would lower morale in the forces.[24] Nonetheless, ten years on, an overall acceptance of homosexuals in the military is apparent. In 2009 a gay soldier appeared on the front cover of *Soldier* magazine[25] and a more tolerant attitude towards homosexuals in the Army can be discerned from commentary and discussion in the media.[26] Thus, on the face of it at least, acceptance of homosexuals within the armed forces has come to be more akin to that of civil society at large.

The success witnessed above in the area of homosexual rights created a political climate which was accommodating to the idea of realising the rights of sexual minorities. The most significant executive measure representing successful implementation is the Gender Recognition Act 2004 (GRA), which establishes the rights of transgender people in UK domestic law. This was preceded by and has been followed up with numerous other legislative instruments.[27] Most recently the Equality Act 2010 includes provisions that further protect transgender rights. Litigation on behalf of transgender individuals in the ECtHR has almost exclusively originated from the British context. This may well be attributable to the fact that gender reassignment operations are available on the National Health Service in the UK, creating a more permissive climate for transgender claims and heightened confidence among the transgender community.

Transgender jurisprudence in the UK was initially based on the BSD ('Biological Sex is Decisive') system,[28] which was articulated by the British courts in *Corbett* v. *Corbett*.[29] It was determined on the basis of purely biological criteria of chromosomes, gonads and genitalia as being indicative of a person's sex, to the exclusion of psychological factors and gender.[30] Despite some initial stumbling blocks, transgender applicants have experienced relative success in convincing the ECtHR to extend protection to their rights.

The transgender community has benefited from centralised structures of civil society mobilisation. Press for Change (PFC) has been the most prominent activist organisation in this field. Their campaigning for the rights of the transgender community is all-encompassing. Not only do they campaign for legislative and policy change but also for a shift in social attitudes. The latter is pursued through a highly organised set of actions aiming at support, education and provision of information. The fact that the transgender community is a concentrated and specific section of society and the existence of one major lobby group spearheading the campaign are significant from a social mobilisation perspective. The education and information process concerning the rights of this minority group is made relatively easy due to its small numbers. Furthermore, the enactment of legislation only affects this specific group of individuals. From the government's perspective, this makes it less controversial as there are no wider-reaching political implications which would provoke reaction and cause political elites to lose votes. If anything, the government stands to gain votes from the group in question.

With the exception of the UK and two cases involving France and Germany, nearly all other countries under study in this volume demonstrate a lack of case law dealing with transgender rights and a corresponding lack of lobbying activity akin to that witnessed in the UK. Stephen Whittle, founder and vice-president of PFC, has noted that many CoE countries do have legislation in place dealing with the rights of the transgender community, including Austria, Germany, Italy and Turkey.[31] However, such legislation has acted in a subversive manner; transgender rights were recognised on the condition that the transgender community remained invisible.

The cases concerning transgender rights can be distinguished on the basis of the issues that they raise in the respective case law. These comprise administrative practices, issues arising as to transgender and 'family life', and one case, not directly implicating the state, about a private health insurer refusing to pay for gender reassignment surgery.[32] The first cluster of cases concerns what must be the most fundamental question for post-operative transsexuals, namely changing their civil status to be in line with their new sex following gender reassignment. *Rees*[33] and *Cossey*[34] were both cases which claimed that the British state was in breach of the ECHR by failing to amend the birth certificates of the applicants to reflect their post-operative gender identity. In *Rees* the applicant, a female-to-male transsexual, claimed a breach of Article 8 ECHR (respect for private life), while in *Cossey* the applicant, a male-to-female transsexual, claimed a breach of Article 12 ECHR (the right to marry), in addition to the Article 8 claim. In both cases, the Court failed to find a breach of the Convention by the British state.

As they had done previously in the cases of *X. and Y. v. Netherlands*, *Dudgeon v. United Kingdom* and *Norris v. Ireland*,[35] the Court in both *Rees* and *Cossey* highlighted the importance of respect for 'the individual's right to his or her sexual life'.[36] At the same time, it also advanced the argument that 'the notion of "respect" is not clear-cut'.[37] Thus it was for the Court to define what 'respect' in this context meant. In *Marckx v. Belgium*[38] it was held that respect does not merely imply negative obligations on the state to refrain from interfering with the private lives of individuals but it can also imply positive obligations to protect. Hence, in the area of sexual orientation, '"respect" covers not only freedom *from* state interference, but also freedom *to* enjoy certain aspects of the human personality'.[39] However, as with the homosexual cases, the Court was not willing to follow through on the promise of positive obligations in this delicate area concerning transgender rights. In the absence of a 'European consensus' on the rights of transgender individuals, the judges at Strasbourg were not willing to step in and define or create such a consensus. The British state was not in violation of the Convention for failing to adjust the birth certificates of the applicants to accord with their current gender identity.

In close succession to these cases the French case of *B. v. France*[40] was brought before the Strasbourg Court. The facts of the case were analogous to those of *Rees* and *Cossey*. The Court asserted that 'the need for appropriate legal measures concerning transsexuals should be kept under review having regard particularly to scientific and societal developments'.[41] The two years that had elapsed between the two UK cases and B. were not a sufficiently long period for significant societal change to have taken place. Yet, in spite of the short passage of time, the ECtHR did in fact find a violation of Article 8 ECHR by the French state. While the two cases were essentially premised upon the same question, namely, whether civil documents can be amended to reflect changes following gender reassignment, they were answered in opposing terms by the Court, whose reasoning was based on the different ways in which the law operates in France and the UK.

The Court distinguished the earlier UK cases from *B. v. France* by highlighting the fact that the systems of civil registration in the two countries differed. In the UK the birth certificate was a factual record of the citizen's gender at the point of birth. In the French system, however, the birth certificate could be changed throughout the individual's life by means of a marginal note or a transcription on the certificate. In the UK, new names could be adopted in the absence of any restrictions or formalities whereas the French system required under Article 57 of the Civil Code that changes in name were subject to judicial permission and a demonstrable 'legitimate interest' on the part of the applicant.[42] Furthermore, the Court distinguished the situations by noting that in the UK, birth certificates are not used as a form of identification, as passports and driving licences suffice. On these latter documents in the UK, the new sex of a transsexual after gender reassignment is duly registered. In France, however, the gender status of an individual is taken from their birth certificate to be reflected in the computerised identity card of the individual. Thus the inconsistency between B's legal sex and actual gender brought her inconvenience on a daily basis.

For the above reasons, the position of the French state regarding transsexuals was found to be in breach of the Convention, in contrast to the UK. Was this a contradiction in the jurisprudence of the Court? Had the Court relied on societal change to justify its position, the judgments in the two cases could well have been incompatible. However, the Court relied purely on the legal differences between the civil registration systems and 'neatly distinguished' one from the other.[43] This improved the situation for transsexuals in France but left the *Rees* and *Cossey* judgments intact, and pre-empted a complete overhaul of the civil registration system in the UK.

Ten years on, the UK government found itself back in Strasbourg in the case of *Goodwin*,[44] concerning the very same question of gender recognition on birth certificates of post-operative transsexuals. The context was slightly different. Christine Goodwin, a male-to-female post operative transsexual, complained that her rights under the Convention had been violated because she was unable to claim a state pension from the age of sixty, as a biological woman can in the UK. Instead, she had to wait until sixty-five, as biological men do in the UK. As gender statuses for the purposes of national insurance were derived from birth certificates, Goodwin argued that her right to private life (Article 8 ECHR) had been violated due to the refusal by the British state, as in *Rees* and *Cossey*, to change the gender status on her birth certificate. The Strasbourg Court found it illogical that Goodwin should have been given gender reassignment surgery on the National Health Service, which recognises the condition of gender dysphoria, only to have the results of the surgery not fully recognised by the state.[45] Thus they found the British state in breach of Article 8. In addition, Goodwin also claimed a breach of Article 12 ECHR, the right to marry; she was unable under British legislation to marry a man, as she was still considered to be a man by reference to her birth certificate. *Rees* and *Cossey* had also questioned this point but their claims under Article 12 had been dismissed by the ECtHR. However, here the Court found that in the light of societal changes in the institution of marriage and in the field of transsexuality 'a test of congruent biological factors can no longer be decisive in denying legal recognition to the change of gender of a post-operative transsexual',[46] and Goodwin 'may therefore claim that the very essence of her right to marry has been infringed'.[47] The Court at Strasbourg declared a breach of Article 12.

Goodwin clarified the status of transgender individuals in the context of the ECtHR. Any contracting state refusing to recognise the post-operative gender of a transsexual will be in breach of the Convention. This decision provided the basis for the political mobilisation that resulted in the GRA in the UK, which gives legal recognition to transgender people. An explanatory note on the PFC website confirms the decision as being 'the minimum line behind which the government cannot retreat. It must provide legal registration for these people.'[48] The Strasbourg Court itself stated that 'the unsatisfactory situation in which post-operative transsexuals live in an intermediate zone as not quite one gender or the other is no longer sustainable'.[49] This was a clear indication and warning to the government that legislative change had to be made. Subsequently, the case of *Grant v. United Kingdom*[50] reinforced the Court's position with regard to post-operative transsexuals as articulated in *Goodwin*. Although finding a breach of Article 8 ECHR by the UK, the Court only rewarded damages for non-payment of state pension to a male-to-female transsexual for the period of time that had elapsed since the *Goodwin* judgment. It was not prepared to open the floodgates by retroactively applying *Goodwin*.

In the meantime a related judgment had been handed down by the Strasbourg Court in *X., Y. and Z. v. United Kingdom*.[51] This case presented conceptual considerations which were not at issue in the cases above. *X., Y. and Z.* also centred upon an alleged breach of Article 8 ECHR but this time in relation to respect for family life instead of private life. X. was a female-to-male transsexual who, along with Y., the female partner of X., had a child, Z., by means of artificial insemination. The question before the Court was whether the British government was in breach of Article 8 by refusing to register X. as the father of Z. Although the Court initially found unanimously that 'de facto family ties'[52] existed between X., Y. and Z., they never once referred to the relationship between the three applicants as 'family life'.[53]

The Court appears to have been distinguishing between biological and non-biological family life. By doing so, it 'seems to be drawing distinctions between the types of relationships protected by Article 8',[54] making choices about *whose* family relationships are to be protected. The relationship between a post-operative transsexual, his partner and their IVF baby appears not worthy of protection in the eyes of the Court. The latter conservatively navigates its way around pronouncing a judgement on a sensitive issue where no European consensus exists coupled with a 'lack of common ground'[55] across contracting states. The Court chose to conceptualise this case in terms of a lack of respect for the rights of transsexuals as opposed to an interference with their rights.[56] This had the effect of placing the burden of proof on the applicant to prove that the state failed to respect their rights as opposed to the state proving that it did not interfere with the right of transsexuals.

The non-interventionist attitude of the Court appears to be making it more difficult for transsexuals in the context of the family to establish their rights. The Court seems to be taking a step back from its judgments in *Rees* and *Cossey* in favour of the state.[57] However, in the wake of *Goodwin*, the situation in the UK at least has been remedied by the GRA, which states: 'The fact that a person's gender has become the acquired gender under this Act does not affect the status of the person as the father or mother of a child.'[58] As for the rest of Europe, the case of *Goodwin*, supportive of the view that the state must facilitate the marriage of post-operative transsexuals to their new opposite sex, can be nothing but promising for the particular issue of the family life of transsexuals as raised in *X., Y. and Z. Goodwin* represents the peak of expansive interpretation of rights providing protection for the transgender community.

Such an expansive interpretation of Convention rights by the Strasbourg Court has come about following growing legal mobilisation on behalf of the transgender community. Such mobilisation has come almost entirely from PFC. PFC was established in 1992 and since then it has led a very successful lobbying campaign to establish equal rights for transgender people. It has acted to effect policy change in the UK by bombarding the ECtHR with test cases, which raised all of the above issues pertinent to transgender identity. Most notably Stephen Whittle, founder and vice-chairman of PFC, played a major role in the drafting of the GRA. Some of the strongest opposition faced by PFC came from the Church, which did not want these rights to be recognised and raised objection to the marriage of transgender people. Its objections were most strongly voiced during the drafting of the GRA. As a result, some of the most emancipatory clauses were omitted, leading some to suggest that the Act did not go as far as it should have. However, in the face of opposition from an institution such as the Church, the GRA represents a milestone and goes a long way in cementing equal rights for the transgender community. The GRA paved the way for further legislation, evidenced in the Equality Act 2010, which buffers the rights protected under the GRA by designating 'gender reassignment' as one of the 'protected characteristics' under the Equality Act.[59]

In sum, the ECtHR together with domestic courts have been inclined to expand their interpretations in part as a result of systematic campaigning on the part of PFC and the transgender community. Their judgments have in turn been important levers in pressuring for legislative reforms and rights-expansive policy change. Outside the legislative arena, further efforts by the UK government can be witnessed. On 8 December 2011, the UK government launched a new initiative to promote human rights for transgender people. Its transgender action plan[60] aims at encouraging equality for transgender people in all governmental departments. This demonstrates an encouraging level of commitment by the UK government not only to assert rights on an administrative abstract level but also to aid the realisation of these rights in practice.

NON-IMPLEMENTATION: JUDGMENTS CONCERNING GYPSIES AND THE ACTIONS OF SECURITY FORCES IN NORTHERN IRELAND

The ECtHR's judgments against the UK concerning Gypsies and the actions of security forces in Northern Ireland are for most part characterised by delayed implementation, as they are left unresolved for long periods. There have been some instances in which the UK government has introduced measures that seemingly satisfy the CoM, and yet the respective cases have remained open without a final resolution for years. However, in most cases the delayed implementation seems to stem from the state's inability to adequately remedy the violation.

Since the mid-1990s, family members of individuals killed by Northern Ireland security forces have been seeking compensation for their losses by taking cases to Strasbourg. Their status as Catholics and their nationalist political views allow us to identify them as both religious and political minorities.[61] The first such case was *McCann and others* v. *United Kingdom*,[62] in which, in 1995, the UK became the first state to be found in violation of Article 2 ECHR (right to life) in the killing of an IRA operative in Gibraltar.[63] This case was implemented quickly, as the only measure required for implementation was the payment of costs and damages to the applicant.[64] In 2000, though, the Court once again found the UK in violation of Article 2 ECHR in four cases (*McKerr*, *Shanaghan*, *Kelly and others* and *Jordan*), again in relation to the killing of suspected terrorists in Northern Ireland.[65] These were joined by *McShane* v. *United Kingdom* in 2002 and *Finucane* v. *United Kingdom* in 2003,[66] both of which involved similar violations and would be considered with the previous four as a group of homogeneous cases in future evaluations of implementation by the CoM.[67] In five of these six cases, applicants also raised Article 14 ECHR in relation to perceived discrimination against the deceased on the basis of their membership of the nationalist and Catholic communities, yet the Court did not find violations of that article in any of the cases.[68]

The Article 2 ECHR violations in these six cases, referred to henceforth as *McKerr et al.*, stemmed largely from the failure of the UK authorities to conduct unbiased, independent investigations into the deaths of suspected terrorists. Implementing the Court's prescribed measures has proven tricky for the UK, as it tries to balance its desire to autonomously govern domestic terrorism with national security issues. As the international law scholar Yutaka Arai-Takahashi suggests, one might generally expect the Court to broaden the margin of appreciation in cases concerning national security threats.[69] Indeed, this has often been the case with applications lodged against the UK.[70] Nevertheless, states must still prove that procedural safeguards are in place to prevent violations of Article 2.[71] The UK violations in *McKerr et al.* stemmed from the failure to ensure such procedural safeguards, as the Court's judgment highlighted the absence of independence in the investigations into the deaths.

Implementing *McKerr et al.* has posed great challenges for the UK government. Three interim resolutions have been drafted by the CoM, and the cases remain open under the supervision of the committee at the time of writing (June 2012). In a 2005 interim resolution, the CoM noted that progress had been made towards implementation, but it did not close its examination of any aspects of the judgments.[72] Another interim resolution in 2007[73] acknowledged significant progress toward implementation in *McKerr et al.* In that resolution, the CoM noted several satisfactory general measures that had been taken,[74] but it also noted that individual measures were still needed to compensate the victims' families.[75] In a third interim resolution, issued in 2009,[76] the CoM noted further progress and closed its examination of additional aspects of the cases that had been effectively addressed by general measures.[77] Individual measures have also been adopted in *McShane* and *Finucane*, and the CoM has closed its examination of those cases with respect to individual measures.[78] All six cases remain open, though, pending complete implementation of every aspect of the Court's judgments. The failure of the British authorities to introduce comprehensive and adequate measures has been ongoing despite repeated recommendations from the British parliamentary Joint Committee on Human Rights (JCHR) to quickly address the violations in these cases.[79]

In a sense, the applicants in the *McKerr et al.* cases did everything right. The initial four sought support from the Northern Ireland Human Rights Commission, which submitted third-party comments on behalf of the applicants to the Court.[80] The applicant in the *McShane* case was represented before the Court by a representative from the Committee on the Administration of Justice, perhaps the leading human rights NGO in Northern Ireland.[81] Her legal representation was well organised,[82] and she emerged from Strasbourg victorious. Yet, a decade later, these cases remain open as the UK has not yet introduced individual and general measures adequate to satisfy the CoM.

Various measures have been introduced by the UK in response to these judgments, but at the time of writing more measures were needed to implement them adequately and terminate the CoM proceedings. For example, the investigations into four of the cases (*Jordan, Kelly and others, McKerr* and *Shanaghan*), as prescribed by the CoM, have yet to be completed. In sensitive cases such as these, reasonable implementation delays are to be expected, but relatives of the deceased in these cases are getting rightfully impatient, as complete implementation has now been pending, in some cases, for nearly twenty years.

Implementation was also pending for many years in another set of judgments related to the conflict in Northern Ireland: *John Murray v. United Kingdom, Murray v. United Kingdom, Quinn v. United Kingdom, Averill v. United Kingdom* and *Magee v. United Kingdom*.[83] The applicants in these cases had been arrested, in different instances, by Northern Ireland security forces under the Prevention of Terrorism (Temporary Provisions) Act of 1989. Following the arrests the applicants had all decided to remain silent during questioning and their silence was subsequently used to incriminate them during their respective trials. They claimed that this use of their silence, combined with their being denied legal advice during the initial forty-eight hours of their detention (twenty-four hours in the *Averill* case) constituted a violation of Article 6 ECHR (right to a fair trial). The UK was found in violation of this provision in each of the five cases and they were subsequently moved to the CoM for implementation monitoring. Released in 1996, the judgment in the first of these cases, *John Murray*, helped pave the way for the other four applicants to bring similar claims before the Court. John Murray's claims were supported by third-party interventions on his behalf by prominent human rights NGOs, including Amnesty International, Liberty, Justice, British–Irish Rights Watch and the Committee on the Administration of Justice.[84]

In 2002, the CoM issued an interim resolution for all five cases, treating them together as a group. The resolution noted policy reforms that had been undertaken to implement the judgments, but lamented the fact that they had not yet entered into force.[85] The CoM did, however, note its intention to re-examine the cases once those policy reforms entered into force or at its meeting in December 2002 at the latest. These implementation measures consisted of the Youth Justice and Criminal Evidence Act of 1999, which essentially banned the drawing of inferences from silence during the questioning of a prisoner in England and Wales, and the Criminal Evidence (Northern Ireland) Order of 1999, which did the same for Northern Ireland. The Youth Justice and Criminal Evidence Act of 1999 came into effect in 2003. The relevant provision (Article 36) of the Criminal Evidence (Northern Ireland) Order of 1999 came into effect in 2007. Together, the introduction of these policy measures effectively satisfied the CoM and they closed the cases in 2010. But it took the UK a staggering 133 months to introduce the general measures necessary to close the *John Murray* case.

While the applicants in the homosexual, transgender and Northern Ireland cases described above have seen their legal efforts in front of the ECtHR result in varying levels of policy reform, British Gypsies' attempts to seek justice in the Strasbourg Court have been thoroughly disappointing. The term 'Gypsy' in the UK is not entirely synonymous with the Roma ethnicity prevailing in the rest of Europe. While it can refer to communities of

Roma ethnicity, in the UK 'Gypsy' also refers to Irish Travellers and anyone who leads or has traditionally led a nomadic lifestyle. Thus, Gypsies in the UK context should be considered a cultural rather than a homogeneous ethnic minority group.

The marginalised status of Gypsies in Europe was definitely apparent to European policy elites by the early 1990s, as is clearly evident in the words of CoE rapporteur Josephine Verspaget, who in 1993 noted:

> The position of many groups of Gypsies can be compared to the situation in the Third World: little education, bad housing, bad hygienic situation, high birth rate, high infant mortality, no knowledge or means to improve the situation, low life expectancy . . . If nothing is done, the situation for most Gypsies will only worsen in the next generation.[86]

The first Gypsies to bring cases to Strasbourg faced an uphill struggle, as the Court tended to grant states a wide margin of appreciation in these cases. In 1996, the Court issued its first-ever ruling in a Gypsy rights case in *Buckley* v. *United Kingdom*.[87] In this case, the applicant claimed that being evicted from her own land, where she lived with her children in her caravan, violated Article 8 ECHR.[88] She also claimed that the UK decision discriminated against her as a Gypsy, which constituted a violation of Article 14 ECHR. The Strasbourg Court found no violation in *Buckley*. It instead accepted the arguments of the UK government claiming that the need to preserve the countryside from development incursions outweighed the applicant's rights guaranteed under Article 8.[89]

At the same time, the *Buckley* case did succeed in raising awareness of Gypsy-related discrimination in the Court. Five years later a group of five cases were brought against the UK, in which the applicants, all Gypsies, again made claims under Articles 8 and 14 ECHR with regard to eviction notices similar to those in the *Buckley* case.[90] These applicants were all represented by the same lawyer and enjoyed support from the European Roma Rights Centre, which submitted a third-party intervention on their behalf. However, this was not enough to convince the Court to find the UK in violation of the Convention. In its judgment in one of the cases (*Chapman* v. *United Kingdom*), though, the Court sent a clear message that it might reconsider its stance in the future. The judgment revealed a split among the Court, which found no violation by ten votes to seven. The seven dissenting judges voiced the opinion that although case law from *Buckley* v. *United Kingdom* applied to this case, it should not bind the Court's decision on issues such as these, and that the Court must constantly consider changing social trends in its judgments.[91] A few years later in 2004, the Court did just that in *Connors* v. *United Kingdom*. The case involved a Gypsy applicant who claimed that his eviction from a site he had occupied with his family for over a decade violated his right to private and family life.[92] This time, the Court found a violation of Article 8 ECHR, conveying that contracting states have a positive obligation to facilitate the Gypsy way of life.

The *Connors* judgment is expected to lead to legislative changes favourable to Gypsy lifestyles; however, at the time of writing (June 2012) its domestic implementation was still pending. To implement *Connors*, the UK introduced Section 318 of the Housing and Regeneration Act 2008, which amends the Mobile Home Act 1983 by giving Gypsy and Traveller residents of mobile home sites the same rights as all other residents of mobile home sites. This is a positive development, but at the time of writing Section 318 had not yet fully entered into force. It should come as no surprise that this issue is low on Parliament's agenda and until it is addressed, the CoM will not close its examination of the *Connors* case.

What accounts for the implementation delay, which now exceeds five years since publication of the judgment? The answer is related, at least in part, to the lack of public support for Gypsies in the UK and the negative image of them portrayed by the media and various politicians. For example, a 9 March 2005 issue of the British tabloid *The Sun* ran a discriminatory cover story declaring 'war on a Gipsy [sic] free-for-all' which described Gypsies as Britain's biggest problem. Helen O'Nions notes also that during the passage of the Criminal Justice and Public Order Act 1994, anti-Gypsy sentiment was expressed by various politicians, with one MP referring to Gypsies as 'mobile spivs'.[93] She also cites a 1993 article from *The Independent*, which quotes a resident of the Somerset village of Middlezoy opposed to the development of a Gypsy site, who says, 'A bullet in the head is what they need . . . If I were dying of cancer I'd buy a shotgun and take out six of them.'[94] This is clearly an extreme statement and does not represent the opinions of the majority, but it nevertheless indicates the extent of the negative sentiment aimed at Gypsies. With such a lack of popular support it is not hard to believe that the *Connors* judgment remains under the monitoring of the CoM. A favourable judgment in Strasbourg is incapable of reforming legislation without the help of legislators and, more broadly, of civil society actors dedicated to advocating the measures necessary to implement rights reform on the ground.

CONCLUSION

The preceding analysis shows that although the UK has on the whole been quick to implement Strasbourg judgments and formalise the rights of the transgender and homosexual communities, in other areas of human rights protection implementation has been uncharacteristically tardy or it has not been realised at all. By the early 1990s the presence of transgender individuals and homosexuals within British society had become acceptable, even if not wholeheartedly welcomed by all. This acceptance was visible in the form of lobby groups such as Stonewall and Press for Change, which attempted to steer policy in their favour by taking test cases to the ECtHR. In the wake of

Strasbourg judgments, the UK government was formalising this wider social acceptance and legitimising the presence of these groups in British society to mirror the situation as it existed on the ground.

Considering that rights of homosexuals and transgender individuals have no further implications for members of society as a whole, the Labour government never really stood to lose a proportion of the vote by consolidating these rights in legislative form. As part of this process the government allowed both the homosexual and transgender communities a substantial input into the drafting of the legal documents. The gay community was involved in the drafting of the new policy about homosexuals in the military, and the Gender Recognition Act 2004 stands at the forefront of legislative instruments within the Council of Europe for the transgender community. In addition to this Act, there has been a proliferation of various other legislative instruments in the area of transgender rights.[95]

The Northern Ireland cases on the other hand display a delayed and reluctant process of implementation. With the exception of prompt implementation in the initial case of *McCann and others*, which involved individual compensation measures, implementation of subsequent judgments in which the UK was found in violation of the Convention has stalled. Even though the CoM has issued three interim resolutions, complete implementation is still pending ten years on. In the cases of *Finucane* and *McKerr et al.* the JCHR stated in its 2008 annual report that it was 'concerned that the adequacy of individual measures remain[s] in question in each of these cases'[96] concerning the use of lethal force in Northern Ireland. In its response to the JCHR, the government attributed such delay to the constant intervention and requests from the families for adjournments, as well as to the Historical Enquiries Team's lengthy historical investigation into the proceedings.

In addition, judgments originating from the situation in Northern Ireland are closely linked to national security issues and raise questions that are embedded in multiple ways in the fabric of UK society as a whole. The position of Northern Ireland with its distinct legal system and its standing between Britain and the Republic of Ireland means that the process of social liberalisation and secularisation there has progressed at a different rate from the rest of the UK. Religion has played a more profound role in the development of Northern Ireland. Ongoing tensions between the Protestant and Catholic communities have reinforced conservative religious ideologies within the community, which does not make Northern Ireland a fertile ground for change. Social and ethno-religious divisions have been more pronounced and despite numerous peace treaties and ceasefires, these divisions persist in violent forms.[97] Thus, to legislate in this area would require the UK government to take an authoritative stance on a politically sensitive issue. It is unlikely that such a complex area, encompassing not only law but social policy, religion, culture and terrorism, can be remedied by a single legislative instrument.

Our review of the domestic implementation in Gypsy-related judgments paints a different picture altogether. Unlike the Northern Ireland cases, the Gypsy community suffers not because its plight is a threat to national security but mainly because of its marked unpopularity in British society. The claims of Gypsies also disclose property issues that have implications for wider society and that often run contrary to land use planning laws. Despite the steps taken in response to the *Connors* judgment the JCHR is still unhappy with the length of time taken by the government to implement these measures.[98] With a lack of centralised lobbying, a lack of funding and continued unpopularity fuelled by the media, the full implementation of judgments and a formalisation of rights for the Gypsy community appear to remain out of reach for the time being.

Some marginalised groups have been more successful than others in achieving a formalisation of their rights. Those which have not been successful in their endeavour to do this are groups whose rights disclose national security or public order issues. The UK has a particular imperial history, embedded in geo-political alliances and conflicts, which makes it a prominent target for terroristic political violence. Under these circumstances it is somewhat understandable that the UK may be more reticent to hand over complete control to Strasbourg in these matters as the implications are undoubtedly far reaching in the extreme. At the same time, the UK's frequent appearances before the Court in Strasbourg also evidences the strong community of human rights lawyers and lobby groups who are active in the UK pursuing test case claims and ensuring adequate implementation of Strasbourg rulings.

British jurists and the UK government were among the chief architects of the Council of Europe and drafters of the European Convention on Human Rights. While such a dedication towards human rights is not diminished by frequent appearances before the Court in Strasbourg, the UK's commitment to the protection of human rights as exemplified in the Human Rights Act 1998 may be on the verge of waning, at least from a governmental perspective. With the recent change in government in 2010 to the Conservative–Liberal Democrat coalition the prospect of the repeal of the Human Rights Act is becoming ever more real. The ultimate question for the minority rights which have been established under the auspices of the ECHR in the UK is therefore: what would become of the status of Strasbourg case law in the domestic system if repeal were to take place? In this case, Prime Minister David Cameron has said that the UK would most certainly remain a member of the Council of Europe. The European Court of Human Rights would still have a role, albeit one which would not have any direct impact on UK law. To reduce Strasbourg's power further a British bill of rights may be on the cards.[99] What form this would take is unclear. However a commission on a bill of rights has been set up by the UK government to ascertain particulars as to the form and content of such a bill.

On 7 November 2011 the UK government took up its six-month

chairmanship of the Council of Europe.[100] The UK promptly published a document stating its top priority to be 'reforming the European Court of Human Rights and strengthening implementation of the European Convention on Human Rights'.[101] Despite the neutral language of this statement of intent, the UK government has been shown to intend to limit the powers of the Strasbourg Court by means of the principle of subsidiarity: the Council of Europe states would have the final word of interpretation on the ECHR, which is supposed to be a check on their own exercise of power.[102] These proposals were followed by a conference held in Brighton in April 2012, from which emerged the 'Brighton Declaration' on the future of the ECtHR.[103] Whatever materialises, it is clear that it would be a shame to see the brave, forward-thinking judgments of both the ECtHR and the domestic courts in the area of marginalised rights and the successful implementation of such judgments fade into futility.

Notes

1. Françoise Tulkens, 'Execution and Effects of Judgments of the European Court of Human Rights: The Role of the Judiciary', in European Court of Human Rights, *Dialogue between Judges* (Strasbourg: Council of Europe, 2006), p. 12.
2. Jill Marshall, *Personal Freedom through Human Rights Law? Autonomy, Identity and Integrity under the European Convention of Human Rights* (Leiden: Martinus Nijhoff, 2009), p. 3.
3. Susan Millns, 'The Jurisprudence of the Strasbourg Court and Protection of Fundamental Rights in the United Kingdom: An Overview of Litigation, Implementation and Domestic Reform' (JURISTRAS Project, 2008), p. 2, available at: http://www.juristras.eliamep.gr/wp-content/uploads/2008/09/britain.pdf (accessed 18 September 2012).
4. This phraseology reflects the title of the Labour Party's consultation paper introduced prior to the general election of May 1997. See Jack Straw MP and Paul Boateng MP, 'Bringing Rights Home: Labour's Plans to Incorporate the European Convention on Human Rights into United Kingdom Law', *European Human Rights Law Review*, no. 1 (1997), pp. 71–80.
5. Stephen Whittle, interview by Kimberley Brayson, Manchester, 27 January 2009.
6. ECtHR, *Dudgeon v. United Kingdom* (no. 7525/76), 26 October 1981.
7. ECtHR *Norris v. Ireland* (no. 10581/83), 26 October 1988.
8. Laurence R. Helfer, 'Finding a Consensus on Equality: The Homosexual Age of Consent and the European Convention on Human Rights', *New York University Law Review*, vol. 65 (1990), p. 1044.
9. Ibid., p. 1056.
10. Ibid., table on p. 1090.
11. ECtHR, *Lustig-Prean and Beckett v. United Kingdom* (nos. 31417/96, 32377/96), 27 September 1999.

12. ECtHR, *Smith and Grady* v. *United Kingdom* (nos. 33985/96, 33986/96), 27 September 1999.

13. ECtHR, *Perkins and R.* v. *United Kingdom* (nos. 43208/98, 44875/98), 22 October 2002.

14. ECtHR, *Beck, Copp and Bazeley* v. *United Kingdom* (nos. 48535/99–48537/99), 22 October 2002.

15. Dia Anagnostou, 'Does European Human Rights Law Matter? Implementation and Domestic Impact of Strasbourg Court Judgements on Minority-related Rights and Policies', *International Journal of Human Rights*, vol. 14, no. 5 (2010), pp. 721–43.

16. See Mark Oakes, 'The Armed Forces Bill', House of Commons Research Paper 01/03, 8 January 2001. Available at http://www.parliament.uk/commons/lib/research/rp2001/rp01-003.pdf (accessed 9 October 2012).

17. 'Armed Forces Guidelines on Homosexuality 1994', in Henry J. Steiner, Philip Alston and Ryan Goodman (eds), *International Human Rights in Context: Law, Politics, Morals*, 3rd edn (Oxford: Oxford University Press, 2008), p. 973.

18. Kimberley Brayson and Susan Millns, 'Gendered Rights on the European Stage: Do Marginalized Groups Find a "Voice" in the European Court of Human Rights?', *European Public Law*, vol. 16, no. 3 (2010), p. 441.

19. Anagnostou, 'Does European Human Rights Law Matter?', p. 8.

20. Clare Saunders, Christopher Rootes and Susan Millns, 'Supranational Rights Litigation, Implementation and the Domestic Impact of Strasbourg Court Jurisprudence: A Case Study of the United Kingdom' (JURISTRAS Project, 2008), p. 28, available at http://www.juristras.eliamep.gr/wp-content/uploads/2008/09/casestudyuk.pdf (accessed 18 September 2012).

21. ECtHR, *B.B.* v. *United Kingdom* (no. 53760/00), 10 February 2004.

22. Anagnostou, 'Does European Human Rights Law Matter?', p. 7. See also CoM, ResDH(2005)99, adopted on 7 July 2004.

23. Rabinder Singh, interview by Kimberley Brayson, Matrix Chambers, London, 3 November 2008; Stephen Whittle, interview by Kimberley Brayson, Manchester, 27 January 2009.

24. 'Delight and despair at gay ban ruling', BBC News website, 27 September 1999, available at http://news.bbc.co.uk/1/hi/uk/458842.stm (accessed 18 September 2012).

25. Aislinn Simpson, 'Armed Forces celebrates diversity with gay serviceman in Soldier magazine.', Telegraph website, 27 July 2009, available at http://www.telegraph.co.uk/news/newstopics/onthefrontline/5917311/Armed-Forces-celebrates-diversity-with-gay-serviceman-in-Soldier-magazine.html (accessed 18 September 2012).

26. Alexandra Topping, 'Gay British soldier talks about coming out to his comrades.' Guardian website, 11 December 2009, available at http://www.guardian.co.uk/uk/2009/dec/11/gay-soldier-ben-rakestrow (accessed 18 September 2012).

27. A list of UK legislation pertaining to the rights of transgender individuals can be found on the Press for Change website at http://www.pfc.org.uk (accessed 18 September 2012).

28. Susan Millns, 'Transsexuality and the European Convention on Human Rights', *Public Law*, vol. 92, no. 4 (1992), p. 565.
29. *Corbett v. Corbett* [1970] 2 All ER, 33.
30. Urfan Khaliq, 'Transsexuals in the European Court of Human Rights: X, Y and Z v. UK', *Northern Ireland Legal Quarterly*, vol. 49, no. 2 (1998), p. 191.
31. Stephen Whittle, interview by Kimberley Brayson, Manchester, 27 January 2009.
32. ECtHR, *Van Kück v. Germany* (no. 35968/97), 12 June 2003.
33. ECtHR, *Rees v. United Kingdom* (no. 9532/81), 17 October 1986.
34. ECtHR, *Cossey v. United Kingdom* (no. 10843/84), 27 September 1990.
35. See ECtHR, *X. and Y. v. Netherlands* (no. 8978/80), 26 March 1985; *Dudgeon v. United Kingdom*; *Norris v. Ireland*.
36. ECtHR, *X. and Y. v. Netherlands*.
37. ECtHR, *Cossey v. United Kingdom*, para. 37.
38. ECtHR, *Marckx v. Belgium* (no. 6833/74), 13 June 1979.
39. Millns, 'Transsexuality and the European Convention on Human Rights', p. 561.
40. ECtHR, *B. v. France* (no. 57/1990/248/319), 25 March 1992.
41. ECtHR, *Cossey v. United Kingdom*, para. 40.
42. Millns, 'Transsexuality and the European Convention on Human Rights', p. 562.
43. Ibid., p. 564.
44. ECtHR, *Christine Goodwin v. United Kingdom* (no. 28957/95) 11 July 2002.
45. Ibid., para. 78
46. Ibid., para. 100.
47. Ibid., para. 101.
48. The note says, 'N.B. The court's endorsement of the rights of "post-operative" transsexual people is the minimum line behind which the government cannot retreat. It must provide legal registration for these people. HOWEVER, it is perfectly possible for the government, when implementing legislation, to go one step further and to make legal recognition available to those who are post-treatment and thus include those trans people who for health, disability or other reason are unable to undergo surgical intervention. This is the position that PFC urges the government to take.' See Stephen Whittle, '*Goodwin & I v. United Kingdom Government*: What Does It Mean?', 2 November 2002, p. 4. Available at http://www.pfc.org.uk/caselaw/Goodwin%20&%20I%20v.%20United%20Kingdom%20Government%20What%20Does%20It%20Mean.pdf (accessed 9 October 2012).
49. ECtHR, *Goodwin v. United Kingdom*, para. 70.
50. ECtHR, *Grant v. United Kingdom* (no. 32570/03), 23 May 2006.
51. ECtHR, *X., Y. and Z. v. United Kingdom* (21830/93), 22 April 1997.
52. Ibid., para. 37.
53. Khaliq, 'Transsexuals in the European Court of Human Rights', p. 194.
54. Ibid., p. 194.
55. ECtHR, *X., Y. and Z. v. United Kingdom*, para. 44.
56. Khaliq, 'Transsexuals in the European Court of Human Rights', p. 196.

57. The majority of the votes, fourteen to six, went in the state's favour. See ibid., p. 199.
58. Gender Recognition Act 2004, Section 12: 'Parenthood', available at http://www.legislation.gov.uk/ukpga/2004/7/section/12 (accessed 18 September 2012).
59. Equality Act 2010, Section 7: Gender Reassignment. See http://www.opsi.gov.uk/acts/acts2010/pdf/ukpga_20100015_en.pdf (accessed 18 September 2012).
60. *Advancing Transgender Equality: A Plan for Action* (HM Government, December 2011), available at http://www.homeoffice.gov.uk/publications/equalities/lgbt-equality-publications/transgender-action-plan?view=Binary (accessed 18 September 2012). Further explanation can be found PFC website: http://www.pfc.org.uk/transactionplan.html (accessed 18 September 2012).
61. All of the individuals concerned were Catholic and members of either the IRA or Sinn Féin, with the exception of Patrick Finucane. Finucane was killed when security forces allegedly mistook him for an IRA officer. He was, in fact, a Catholic human rights lawyer who had represented IRA members in domestic civil rights cases, including high-profile individuals such as Bobby Sands.
62. ECtHR, *McCann and others v. United Kingdom* (no. 18984/91), 27 September 1995.
63. Christine Bell and Johanna Keenan, 'Lost on the Way Home? The Right to Life in Northern Ireland', *Journal of Law and Society*, vol. 32, no. 1 (2005), p. 73.
64. CoM, Res DH(96)102, 'Case of McCann and Others against United Kingdom' (1996).
65. See ECtHR, *McKerr v. United Kingdom* (no. 28883/95), 4 May 2001; *Hugh Jordan v. United Kingdom* (no. 24746/94), 4 May 2001; *Kelly and others v. United Kingdom* (no. 30054/96), 4 May 2001; *Shanaghan v. United Kingdom* (no. 37715/97), 4 May 2001.
66. ECtHR, *McShane v. United Kingdom* (no. 43290/98), 28 May 2002; *Finucane v. United Kingdom* (no. 29178/95), 1 July 2003.
67. For a thorough explanation of the specific details of the violations of each individual application see CoM Interim Resolution, ResDH(2005)20, 'Action of the Security Forces in Northern Ireland (Case of McKerr against the United Kingdom and five similar cases)' (2005).
68. The applicant in *Finucane v. United Kingdom* did not claim discrimination in her application to the Court.
69. See Yutaka Arai-Takahashi, *The Margin of Appreciation Doctrine and the Principle of Proportionality in the Jurisprudence of the ECHR* (Oxford: Intersentia Press, 2002).
70. In *McLaughlin v. United Kingdom*, the Commission found inadmissible to the Court an application claiming that a broadcasting ban on material supporting Sinn Féin violated ECHR Article 10 (freedom of speech). ECtHR, *McLaughlin v. United Kingdom* (no. 18759/91), 9 May 1994
71. Arai-Takahashi, *The Margin of Appreciation Doctrine and the Principle of Proportionality in the Jurisprudence of the ECHR*, p. 84.
72. See CoM Interim Resolution, ResDH(2005)20.
73. CoM Interim Resolution, ResDH(2007)73, 'Action of the Security Forces in

Northern Ireland (Case of McKerr against the United Kingdom and five similar cases)' (2007).

74. These included legislation that set new guidelines for deciding whether or not to prosecute state agents, and assurances from the UK government that, in future cases suggesting that an investigation by the Police Service of Northern Ireland cannot be fully independent, the chief constable of that service will call in another police force to investigate. The CoM also noted the establishment of the Police Ombudsman for Northern Ireland in 2000 and acknowledged that a five-year review of the operation of the legislation governing that office was under way.

75. The individual measures called for here are effective, independent investigations into the historical events of the cases, carried out in a way that will hold those responsible (if any) for unlawful actions.

76. CoM Interim Resolution, ResDH(2009)44, 'Action of the Security Forces in Northern Ireland (Case of McKerr against the United Kingdom and five similar cases)' (2009).

77. Satisfactory general measures included the establishment of the Historical Enquiries Team in 2005 to replace the Serious Crime Review Team, which has now begun to provide concrete results in investigations of historical cases. Although the CoM accepted this as a general measure, investigations into the cases at hand are still outstanding and will have to be carried out as an individual measure in each case.

78. *McKerr*, *Kelly and others*, *Shanaghan* and *Jordan* are all still awaiting individual measures, which is very problematic given the fact that twenty-seven years have now passed since the death of Gervaise McKerr and his family is still awaiting answers into the details of his death. The applicants in the other cases died in 1987, 1991and 1992 respectively.

79. Joint Committee on Human Rights, *Monitoring the Government's Response to Human Rights Judgments: Annual Report 2008*, Thirty-first Report, Session 2007–8 (HL Paper 173/HC 1078), p. 16, available at http://www.publications. parliament.uk/pa/jt200708/jtselect/jtrights/173/173.pdf (accessed 18 September 2012). See also Joint Committee on Human Rights, Nineteenth Report, Session 2005–6, para. 137, available at http://www.publications.parliament.uk/ pa/jt200506/jtselect/jtrights/185/18502.htm (accessed 18 September 2012).

80. See ECtHR, *McKerr v. United Kingdom*; *Kelly and others v. United Kingdom*; *Hugh Jordan v. United Kingdom*; *Shanaghan v. United Kingdom*, para. 7 in each.

81. ECtHR, *McShane v. United Kingdom*, para. 2.

82. Kelly and Shanaghan were both represented by the same solicitors, as were McKerr and Jordan (although by different solicitors from Kelly and Shanaghan).

83. ECtHR, *John Murray v. United Kingdom* (no. 18731/91), 8 February 1996; *Murray v. United Kingdom* (no. 22384/93), 21 October 1996; *Quinn v. United Kingdom* (no. 23496/94), 21 October 1996; *Averill v. United Kingdom* (no. 36408/97), 6 June 2000; *Magee v. United Kingdom* (no. 28135/95), 6 June 2000.

84. ECtHR, *John Murray v. United Kingdom*, para. 5.

85. CoM Interim Resolution, ResDH(2002)85.

86. Josephine Verspaget, *Gypsies in Europe*, Council of Europe Parliamentary

Assembly Doc. 6733 (11 January 1993), para. 29, quoted in Helen O'Nions, *Minority Rights Protection in International Law: The Roma in Europe* (Aldershot: Ashgate, 2007), p. 8.

87. ECtHR, *Buckley* v. *United Kingdom* (no. 20348/92), 25 September 1996.
88. British case law has determined that parking caravans on land constitutes development. See *Restormel Borough Council* v. *Secretary of State for the Environment and Rabey* [1982] JPL 785.
89. Ibid., para. 84.
90. ECtHR, *Chapman* v. *United Kingdom* (no. 27238/95), 18 January 2001; *Beard* v. *United Kingdom* (no. 24882/94), 18 January 2001; *Coster* v. *United Kingdom* (no. 24876/94), 18 January 2001; *Lee* v. *United Kingdom* (no. 25289/94), 18 January 2001; *Jane Smith* v. *United Kingdom* (no. 25154/94), 18 January 2001.
91. See 'Joint Dissenting Opinion of Judges Pastor Ridruejo, Bonello, Tulkens, Stránická, Lorenzen, Fischbach and Casadevall', ECtHR, *Chapman* v. *United Kingdom*, para. 1.
92. ECtHR, *Connors* v. *United Kingdom* (no. 66746/01), 27 May 2004.
93. O'Nions, *Minority Rights Protection in International Law*, pp. 13–14.
94. Helen O'Nions, 'The Marginalisation of Gypsies', *Web Journal of Current Legal Issues*, no. 3 (1995), available at http://webjcli.ncl.ac.uk/articles3/onions3.html (accessed 18 September 2012).
95. All legislative instruments dealing with transgender issues in the UK can be accessed at http://www.pfc.org.uk (accessed 18 September 2012).
96. Joint Committee of Human Rights, *Monitoring the Government's Response to Human Rights Judgments*.
97. Henry McDonald, 'Catholic youth worker's widow blames UDA for killing', Guardian website, 26 May 2009, available at: http://www.guardian.co.uk/uk/2009/may/26/catholic-youth-worker-widow-uda (accessed 18 September 2012).
98. Joint Committee of Human Rights, *Monitoring the Government's Response to Human Rights Judgments*, p. 29.
99. Conor Gearty, interview by Kimberley Brayson, London School of Economics and Political Science, 25 March 2009.
100. Coincidentally, the British judge Sir Nicholas Bratza took up his post as the president of the ECtHR just three days previously, on 4 November 2011.
101. 'United Kingdom Chairmanship of the Council of Europe: Priorities and Objectives', available at http://www.coe.int/lportal/c/document_library/get_file?uuid=46e525f1-23ca-4cff-ab23-e8eb9b183ed2&groupId=10227 (accessed 19 September 2012).
102. Joshua Rozenberg, 'Dominic Grieve takes on the European Court of Human Rights', Guardian website, 27 October 2011, available at http://www.guardian.co.uk/law/2011/oct/27/dominic-grieve-european-human-rights (accessed 19 September 2012).
103. 'High Level Conference on the Future of the European Court of Human Rights: Brighton Declaration', Council of Europe website, available at http://www.coe.int/en/20120419-brighton-declaration/ (accessed 18 September 2012).

Chapter 9

Politics, courts and society in the national implementation and practice of European Court of Human Rights case law

Dia Anagnostou

Since the Second World War, and especially over the past twenty years, the evolution of the transnational human rights regime centred on the Convention has been one of the most remarkable institutional transformations in Europe. It embodies a highly successful transnational legal system with far-reaching consequences for European and national governance. In its genesis, the Convention regime was the creature of state governments, which also determined with their decision-making its institutional remoulding over time. At the same time, though, its evolution into a 'constitutional instrument of European public order' has been a multi-dimensional phenomenon. Its construction and operation has involved dynamic processes of interaction engaging various national authorities but also non-state social actors, both individual and collective.

The present volume has sought to identify and explore the factors and conditions that determine the implementation and domestic impact of the ECtHR's judgments, and the variable patterns of influence that they exert upon national laws and policies. While national authorities promptly institute measures and pursue reforms called for by the ECtHR's judgments in some cases, they procrastinate or resist doing so in others. But variation is also qualitative, as the adopted measures in response to some judgments may be directly appropriate to the underlying rights issue or dispute at stake, or conversely, they may be extraneous or only tangentially related to it. By contextualising implementation in its domestic institutional and societal context, the contributions shed light on the multi-faceted ways in which the ECHR system and its Strasbourg-based judicial arm penetrate and impact upon national legal and political orders.

This concluding chapter discusses and analyses the patterns of variation in the domestic implementation of the ECtHR's judgments and seeks to understand the attitudes of national officials, judges and government actors towards the ECtHR's case law across and within the different countries under study. National judges, especially those sitting in higher and constitutional courts, are central and often dominant actors in this regard. The responses of national authorities, including judges, vary across countries, across different categories of rights claims, and often across time. The purpose of this volume is not to compare systematically and to evaluate alternative theories regarding the factors that influence domestic implementation of the ECtHR's judgments. Instead, drawing from the country case studies, it identifies and explores distinct approaches for systematically studying the domestic implementation of human rights case law.

The implementation of the ECtHR's judgments and their potential for prompting reform and policy change domestically can be approached through different perspectives, which may also be relevant for understanding compliance with international law more broadly: the political and policy process, a judicial politics perspective, and a social mobilisation perspective. Following an overview of the findings of the country case studies in this volume, this chapter outlines and discusses these three perspectives. Finally, this chapter's last section reflects on the current challenges facing the Strasbourg Court, as well as on measures to improve the domestic enforcement mechanism of the convention system.

OVERVIEW OF FINDINGS

The preceding chapters bring to light an extremely rich and highly diverse landscape regarding the domestic implementation of the ECtHR's judgments, which at first glance appears to defy broad generalisations. On the whole, as other studies have also noted, national authorities take seriously their obligation to give effect to the ECtHR's adverse judgments. The vast majority of them do so, sooner or later. Instances of persistent and outright refusal to implement are indeed rare. At the same time, though, national governments accord a medium to low political priority to the implementation of the ECtHR's judgments, which is often assigned to administrative-executive bodies lacking sufficient political clout. In the broad picture, the nature and scope of measures that national authorities adopt vary tremendously. To begin with, it is clear that the status of the Convention in the domestic hierarchy of legal norms is not consequential for the applicability of the Convention or of the ECtHR's case law. This factor may even be considered nearly irrelevant as national courts, especially higher and constitutional courts, have developed various interpretations and jurisprudential techniques to grant the Convention supra-legislative status. They have tended to interpret national rights guarantees in the light of the ECHR norms and ECtHR case law, even if the Convention does not formally override constitutional norms.

The overall impact of the Strasbourg Court's case law in different legal and political orders varies tremendously depending on the scope and effectiveness of national-level rights protection and judicial review. Germany is a case in point. An elaborate system of judicial rights review domestically, a highly authoritative Federal Constitutional Court (FCC) with individual access, and by and large the congruence of rights norms contained in the Basic Law with those of the Convention, all contribute to the fact that the impact of the ECtHR's case law is secondary, highly subsidiary and for most part peripheral. National authorities in Germany closely follow relevant Strasbourg Court case law issued against other states. They also engage in a kind of pre-emptive review of national draft legislation in order to verify its compatibility with the Convention and the ECtHR's case law. The cumulative effect of all this is a small number of adverse judgments against Germany, relatively few of which require substantial legal or policy change.

The emphasis of this volume is mainly in the general (less so in the individual) measures that national authorities undertake. General measures encapsulate the potential for the Strasbourg Court's case law to exert legal and policy impact domestically. Even if they may at times result in significant legislative and other changes, single judgments usually do not lead to any broad and substantial reform. More frequently, they raise particular aspects of a problem rather than challenge a whole area of law and policy. Pressures for implementing general measures and pursuing reforms are compounded when there are repeat condemnations of a country in similar or related issues. In so far as the ECtHR's judgments manage to exert broader impact on laws and policies, they do so as one factor in a complex policy-making process, rather than as the decisive trigger and influence on the policy outcome.[1] Therefore, in order to understand the potential of the ECtHR's judgments to influence broader policy reform in an area, their influence must be traced within the frame of broader policy processes.

It must be noted, though, that establishing causality between the Court's judgments and legislative or other reforms is often tricky and far from straightforward, even when the relevant reforms are recorded in the CoM resolutions as being taken in response to specific Court rulings. Not infrequently, national authorities may submit reform initiatives, which are taken in response to a variety of other factors and imperatives, as measures to implement the ECtHR's judgments. For instance, an important constitutional amendment in 2001 in Greece reinforced the administration's obligation to enforce domestic court judgments, and allowed for compulsory execution of judgments against the state. While such a reform was submitted by national authorities as a measure to implement the ECtHR's judgment in *Hornsby* v. *Greece*, it is clear that the latter by no means caused this constitutional amendment.[2] Instead, this judgment only added to a momentum for reform that had been gathering for some time. It was driven by a variety of pressures to remedy the generalised resistance of the Greek administration to respond to the legitimate demands of citizens who had been vindicated in court.

Notwithstanding the difficulty of establishing causality, the country-based case studies in this volume show that in a variety of different areas of policy and rights claims, the ECtHR's judgments have been important triggers or causes. They have also provided leverage for domestic actors to pressure for substantial reforms. While filling relatively minor gaps in the judicial system in Germany, they exposed the systemic problems with the administration of justice in Italy, as well as with the deficient protection that private property as a constitutional right has enjoyed domestically. The ECtHR's judgments were also a fundamental motor for reform of various aspects of the justice system in ex-communist countries such as Romania and Bulgaria. They played a no less catalytic role in bringing an end to the restrictions imposed upon the rights of marginalised individuals and minorities, such as Jehovah's Witnesses (JWs), and expanding the rights of homosexuals and transgender individuals in countries such as Greece, the UK, Austria and France, among others. At the same time, though, the ECtHR's adverse rulings that criticised state attitudes towards minorities or raised issues that pertained to a state's internal and external security concerns (Turkey, the UK, Bulgaria, Greece etc.) have been met with non-implementation, or with minimal or extraneous remedial measures.

One generalisation that can be drawn from the case studies is that the implementation of the ECtHR's judgments is less likely to be resisted when they raise procedural or technical aspects pertaining, for instance, to the justice system. Such examples are the legislative amendments to the Criminal Procedure Code linked to effective judicial control of pre-trial detention in 2000 in Bulgaria, as well as amendments that allowed for judicial review of administrative decisions about social welfare and the welfare of persons with disabilities. Still, not all procedural issues are smoothly implemented or are devoid of conflict, as they may be embedded in legal culture and tradition and/or challenge vested interests of judicial or state officials. For instance, as the chapter on Romania shows, those parts of the Criminal Procedure Code that pertained to the powers of the prosecutor in criminal procedure have actually been strongly contested and difficult to reform. Overall, however, it can be observed that judgments that do not involve politically sensitive issues are eventually implemented, even if with delays. By contrast, ECtHR judgments that raise sensitive issues about who is and who can be defined as an ethnic minority, or that interfere with the ability of national authorities to expel immigrants or other individuals whom they consider suspect on national security grounds, are least likely to be aptly and completely implemented.

A further broad distinction can be made between rights claims (and relevant issue areas or policies) that pertain to progressive social values and pluralism on the one hand, and those that pertain to the rights of minorities and immigrants and are seen as crucial for state security and national sovereignty on the other. The national implementation and the domestic impact of the ECtHR's judgments have been much more notable and satisfactory in the former set of cases than in the latter, in which they range from non-existent to highly compromised. For instance, the Strasbourg Court judgments have promoted religious freedom, even if in a piecemeal fashion, and therefore pluralism, by extending the relevant rights to non-majoritarian religious groups. They have also contributed to a more progressive approach and to legal changes that over time expanded the rights of homosexuals and transgender individuals domestically.

The ECtHR's immigration-related judgments have also defined certain limits to unfettered state discretion regarding the expulsion or deportation of aliens. Their implementation at the national level has contributed to improvements in the procedural aspects of asylum-seeking, the ability of non-nationals to access social benefits and the legal rights of non-nationals. Even though changes have not expanded the rights of immigrants and foreigners to enter or stay in a country, they have nonetheless enhanced certain safeguards as to how they are treated by national authorities.

Since the 1990s, the political and geographical composition of the Council of Europe's membership has extended well beyond the original core of established European democracies. Currently 50 per cent of the ECtHR's judgments involve Turkey, the western Balkans and the ex-Soviet states, where democracy and the rule of law encounter serious structural problems or have yet to take hold.[3] In the recently democratised ex-communist states of central, eastern and south-eastern Europe (CESE), the role of the ECtHR's case law has so far been less that of an 'evolutive standard setter' and more that of a democratic agenda setter. Among the eight country-based case studies that are included in this volume, the effect of the ECtHR's case law in promoting legislative reforms and policy change appears to be greatest in Turkey, as well as in Romania and Bulgaria prior to their accession to the EU. The domestic implementation and influence of the ECtHR's judgments cannot be separated from the broader EU integration processes, as the chapters on Romania and Turkey show.

During its accession process prior to membership in 2007, pressures on implementing the ECtHR's judgments in Romania were pronounced. Their normative prescriptions were reinforced by the tremendous influence and leverage exerted by the EU accession conditionality. In defining the democratic reforms that Romania had to undertake in order to meet the democracy and human rights *acquis* (in judicial reform, the role of the prosecutor, freedom of expression for journalists etc.), the European Commission drew heavily on the ECtHR's judgments and the infringements of the Convention identified by them. As a transnational mechanism of norm adaptation, the obligation and pressures to implement the ECtHR's judgments were augmented through the intergovernmental enforcement inherent in the EU accession process.[4] In addition, the EU accession process provided tremendous infrastructure support to undertake or facilitate reforms explicitly recommended or indirectly implied by the ECtHR's judgments. It also proved instrumental in promoting reforms to strengthen the independence of the judiciary and to safeguard the rule of law in general. In sum, the EU accession process added 'teeth' to the obligation of Romania to implement the ECtHR's judgments. At the same time, important differences must be noted. For instance, these judgments have had a reformist effect in freedom of expression issues, but not in issues linked to the powers of the secret service in the country.

External reinforcement of human rights norms through the ECtHR's judgments has arguably been most effective in countries like Romania, despite the fact that the political will to undertake reforms in line with these judgments has been wavering. After 1989, the domestic constellation of political forces in the country was mixed, defined by the absence of an elite consensus on liberal reforms and Western integration. The main political parties have equally included both liberal democratic forces and parties with strong nationalist and authoritarian tendencies.[5]

In countries with an ambivalent reformist orientation domestically, such as post-communist Romania, a strong external impetus is decisive for government action to comply with human rights norms. In Romania, the ECtHR's judgments became simultaneously a point of reference both for civil society actors such as APADOR (the Association for the Defence of Human Rights in Romania – The Helsinki Committee) to exert pressures from below (i.e. in the area of freedom of expression) and for the European Commission's monitoring in assessing progress with human rights reform. By 2004–5, twin pressures from civil society and the EU were strong enough to compel even President Iliescu, who had earlier been opposed to it, to seek to abolish the prison sentence for calumny and offence against authority. Even though they are a product of external pressure, the relevant reforms are arguably still sustainable in the longer run and pave the way for eventual internalisation.[6] However, the Romanian chapter points out that following the country's EU membership in 2007, the momentum in the implementation of the ECtHR's judgments and the democratic reforms that are linked to them have subsided.

The role of the ECtHR's case law as a democratic agenda setter has been even more pronounced in countries like Turkey where the presence and role of the military in political life creates fundamental incompatibilities with the Convention and its democratic precepts. This finding is in accord with recent studies that identify the domestic impact of human rights treaties to be greatest in countries at an intermediate stage, which are neither firmly rooted democracies nor stable authoritarian polities. While in the former most rights are already well protected and the motive for social mobilisation is low, the likelihood of successful mobilisation in the latter is also low.[7] Even though the salience of the ECtHR's judgments in triggering legislative reforms has been high in non-consolidated democracies like Turkey, their routine implementation in practice, as well as the ability of the relevant reforms to take root in the longer run, are nonetheless questioned. Legal reforms in accordance with human rights and the rule of law are a necessary but not a sufficient condition for embedding democracy. They also require sustained political and governmental will and the growth of a legal and judicial culture conducive to them. As the case study on Turkey argues, legal reforms imposed from above have failed to solve the Kurdish question in the absence of a political solution on the ground.

IMPLEMENTATION OF THE ECtHR'S JUDGMENTS AND THEIR POTENTIAL TO INFLUENCE REFORM AND POLICY CHANGE

The domestic influence of the ECtHR's case law can be approached and traced through three distinct perspectives. These are not necessarily mutually exclusive. Instead, some may be more appropriate for understanding and explaining variable (intra-state and cross-state) implementation of the ECtHR judgments in some categories of rights claims and issue areas than in others. Each of these perspectives is defined by the dominance of specific actors whose role is decisive in complying with and implementing the ECtHR's judgments and the Convention in particular issue areas.

The political and policy process

One way to understand the implementation of the ECtHR's judgments is to view it as part of the policy process in each country. Understanding why particular measures were adopted (or not adopted) would require tracing the actions and interactions, motives and preferences of the different institutional and political actors in the respective area of law and policy that is touched upon by an ECtHR judgment. In each country, the policy process is shaped by a particular constellation of institutions: state organisations or bodies specialising in human rights with a consultative or other role (i.e. ombudsman, human rights commissions or related committees); the ministries with competence in the area that is touched upon by a judgment; and the government and the legislature, with their specific configuration of political forces. The policy process in each country also intersects with the institutions that are specifically assigned the task of execution of the ECtHR's judgments. While centring on the executive, in some countries (such as the UK and Germany) execution also involves parliamentary actors. The different institutions and actors that are involved in national policy processes are characterised by various power and other resource endowments, and they may have distinct preferences as to whether and how to implement particular ECtHR judgments. To be sure, in most instances, the implementation of the ECtHR's judgments does not activate the entire policy process, as it may involve legislative or administrative interventions of secondary importance or technical issues that are undertaken with little discussion or controversy by the respective ministries.

One influential theory from a rational choice approach in new institutionalism conceptualises the policy process in relation to the number of veto players (both institutional and partisan) with specific preferences, and a certain degree of internal cohesion but also distance among them. Veto players are all those actors whose agreement is necessary for a legislative change to take place and for a change in the status quo more broadly. Some veto players have prime position in the process as they are the ones that can set the agenda.[8] Drawing from this theory, Mary Volcansek argues that constitutional courts must also be conceptualised as veto players. They are integral, rather than external, to the policy process along with executives and legislatures. When courts can exercise the power of constitutional review, they can influence in a variety of direct and indirect ways the policy-making process. Beyond the nullification of policies, a court can exert such an influence by eliminating options and narrowing the range of acceptable policies, granting legitimacy to some and withholding it from others.[9]

A telling example of courts as influential policy actors can be drawn from the case study of Italy. Notwithstanding intra-court differences across various issue areas, on the whole, the Italian higher courts seem to have taken the lead and initiative with respect to executive and parliamentary actors in upgrading domestic implementation of the ECtHR's case law. Executive and parliamentary actors have been more cautious and even unable – for political reasons – to adopt the measures necessary to bring Italian law in line with the ECHR provisions and the Court's case law in areas such as property rights and length of judicial proceedings. The political failure to improve compliance with the ECtHR's judgments in part prompted the judicial branch to assume a more proactive role, at times acting instead of the legislator. As the *Dorigo* judgments issued by the Constitutional Court and the Court of Cassation show, the Italian judiciary has encouraged the legislator to bring national law in line with the Convention. Still, beyond the overall assessment of the judiciary's changing attitudes towards the ECHR and the Strasbourg Court's case law, it is imperative to examine the important differences and conflicts that exist among different courts, which is taken up in the next section of this chapter.

The domestic implementation and influence of human rights case law may be constrained by separation of powers doctrines that may hinder the judicial review of legislative and executive acts in reference to higher norms. Generally, it is argued that 'in virtually every country, the Convention has enhanced judicial authority vis-à-vis the legislative and executive branches'.[10] Besides the configuration of and interaction among legislative, executive and judicial institutions and actors involved in policy-making, as well as the balance of power among them, the policy process may be influenced by the institutional architecture of the state, such as its federal structure. For instance, in Germany, even though implementation is assigned to the

Ministry of Justice, in practice, the execution of the ECtHR's judgments is a highly dispersed task that involves different federal and state actors depending on the area or issue at hand. Other institutional features of the state that are highly relevant to the implementation of the ECtHR's judgments include the relationship between parliaments and executives, the organisation of the judiciary and the presence of higher (and/or constitutional) courts.

Human rights treaties can arguably empower, even if in subtle ways, the executive in favour of the legislature to set the agenda and pursue reforms.[11] We can observe this in some cases, particularly in the post-communist countries, as well as in countries such as Turkey. However, as a mechanism for human rights treaties to influence domestic rights-expansive legal and policy change, it is premised on the questionable assumption that governments have stronger preferences for rights than legislatures. External human rights norms may indeed enable the executive to push through with domestic reforms against internal opposition, provided that sufficient government will is there to implement the Convention and the ECtHR's case law. In the post-communist context, the process of accession in the EU also contributed to strengthening the executive over Parliament, including in rule-of-law reforms. Under pressure to pass laws speedily to transpose the EU *acquis* into national law, governments like the one in Romania made use of extraordinary government decrees that required only retrospective approval of Parliament. Parliamentarians have often been only minimally involved in the process and they have had insufficient knowledge regarding the details of the laws being passed.[12]

At the same time, constitutional courts have also played important roles, often as independent and active players in the law- and policy-making processes of post-transition states in CESE. Parliamentary minorities have often found in courts useful allies in their struggle to overturn laws on which they were outvoted.[13] Nonetheless, the case studies included in this volume show that national courts, especially higher and constitutional courts (for instance the Romanian Constitutional Court or RCC) have on the whole been highly ambivalent vis-à-vis the Convention and the ECtHR's case law – for instance, when the 2004 reform of the Criminal Code adopted by the Romanian Parliament repelled 'insult' and abolished the prison sentence for slander, thereby aligning domestic law more closely with ECtHR case law, the RCC rolled back the reform. It declared unconstitutional the law decriminalising insult and defamation in 2007, on the grounds that there should be an effective remedy for interference with the private life and reputation of persons.

The nature and scope of implementation of the ECtHR's judgments is closely linked to the domestic and interest group politics in the issue area in question. A number of the contributions to this volume highlight that the implementation of the ECtHR's judgments may be decisively influenced

by power struggles among different groups that see their interests and positions being challenged by reforms that may be called for by these judgments.
For instance, in Romania a series of ECtHR judgments have been critical
of the extraordinary powers of the prosecutor (to arrest, to strike down
final court judgments etc.). The hurdles encountered in the process of their
implementation have brought to light a strong conflict between judges and
prosecutors (as representatives of the state) over the transfer of powers from
the latter to the former, who are viewed as more independent. The stance
of the RCC on this issue has been highly contradictory, aligning itself with
ECtHR jurisprudence but also rolling back in 2003 the reformist nature of
the measures undertaken by the government. A policy process approach
could investigate the conflicting views and interests of judges, prosecutors,
the government and Parliament in order to understand the implementation
outcome. Eventually, following the *Pantea* judgment, and under strong pressure from the EU in the process of accession, in 2004 the Romanian government proceeded with reforms that fundamentally undercut the powers of the
prosecutors.

Patterns of public support or opposition, as well as the ability of interested social actors to enlist the support of influential elites and policy
makers, can also influence the government's willingness to decisively and
effectively implement the ECtHR's judgments and to engage in reforms. The
salience of public attitudes is exemplified in the non-implementation of the
ethnic minority judgments issued by the ECtHR against Greece and Bulgaria.
The failure of national authorities in the two countries to implement these
judgments is no doubt closely linked to the thorough lack of public support
for a policy that in any way would move closer to recognising the self-
definition (and thereby existence) of Turkish or Macedonian minorities. On
the other hand, the Greek and Bulgarian governments undertook reforms
that expanded the rights of JWs. JWs were able to exercise sufficient leverage
on the government to persuade it to undertake reforms that removed restrictions on religious freedom, while members of ethnic minorities have been
unable to do so. Social science research could explore the ways in which, and
the conditions under which, particular social actors and domestic constituencies manage to leverage the ECtHR's judgments in order to pressure the
government to undertake rights-expansive reforms.

According to Lisa Conant, governments are likely to align their policies
with European court decisions only in so far as their interpretations of these
decisions enjoy sufficient public, political and/or institutional support.
Implementation of such decisions also depends on government responsiveness to the preferences of actors with structural power, in addition to legal
and political mobilisation by organised groups.[14] The empirical material presented in some of the chapters shows that political and institutional support
is decisive for the domestic implementation of the ECtHR judgments and
their potential to exert legislative and policy impact. In Austria, for instance,

the government has preferred to implement the ECtHR's judgments pertaining to the expulsion of non-citizens on a case-by-case basis so as not to attract the extent of public attention that any amendment in aliens legislation would trigger. The latter would most likely fuel reactions from right-wing conservative parties calling for an end to migration for reasons of public interest and security.

National judicial politics

Domestic courts are the pre-eminent actors in the implementation of the ECtHR's judgments. They are so both indirectly, by interpreting the status and authority of the Convention in relation to national constitutional norms, and directly, by their readiness to align their jurisprudence to that of the Strasbourg Court. Probing into the interaction between national courts (especially higher and constitutional courts) and the ECtHR, studies have exposed the complexity, flexibility and pluralism that characterise such relations. On the whole, and over time, a remarkable level of consensus and mutual accommodation has been achieved. Yet there have been occasions when national constitutional courts have resisted the ECtHR's judgments and asserted their power to determine the limits of the Convention and the Strasbourg Court's case law as against national law.[15] Such an act of resistance is reflected in the Federal Constitutional Court's reaction to the *Görgülü* judgment, as is shown in the case study of Germany. While the relations between national courts and the ECtHR, as well as their implications for the Strasbourg Court's case law, have received scholarly attention, much less attention has been paid to inter-court relations and competition among different courts within each country. Such relations, as they surface in some of the country case studies in this volume, emerge as highly consequential for the implementation of the ECtHR's judgments.

Scholars studying legal integration in the EU context have shed light on the differentiated attitudes of various domestic courts towards Community law and the jurisprudence of the Court of Justice of the EU (CJEU). They have explored the role of national judiciaries in promoting legal integration and the acceptance and diffusion of the supremacy and direct effect of EU law.[16] The penetration and supremacy of EU law has introduced highly competitive dynamics among lower and higher courts within member states. Departing from neo-functionalist accounts that saw the interests of legal and judicial actors inexorably driving forward the process of integration,[17] subsequent studies elaborated on and qualified the interests and responses of national courts in their interactions with the CJEU.[18] They modified the initial assumption that EU law uniformly empowers national courts by allowing them to conduct judicial review. Far from universal, such a sense of self-empowerment is instead highly variable among different national courts within a country. Indeed, high courts have often found that their overarching influence to interpret and apply national law diminishes because of the supremacy of EU law. Different courts have different interests vis-à-vis EC law, which they have used in struggles between different levels of the judiciary, as well as between the judiciary and political actors. In the process, they have inadvertently tended to facilitate the process of legal integration. Indeed, it is the differences between the lower and higher court interests that have provided the motor for legal integration to proceed.[19]

Dynamics of inter-court competition also appear to fundamentally shape domestic judicial attitudes towards the Convention and the ECtHR's case law. They generally run parallel to but sometimes intersect with those that have emerged with regard to EU law, as some of the chapters in this volume show. The preliminary reference ruling, an element of institutional architecture that has been instrumental in triggering a dynamic of intra-court competition in the case of the CJEU, is absent in the ECHR system. Nonetheless, the national intra-court competition that has emerged in relation to the CJEU seems to also have repercussions for the national judicial reception of the ECHR and the implementation of the ECtHR's case law. These two parallel supranational/transnational orders interact and distinctly influence legal norms and judicial approaches towards Community and human rights law at the national level.

The progressive incorporation of human rights principles in EU law prompted national judges to also search for and adopt new interpretations of the domestic status and authority of the Convention and the Strasbourg Court's case law. This can be illustrated very clearly in the case of Italy, as is discussed in the respective country chapter. Overlooking the domestic status of the Convention as ordinary law, over the past years higher courts have attributed to it supra-legislative status. As early as 1993, both the Italian Constitutional Court (ICC) and the Court of Cassation (CC) independently issued decisions that recognised in the ECHR some kind of 'atypical' and special quality that distinguished it from ordinary legislation. This was far from coincidental or fortuitous. The two courts found a basis to do so in reference to the Maastricht Treaty, which had been recently ratified, and vowed respect for the rights guaranteed by the ECHR as general principles of Community law (Art. 6(2)).[20] This step, however, did not translate into a full-blown recognition of the Convention's supra-legislative status until much later and only after the 2001 constitutional revision that explicitly provided for it. Article 117 of the amended 2001 Constitution explicitly stipulated that a domestic law that contradicts the Convention principles as interpreted by the ECtHR must be declared unconstitutional by the ICC.

Relying on the explicit reference of the Treaty of the European Union to the ECHR as a source of general principles of Community law, some ordinary judges in Italy, supported by the highest ordinary and administrative courts, began to treat the ECHR as on a par with EU law. They took the initiative to handle questions themselves of the ECHR's compatibility with the

Constitution.[21] Such a move, though, would have effectively allowed ordinary judges once more to bypass the ICC, in a similar way as they had been able to do under EU law. Using the preliminary reference ruling procedure, ordinary judges have directly raised constitutionality issues with the CJEU rather than with the ICC. In interpreting Article 117 of the amended Italian Constitution (in 2001), decisions nos. 248 and 249, issued by the ICC in 2007, were in large part a response to pre-empt such a possibility from recurring. In these decisions, the ICC declared unconstitutional an Italian statute that provided awards of compensation for the expropriation of land, because it was found to be incompatible with the ECHR and the ECtHR's case law. Besides boosting the domestic status of the Convention, which was attributed with supra-legislative force, these decisions, confirmed and elaborated in subsequent decisions of the ICC, also greatly augmented the authority and binding nature of the ECtHR's case law. They acknowledged that it could even prevail over the Italian Constitution, if the protection of the relevant fundamental rights is higher in Strasbourg than at the constitutional level.[22]

Underneath the elevated authority and enforcement power of the Convention and the ECtHR's case law, the 2007 judgments were an act of initiative and assertion by the ICC that departed from its own earlier position. While the ICC recognised that the ECHR and Strasbourg case law are part of the general principles of EU law (pursuant to Article 6 of the Treaty of the European Union), it also distinguished the Community legal order from that of the Convention. While it considered as justifiable the control of conformity with EU law by ordinary courts, it questioned the legitimacy for ordinary judges to engage in an equivalent kind of control with regard to the ECHR.[23] Significantly, by drawing this distinction, the ICC put a halt to the trend that had been inaugurated by ordinary judges of setting aside domestic national legislation in conflict with the ECHR and the Strasbourg Court's case law. Instead, ordinary judges are now obliged to refer a question about the constitutionality of a national law in conflict with the ECHR to the ICC. Italian Constitutional Court judges must in turn verify if the protection offered by the Convention and the ECtHR's case law is equivalent to that guaranteed by the Italian Constitution.

In sum, the 2007 judgments enabled the ICC to exclusively assume the competence of ascertaining an incompatibility between the ECHR and national law.[24] They enabled it to establish its centralised control and leading role over conventionality review, and to discard a national law that is contrary to the Convention and the ECtHR's case law. In exclusively asserting for itself the power to do so, the ICC simultaneously refused to give any national court the power to engage in such a review.

While Community and Convention law are undoubtedly rooted in different kinds of relationship with national law (supremacy and subsidiarity, respectively), which indeed sets them apart, the distinction drawn by the ICC must be attributed to more than this. Under the direct effect and supremacy of Community law, Italy's Constitutional Court lost its control as the sole arbitrator on questions of constitutionality, since these now also involved a supranational court. More importantly, and particularly with the preliminary ruling mechanism, it also lost its role vis-à-vis ordinary courts domestically, which were able to refer such questions to the CJEU as they wished. With the two abovementioned decisions issued in 2007, the ICC also asserted itself against the Strasbourg Court and the growing influence of the latter in developing the domestic constitutional case law on human rights. As Silvia Mirate states:

> What the Italian [Constitutional Court] seems to express . . . is the need for a leading role in protecting human rights in the domestic law . . . which discloses a natural vocation of the Italian Court to protect the national boundaries in the face of the influence coming from the European case law.[25]

The above discussion of the Italian case shows that in order to understand the activist but also ambivalent role that the Italian courts have on the whole assumed in the implementation of ECtHR judgments with respect to the executive, one must explore the inter-court dynamics. Other chapters also provide clues to similar dynamics present in other countries. For instance, similarly to the Italian CC, the Romanian Constitutional Court advised the ordinary courts to refer to it questions of compatibility of domestic law with the Convention.[26] Furthermore, and in spite of the RCC's 2007 decision that challenged the constitutionality of the law decriminalising insult and defamation, domestic ordinary courts started to appeal to the ECtHR's case law in order to acquit journalists in freedom of expression cases. Such a major shift has been particularly evidenced among the younger generation of Romanian judges, as the case study chapter on Romania suggests. In sum, inter-judicial interactions and antagonisms are highly consequential in shaping the stances of different courts to implementing the ECtHR's judgments.

Social and legal mobilisation

Processes of social mobilisation have been instrumental and increasingly important components of litigation in the ECtHR, as well as influential in the domestic implementation of its case law. They are variably evidenced in established and consolidated democracies like the UK, France or Greece, in recently democratised ex-communist countries, and in democratising states like Turkey. Individuals, at times on behalf of collective actors, have strategically and systematically deployed ECtHR litigation after exhausting all domestic remedies. They have done so in the frame of a broader array of political actions to pressure governments to redefine their policy towards particular minorities. Cases that exemplify this are JWs in Greece (and elsewhere in Europe), homosexuals in the UK and Austria, transgender individuals in the UK, and Kurds in Turkey. Large-scale strategic use of litigation before the ECtHR, for instance, was incorporated as the centrepiece of an alternative Kurdish politics that distanced itself from armed struggle. Besides seeking individual redress, its goals have been to pressure Turkey to change its policies towards minorities and undertake reforms, as well as to raise public awareness about the situation of Kurds in the south-eastern parts of the country.

Litigation in the ECtHR has been a part of multi-pronged mobilisational tactics by the abovementioned minority actors, who have taken recourse in Strasbourg in order to pursue more favourable and expansive interpretations of their rights. Favourable ECtHR judgments have been important sources of leverage and they have been employed by minorities to pressure their governments for change, as some of the case study chapters in this volume show, with variable degrees of success for the enforcement and implementation of the relevant rights. Therefore, it is instructive to inquire into why some groups take recourse in the ECtHR, and under what conditions their mobilisation is likely to promote or facilitate the implementation of the Court's judgments and to redefine government policy.

The degree to which particular groups have access to and can influence formal channels of decision-making at the national level significantly determines their willingness to engage in litigation in the ECtHR.[27] However, such access, which for instance was enjoyed to some degree by homosexuals in the UK and Austria, does not exclude simultaneous resort to human rights litigation. Resort to the latter is particularly likely if access to decision makers does not necessarily translate into political strength and a corresponding ability to effectively pressure for change. Secondly, the willingness and ability of individuals (on behalf of groups) to mount a successful litigation campaign in the ECtHR is influenced by the nature of the group. As is also shown in studies on litigation in the CJEU, the narrower the interest group's mandate and constituency, the more likely it is to turn to a human rights litigation strategy.[28] This is evidenced in the case of homosexuals and transsexuals in the UK and in Austria, as well as in the case of JWs in Greece. All of these groups had a narrow mandate that did not have repercussions beyond the confines of these groups, notwithstanding the fact that they challenged dominant societal views and values. A group's mandate is also usually linked to the nature of its organisation. Groups like homosexuals in the UK or JWs in Greece are characterised by relatively cohesive and centralised rather than dispersed organisational and leadership structures, which determined their priorities and agendas in terms of the rights to be pursued. Thirdly, all of these groups enjoyed access to legal support from lawyers who were well versed in human rights developments in Europe and beyond.

The substantial influence that the ECtHR's case law has had on the rights of sexual minorities in the UK, France and Austria cannot be understood independently of the active engagement of national and transnational organisations with European human rights law and their legal mobilisation.[29]

Organisations like Press for Change in the UK and LAMBDA in Austria have been significantly influential in promoting the rights of homosexuals and transgender people. Helmut Graupner, a lawyer and president of the Austrian lesbian and gay rights organisation Rechtskomitee LAMBDA, and founder of Platform gegen § 209, encouraged convicted homosexuals to take their cases to the ECtHR. Taking the cases to the ECtHR was part of a broader campaign by NGOs and certain politicians pressuring for the abolition of Section 209 of the Austrian Criminal Code, which defined a different age of consent for male homosexuals in Austria. Such a campaign gained further momentum by publicity at the EU level.

Notably, the litigation and political mobilisation campaigns mounted by the abovementioned groups have had a significant transnational dimension. They have involved networks of actors and organisational tactics that spread across states. International human rights NGOs and interest-specific organisations have assumed an important role in identifying cases and supporting their submission to the Strasbourg Court. Domestic and international NGOs supporting the rights of homosexuals such as the International Lesbian and Gay Association have provided the ECtHR with information about international developments in human rights related to sexual orientation. They have done so by submitting written comments as third-party interveners in a number of cases. Their mobilisation of Convention legal norms as part of their political strategy has spread transnationally, coordinating national initiatives and transmitting relevant legal expertise, political skills and advocacy work across states.

While sustained and effective legal challenge before the ECtHR by interested social and minority actors is an important prerequisite, it does not necessarily translate into national implementation of the relevant judgments. Crucial for national implementation of an adverse ECtHR judgment that is favourable to a particular set of rights claims is that the petitioners 'follow through' and capitalise upon their legal victory in order to pressure their government.[30] One way that minority actors studied in this volume have sought to achieve this is by combining legal mobilisation in the Strasbourg Court with campaigning strategies to inform and influence public opinion, as well as the views of policy makers, not only domestically but also internationally.

Most importantly, social and minority actors who have been vindicated by the ECtHR need, in turn, to find allies within national institutions responsible for implementing human rights but also with the political weight to initiate change.[31] They must at the same time engage in lobbying in legislatures and bureaucratic agencies in order to mobilise the broader political support that is necessary for implementation and policy change.[32] The country case studies in the second part of this book show that the electoral leverage of socially marginalised and minority groups is generally limited. An information campaign to solicit greater public support does not necessarily help, unlike in other areas such as environmental protection, where compliance with international law may have diffuse benefits which can be capitalised upon by dispersing information in order to expand public awareness and support. [33] By contrast, expanding the rights of sexual, ethnic or religious minorities or immigrants does not involve any diffuse societal benefits; if anything, it may run up against strong majority opposition.

Political elite support for the rights of various marginalised and minority actors, however, may also be solicited even in issues for which public support is limited. Indeed, the ECtHR's judgments can be especially catalytic in such issue areas in which progressive legal and policy change is broadly unpopular. The Greek case shows that domestic political support for expanding the rights of JWs has had – at best – a narrow base, while public opposition has been extensive. Nonetheless, the ECtHR's judgments became a pretext for administrators and elected officials who for historical reasons had a distaste for the privileges of the Greek Orthodox Church but who were also fearful of public reaction and unpopularity to support reforms without openly declaring it. By contrast, the close association of ethnic minority issues with national security prevented even liberal-minded political officials and academics from supporting openly or even tacitly policy change in line with the ECtHR's relevant judgments. Considerations of electoral cost proved paramount among parliamentary and party representatives, as well as among government officials on this issue.

CONCLUDING REMARKS

The domestic implementation of the ECtHR's case law involves a multifaceted set of processes, in which governments and state authorities, national courts and societal actors are variably but extensively involved. The ECtHR's judgments that vindicate individuals enable human rights defenders and minority activists to draw legitimacy to expose infringements, as well as to pressure for change in ongoing struggles to (re)define the nature and scope of fundamental rights and freedoms. The Strasbourg Court embodies *par excellence* the judicialisation of human rights at the European level. Its judgments are a most authoritative source of pressure that are continuously monitored by the EU, and by bodies such as the Committee for the Prevention of Torture and other international and European organisations that draw upon them to define their approach to rights and their position vis-à-vis different states. Today, the battles over the rights of individual citizens and the interests of state security in Europe have as an inescapable frame of reference the transnational human rights regime centred on the ECtHR to an extent and in a manner far more pervasive and consequential than it was originally willed or anticipated.

Notwithstanding the resisting or evasive responses to its implementation by national authorities, the normative pull of the ECtHR's jurisprudence has been far reaching. Over time, it has substantially upgraded national standards of rights protection across Europe. Most of the countries that originally became parties to the Convention and submitted to the jurisdiction of the Strasbourg Court are robust democracies that firmly guarantee rights contained in the Convention. Still, rapidly changing, pluralist and multicultural European societies continuously generate conflicting claims that necessitate ongoing review of the content of rights, as well as a redrawing of the boundaries between individual rights and public interests. As has been rightly pointed out, the distinctive contribution of the Convention and the ECtHR's case law in consolidated European democracies is that of 'establishing and periodically reassessing the boundaries of a "European consensus" on human rights norms in light of evolving social realities'.[34] At the same time, structural problems, largely pertaining to the length of civil, criminal and administrative proceedings, persist in well-established democracies.

Following the accession of many ex-communist states to the Council of Europe, the ECtHR's original role, function and identity has come under challenge and reconsideration. The Court is now called to review a growing volume of pervasive human rights abuses, such as extra-judicial killings, disappearances and arbitrary detention, among others, in countries where democracy and the rule of law are not well entrenched. In this regard, the Strasbourg judiciary finds itself in a position not of a secondary guarantor of individual liberties but of a front-line protector of flagrant violations in cases where it cannot rely on the government's ability to investigate alleged abuses or to pursue effective remedies. This has both overburdened the Strasbourg Court with a huge number of petitions and prompted a search for reforms in its adjudicatory approach, judicial procedure and institutional design. A widely acclaimed innovation has been the adoption of the so-called pilot procedure, grouping together similar judgments that underscore the systemic nature of a problem. By specifically indicating the general measures that must be adopted in response, the pilot procedure profoundly departs from the earlier practice of the Court to defer to national authorities, and reflects the tribunal's willingness to enhance its remedial powers.

Improving remedies and implementation of the ECtHR's judgments at the national level is undoubtedly central for guaranteeing the longer-term effectiveness and credibility of the Convention system, as the Parliamentary Assembly, among other CoE actors, has time and again recognised.[35] At the national level, the implementation of the ECtHR's judgments is not merely or mainly a matter of inadequate statutory and constitutional guarantees or insufficient legal awareness of the Convention and the Court among lawyers and judges at the national level, as some recent studies seem to suggest.[36] As a number of the contributions in this volume show, domestic implementation has a profoundly qualitative dimension that is exhausted not in whether or not national authorities execute the Strasbourg Court's rulings but in how aptly, effectively, and completely they do so. For this reason, the search for improving domestic implementation of the ECtHR's judgments must also involve the active engagement of actors with a direct interest in and commitment to human rights. These may be national human rights institutions (NHRIs), parliamentary representatives and civil society actors, who are willing to scrutinise the adopted remedial, legislative and policy measures and to delve into their substantive content and their actual consequences for human rights protection.

It is convincingly argued that effectively improving the domestic implementation of the Strasbourg Court's judgments is premised on structurally embedding the Court in the national legal systems of the contracting states.[37] The idea of embeddedness is distinguished from both the individual and the constitutional justice models, which are offered as competing visions as to how the ECtHR should develop. It calls for a more assertive interventionist and supervisory role for the Court, at least in cases where deference to national authorities to effectively execute judgments is little more than wishful thinking. It also envisions introducing more systematic and institutionalised interaction between Strasbourg and national court judges, extending the practice of preventive review of national statutes and policies with the Convention, channelling more resources and energy into training government authorities, domestic judges and law enforcement officials, and bolstering the role of NHRIs, as ways to strengthen embeddedness.[38] The idea of embeddedness is not entirely clear and needs to be further expounded and concretised, but overall it appears to offer an appropriate and promising vision. In practice, though, it cannot merely be achieved through institutional redesigning but also through actions and initiatives, at both the national and the European levels, aimed at soliciting and mobilising the support of national judges as well as governmental, parliamentary and rights-committed societal and institutional actors.

Notes

1. Lisa Conant, *Justice Contained: Law and Politics in the European Union* (Ithaca, NY: Cornell University Press, 2002), p. 13.
2. ECtHR, *Hornsby* v. *Greece* (18357/91), 19 March 1997.
3. For instance, between 2005 and 2009, the proportion of the ECtHR's judgments concerning the original EU-15 member states dropped from 31.3 per cent to 18.9 per cent. By contrast, in the same period, the proportion of the ECtHR's judgments issued vis-à-vis the other twelve member states (mostly in central, eastern and south-eastern Europe) grew from 17.3 per cent to 29 per cent. In 2009, 50 per cent of all ECtHR judgments concerned Turkey, the western Balkans (Albania, Bosnia-Herzegovina, Croatia, the Former Yugoslav Republic of Macedonia, Montenegro and Serbia) and the ex-Soviet states (Armenia, Azerbaijan, Georgia, Moldova, Russia and Ukraine). See Robert Harmsen, 'The Transformation of the ECHR Legal Order and the Post-enlargement Challenges Facing the European Court of Human Rights', in Giuseppe Martinico and Oreste Pollicino

(eds), *The National Judicial Treatment of the ECHR and EU Laws* (Groningen: Europa Law Publishing, 2010), p. 31.

4. Frank Schimmelfennig, 'Strategic Calculation and International Socialization: Membership Incentives, Party Constellations, and Sustained Compliance in Central and Eastern Europe', *International Organization*, vol. 59, no. 4 (2005), pp. 827–60.

5. Ibid., p. 856.

6. Ibid., p. 837.

7. Beth A. Simmons, *Mobilizing for Human Rights: International Law in Domestic Politics* (New York: Cambridge University Press, 2009), p. 15.

8. George Tsebelis, *Veto Players: How Political Institutions Work* (Princeton: Princeton University Press, 2002).

9. Mary L. Volcansek, 'Constitutional Courts as Veto Players: Divorce and Decrees in Italy', *European Journal of Political Research*, vol. 39, no. 3 (2001), p. 368.

10. Helen Keller and Alec Stone Sweet, 'Introduction: The Reception of the ECHR in National Legal Orders', in Helen Keller and Alec Stone Sweet (eds), *A Europe of Rights: The Impact of the ECHR on National Legal Systems* (Oxford: Oxford University Press, 2008), pp. 28–9.

11. This is the argument advanced by Beth Simmons in *Mobilizing for Human Rights*, pp. 127–9.

12. Wojciech Sadurski, 'Accession's Democracy Dividend: The Impact of the EU Enlargement upon Democracy in the New Member States of Central and Eastern Europe', *European Law Journal*, vol. 10, no. 4 (2004), pp. 383–4.

13. Ibid., p. 389.

14. Conant, *Justice Contained*, p. 31.

15. Nico Krisch, 'The Open Architecture of European Human Rights Law', LSE Law, Society and Economy Working Papers 11/2007, available at http://papers.ssrn.com/sol3/papers.cfm?abstract_id=1018991 (accessed 19 September 2012).

16. Anne-Marie Slaughter, Alec Stone Sweet and J. H. H. Weiler (eds), *The European Court and National Courts – Doctrine and Jurisprudence: Legal Change in Its Social Context* (Oxford: Hart, 1998).

17. Anne-Marie Burley and Walter Mattli, 'Europe before the Court: A Political Theory of Legal Integration', *International Organization*, vol. 47, no.1 (1993), pp. 53–4.

18. Karen J. Alter, *Establishing the Supremacy of European Law: The Making of an International Rule of Law in Europe* (Oxford: Oxford University Press, 2001).

19. Karen J. Alter, *The European Court's Political Power: Selected Essays* (Oxford: Oxford University Press, 2009), pp. 241–2.

20. Silvia Mirate, 'A New Status for the ECHR in Italy: The Italian Constitutional Court and the New "Conventional Review" on National Laws', *European Public Law*, vol. 15, no. 1 (2009), p. 97.

21. Giuseppe Martinico and Oreste Pollicino, 'Report on Italy', in Giuseppe Martinico and Oreste Pollicino (eds), *The National Judicial Treatment of the ECHR and EU Laws* (Groningen: Europa Law Publishing, 2010), p. 285.

22. Ibid., p. 295.

23. Mirate, 'A New Status for the ECHR in Italy', p. 100.
24. Martinico and Pollicino, 'Report on Italy', p. 289.
25. Mirate, 'A New Status for the ECHR in Italy', p. 103.
26. Elena Raducu, 'Report on Romania', in Giuseppe Martinico and Oreste Pollicino (eds), *The National Judicial Treatment of the ECHR and EU Laws* (Groningen: Europa Law Publishing, 2010), p. 372.
27. Karen J. Alter and Jeannette Vargas, 'Explaining Variation in the Use of European Litigation Strategies', *Comparative Political Studies*, vol. 33, no. 4 (2000), p. 472.
28. Ibid., p. 474.
29. See Loveday Hodson, *NGOs and the Struggle for Human Rights in Europe* (Oxford: Hart, 2011).
30. Alter, *The European Court's Political Power*, p. 203.
31. Virginie Guiraudon, 'European Courts and Foreigners' Rights: A Comparative Study of Norms Diffusion', *International Migration Review*, vol. 34, no. 4 (2000), p. 1094.
32. Conant, *Justice Contained*, pp. 22–3.
33. Xinyuan Dai, 'Why Comply? The Domestic Constituency Mechanism', *International Organization*, vol. 59, no. 2 (2005), pp. 363–98.
34. Harmsen, 'The Transformation of the ECHR Legal Order and the Post-Enlargement Challenges facing the ECtHR', p. 33.
35. See 'The Effectiveness of the ECHR at National Level', PACE Committee on Legal Affairs and Human Rights, AS/Jur (2007) 35 rev, 20 July 2007.
36. See Frank Emmert, 'The Implementation of the ECHR and Fundamental Freedoms in New Member States of the Council of Europe: Conclusions Drawn and Lessons Learned', in Leonard Hammer and Frank Emmert (eds), *The European Convention on Human Rights and Fundamental Freedoms in Central and Eastern Europe* (The Hague: Eleven International, 2011).
37. Laurence R. Helfer, 'Redesigning the European Court of Human Rights: Embeddedness as a Deep Structural Principle of the European Human Rights Regime', *European Journal of International Law*, vol. 19, no.1 (2008), pp. 125–59.
38. Ibid., pp. 155–9.

European Court of Human Rights judgments and European Commission on Human Rights cases

ECtHR JUDGMENTS

ECtHR, *Ahmed* v. *Austria* (no. 25964/94), 17 December 1996

ECtHR, *Gaygusuz* v. *Austria* (no. 17371/90), 16 September 1996

ECtHR, *H.G. and G.B.* v. *Austria* (nos. 11084/02, 15306/02), 2 June 2005

ECtHR, *Jakupovic* v. *Austria* (no. 36757/97), 6 February 2003

ECtHR, *Jancikova* v. *Austria* (no. 56483/00), 7 April 2005

ECtHR, *Jurisic and Collegium Mehrerau* v. *Austria* (no. 62539/00), 27 July 2006

ECtHR, *Kamasinski* v. *Austria* (no. 9783/82), 19 December 1989

ECtHR, *Karakurt* v. *Austria* (no. 32441/96), 14 September 1999

ECtHR, *Karner* v. *Austria* (no. 40016/98), 24 July 2003

ECtHR, *Kobenter and Standard Verlags GmbH* v. *Austria* (no. 60899/00), 2 November 2006

ECtHR, *L. and V.* v. *Austria* (nos. 39392/98, 39829/98), 9 January 2003

ECtHR, *Ladner* v. *Austria* (no. 18297/03), 3 February 2005

ECtHR, *Maslov* v. *Austria* (no. 1638/03), 23 June 2008

ECtHR, *Moser* v. *Austria* (no. 12643/02), 21 September 2006

ECtHR, *Oberschlick* v. *Austria* (no. 11662/85), 23 May 1991

ECtHR, *Oberschlick* v. *Austria* (No. 2) (no. 20834/92), 1 July 1997

ECtHR, *Palaoro* v. *Austria* (no. 16718/90), 23 October 1995

ECtHR, *P.B. and J.S.* v. *Austria* (no. 18984/02), 22 July 2010

ECtHR, *Radovanovic* v. *Austria* (no. 42703/98), 22 April 2004

ECtHR, *R.H.* v. *Austria* (no. 7336/03), 19 January 2006

ECtHR, *Rusu* v. *Austria* (no. 34082/02), 2 October 2008

ECtHR, *S.L.* v. *Austria* (no. 45330/99), 9 January 2003

ECtHR, *Unabhängige Initiative Informationsvielfalt* v. *Austria* (no. 28525/95), 26 February 2002

ECtHR, *Woditschka and Wilfling* v. *Austria* (nos. 69756/01, 6306/02), 21 October 2004

ECtHR, *Wolfmeyer* v. *Austria* (no. 5263/03), 26 May 2005

ECtHR, *Yildiz* v. *Austria* (no. 37295/97), 31 October 2002

ECtHR *Marckx* v. *Belgium* (no. 6833/74), 13 June 1979

ECtHR, *M.S.S.* v. *Belgium and Greece* (no. 30696/09), 21 January 2011

ECtHR, *Al-Nashif and others* v. *Bulgaria* (no. 50963/99), 20 June 2002

ECtHR, *Angelova and Iliev* v. *Bulgaria* (no. 55523/00), 26 July 2007

ECtHR, *Anguelova* v. *Bulgaria* (no. 38361/97), 13 June 2002

ECtHR, *Assenov and others* v. *Bulgaria* (no. 24760/94), 28 October 1998

ECtHR, *Bashir and others* v. *Bulgaria* (no. 65028/01), 14 June 2007

ECtHR, *C.G. and others* v. *Bulgaria* (no. 1365/07), 24 April 2008

ECtHR, *Hasan* v. *Bulgaria* (no. 54323/00), 14 June 2007

ECtHR, *Hasan and Chaush* v. *Bulgaria* (no. 30985/96), 26 October 2000

ECtHR, *Holy Synod of the Bulgarian Orthodox Church (Metropolitan Inokentiy) and others* v. *Bulgaria* (nos. 412/03, 35677/04), 16 September 2010

ECtHR, *Ivanov and others* v. *Bulgaria* (no. 46336/99), 24 November 2005

ECtHR, *Musa and others* v. *Bulgaria* (no. 61259/00), 11 January 2007

ECtHR, *Nachova and others* v. *Bulgaria* (nos. 43577/98, 43579/98), 6 July 2005

ECtHR, *Neshev* v. *Bulgaria* (no. 40897/98), 28 October 2004

ECtHR, *Ognyanova and Choban* v. *Bulgaria* (no. 46317/99), 23 February 2006

ECtHR, *Pramov* v. *Bulgaria*, (no. 42986/98), 30 September 2004

ECtHR, *Supreme Holy Council of the Muslim Community* v. *Bulgaria* (no. 39023/97), 16 December 2004

ECtHR, *Tzekov* v. *Bulgaria* (no. 45500/99), 23 February 2006

ECtHR, *United Macedonian Organisation Ilinden and Ivanov* v. *Bulgaria* (no. 44079/98), 20 October 2005

ECtHR, *United Macedonian Organisation Ilinden and others* v. *Bulgaria* (no. 59491/00), 19 January 2006

ECtHR, *United Macedonian Organisation Ilinden – PIRIN and others* v. *Bulgaria* (no. 59489/00), 20 October 2005

ECtHR, *Varbanov* v. *Bulgaria* (no. 31365/96), 5 October 2000

ECtHR, *Velikova* v. *Bulgaria* (no. 41488/98), 18 May 2000

ECtHR, *D.H.* v. *Czech Republic* (no. 57325/00), 13 November 2007

ECtHR, *B.* v. *France* (no. 13343/87), 25 March 1992

ECtHR, *Elsholz* v. *Germany* (no. 25735/94), 13 July 2000

ECtHR, *Garcia Alva* v. *Germany* (no. 23541/94), 13 February 2001

ECtHR, *Görgülü* v. *Germany* (no. 74969/01), 26 February 2004

ECtHR, *Heinisch* v. *Germany* (no. 28274/08), 21 July 2011

ECtHR, *Jalloh* v. *Germany* (no. 54810/00), 11 July 2006

ECtHR, *Karlheinz Schmidt* v. *Germany* (no. 13580/88), 18 July 1994

ECtHR, *Keles* v. *Germany* (no. 32231/02), 27 October 2005

ECtHR, *Kirsten* v. *Germany* (no. 19124/02), 15 February 2007

ECtHR, *Luedicke, Belkacem and Koç* v. *Germany* (no. 6210/73), 28 November 1978

ECtHR, *M.* v. *Germany* (no. 19359/04), 17 December 2009

ECtHR, *Mooren* v. *Germany* (no. 11364/03-Chamber), 13 December 2007

ECtHR, *Mooren* v. *Germany* (no. 11364/03-Grand Chamber), 9 July 2009

ECtHR, *Öztürk* v. *Germany* (no. 8544/79), 21 February 1984

ECtHR, *Rumpf* v. *Germany* (no. 46344/06), 2 September 2010

ECtHR, *Stambuk* v. *Germany* (no. 37928/97), 17 October 2002

ECtHR, *Sürmeli* v. *Germany* (no. 75529/01), 8 June 2006

ECtHR, *Van Kück* v. *Germany* (no. 35968/97), 12 June 2003

ECtHR, *Von Hannover* v. *Germany* (no. 59320/00), 24 June 2004

ECtHR, *Yilmaz* v. *Germany* (no. 52853/99), 17 April 2003

ECtHR, *Agga* v. *Greece* (No. 1) (no. 37439/97), 25 January 2000

ECtHR, *Agga v. Greece* (No. 2) (nos. 50776/99, 52912/99), 17 October 2002

ECtHR, *Agga v. Greece* (No. 3) (no. 32186/02), 13 July 2006

ECtHR, *Agga v. Greece* (No. 4) (no. 33331/02), 13 July 2006

ECtHR, *Agko v. Greece* (no. 31117/96), 20 October 1997

ECtHR, *Ahmet Sadik v. Greece* (no. 18877/91), 15 November 1996

ECtHR, *Bekir-Ousta and others v. Greece* (no. 35151/05), 11 October 2007

ECtHR, *Canea Catholic Church v. Greece* (no. 25528/94), 16 December 1997

ECtHR, *Efstratiou v. Greece* (no. 24095/94), 18 December 1996

ECtHR, *Emin and others v. Greece* (no. 34144/05), 27 March 2008

ECtHR, *Galanis v. Greece* (no. 69333/01), 6 February 2003

ECtHR, *Georgiadis v. Greece* (no. 21522/93), 29 May 1997

ECtHR, *Hornsby v. Greece* (18357/91), 19 March 1997

ECtHR, *Imam and others v. Greece* (no. 29764/96), 20 October 1997

ECtHR, *Kokkinakis v. Greece* (no. 14307/88), 25 May 1993

ECtHR, *Larissis and others v. Greece* (nos. 23372/94, 26377/94, 26378/94), 24 February 1998

ECtHR, *Manoussakis and others v. Greece* (no. 18748/91), 26 September 1996

ECtHR, *Nurioglu v. Greece* (no. 18545/91), 17 May 1995

ECtHR, *Ouranio Toxo and others v. Greece* (no. 74989/01), 20 October 2005

ECtHR, *Pentidis and others v. Greece* (no. 23238/94), 9 June 1997

ECtHR, *Raif Oglu v. Greece* (no. 33738/96), 27 June 2000

ECtHR, *Sadik Ahmet and others v. Greece* (no. 64756/01), 3 February 2005

ECtHR, *Serif v. Greece* (no. 38178/97), 14 December 1999

ECtHR, *Sidiropoulos and others v. Greece* (no. 26695/95), 10 July 1998

ECtHR, *Thlimmenos v. Greece* (no. 34369/97), 6 April 2000

ECtHR, *Tourkiki Enosi Xanthis and others v. Greece* (no. 26698/05), 27 March 2008

ECtHR, *Tsavachidis v. Greece* (no. 28802/95), 21 January 1999

ECtHR, *Tsilis and Kouloumpas v. Greece* (nos. 19233/91, 19234/91), 29 May 1997

ECtHR, *Tsingour v. Greece* (no. 40437/98), 6 July 2000

ECtHR, *Valsamis v. Greece* (no. 21787/93), 18 December 1996

ECtHR, *Vergos v. Greece* (no. 65501/01), 24 June 2004

ECtHR, *Norris v. Ireland* (no. 10581/83), 26 October 1988

ECtHR, *Argenti v. Italy* (no. 56317/00), 10 November 2005

ECtHR, *Artico v. Italy* (no. 6694/74), 13 May 1980

ECtHR, *Bastone v. Italy* (no. 59638/00), 11 July 2006

ECtHR, *Bifulco v. Italy* (no. 60915/00), 8 February 2005

ECtHR, *Bottazzi v. Italy* (no. 34884/97), 28 July 1999

ECtHR, *Bronda v. Italy* (no. 22430/93), 9 June 1998

ECtHR, *Calogero Diana v. Italy* (no. 15211/89), 15 November 1996

ECtHR, *Capuano v. Italy* (no. 9381/81), 25 June 1987

ECtHR, *CGIL and Cofferati v. Italy* (no. 46967/07), 24 February 2009

ECtHR, *Ciricosta and Viola v. Italy* (19753/92), 4 December 1995

ECtHR, *Colozza v. Italy* (no. 9024/80), 12 February 1985

ECtHR, *Cordova v. Italy* (No. 1) (no. 40877/98), 30 January 2003

ECtHR, *Cordova v. Italy* (No. 2) (no. 45649/99), 30 January 2003

ECtHR, *Covezzi and Morselli* v. *Italy* (no. 52763/99), 9 May 2003
ECtHR, *Craxi* (no. 2) v. *Italy* (no. 25337/94), 17 July 2003
ECtHR, *De Jorio* v. *Italy* (no. 73936/01), 3 June 2004
ECtHR, *Di Giovine* v. *Italy* (no. 39920/98), 26 July 2001
ECtHR, *Di Mauro* v. *Italy* (no. 34256/96), 28 July 1999
ECtHR, *Domenichini* v. *Italy* (no. 15943/90), 15 November 1996
ECtHR, *Ferrari* v. *Italy* (no. 33440/96), 28 July 1999
ECtHR, *Ganci* v. *Italy* (no. 41576/98), 30 October 2003
ECtHR, *Giacomelli* v. *Italy* (no. 59909/00), 2 November 2006
ECtHR, *Guerra and others* v. *Italy* (no. 14967/89), 19 February 1998
ECtHR, *Ielo* v. *Italy* (no. 23053/02), 6 December 2005
ECtHR, *Immobiliare Saffi* v. *Italy* (no. 22774/93), 28 July 1999
ECtHR, *Indelicato* v. *Italy* (no. 31143/96), 18 October 2001
ECtHR, *Labita* v. *Italy* (no. 26772/95), 6 April 2000
ECtHR, *Leo Zappia* v. *Italy* (no. 77744/01), 29 September 2005
ECtHR, *L.M.* v. *Italy* (no. 60033/00), 8 February 2005
ECtHR, *Madonia* v. *Italy* (no. 55927/00), 6 July 2004
ECtHR, *Messina* v. *Italy* (No. 2) (no. 25498/94), 28 September 2000
ECtHR, *Messina* (No. 3) v. *Italy* (no. 33993/96), 24 October 2002
ECtHR, *Moni* v. *Italy* (no. 35784/97), 11 January 2000
ECtHR, *Musumeci* v. *Italy* (no. 33695/96), 11 January 2005
ECtHR, *Natoli* v. *Italy* (no. 26161/95), 9 January 2001
ECtHR, *Ospina Vargas* v. *Italy* (no. 40750/98), 14 October 2004
ECtHR, *Patrono, Cascini and Stefanelli* v. *Italy* (no. 10180/04), 20 April 2006
ECtHR, *Rinzivillo* v. *Italy* (no. 31543/96), 21 December 2000
ECtHR, *Roda and Bonfatti* v. *Italy* (no. 10427/02), 21 November 2006
ECtHR, *Salvatore* v. *Italy* (no. 42285/98), 6 December 2005
ECtHR, *Scordino and others* (No. 1) v. *Italy* (no. 36813/97), 29 March 2006
ECtHR, *Scozzari and Giunta* v. *Italy* (nos. 39221/98, 41963/98), 13 July 2000
ECtHR, *Spadea and Scalabrino* v. *Italy* (no. 12868/87), 28 September 1995
ECtHR, *X. and Y.* v. *Netherlands* (no. 8978/80), 26 March 1985
ECtHR, *Broniowski* v. *Poland* (no. 31443/96), 22 June 2004
ECtHR, *Kudla* v. *Poland* (no. 30210/96), 26 October 2000
ECtHR, *Comingersoll SA* v. *Portugal* (no. 35382/97), 6 April 2000
ECtHR, *Brumărescu* v. *Romania* (no. 28342/95), 28 October 1999
ECtHR, *Brumărescu* v. *Romania* (Article 41) (no. 28342/95), 23 January 2001
ECtHR, *Cotleţ* v. *Romania* (no. 38565/97), 3 June 2003
ECtHR, *Cumpănă and Mazăre* v. *Romania* (no. 33348/96), 17 December 2004
ECtHR, *Dalban* v. *Romania* (no. 28114/95), 28 September 1999
ECtHR, *Dumitru Popescu* v. *Romania* (No. 2) (no. 71525/01), 26 April 2007
ECtHR, *Falcoianu* v. *Romania* (no. 32943/96), 9 July 2002
ECtHR, *Kaya* v. *Romania* (no. 33970/05), 12 October 2006
ECtHR, *Lupsa* v. *Romania* (no. 10337/04), 8 June 2006
ECtHR, *Păduraru* v. *Romania* (no. 63252/00), 1 December 2005
ECtHR, *Pantea* v. *Romania* (no. 33343/96), 3 June 2003

ECtHR, *Partidul Comunistilor (Nepeceristi) and Ungureanu v. Romania* (no. 46626/99), 3 February 2005

ECtHR, *Petra v. Romania* (no. 27273/95), 23 September 1998

ECtHR, *Popescu Nasta v. Romania* (no. 33355/96), 7 January 2003

ECtHR, *Rotaru v. Romania* (no. 28341/95), 4 May 2000

ECtHR, *Sabou and Pîrcălab v. Romania* (no. 46572/99), 28 September 2004

ECtHR, *SC Maşinexportimport Industrial Group SA v. Romania* (no. 22687/03), 1 December 2005

ECtHR, *Vasilescu v. Romania* (no. 27053/95), 22 May 1998

ECtHR, *Akbayır and others v. Turkey* (no. 30415/08 and 108 others), 28 June 2011

ECtHR, *Akdıvar and others v. Turkey* (no. 21893/93), 16 September 1996

ECtHR, *Aksoy v. Turkey* (no. 21987/93), 18 December 1996

ECtHR, *Boğuş and others v. Turkey* (no. 54788/09 and 91 others), 28 June 2011

ECtHR, *Çıraklar v. Turkey* (no. 19601/92), 28 October 1998

ECtHR, *Demir and others v. Turkey* (nos. 21380/93, 21381/93, 21383/93), 23 September 1998

ECtHR, *Demirel v. Turkey* (no. 39324/98), 28 January 2003

ECtHR, *Democracy and Change Party and others v. Turkey* (nos. 39210/98, 39974/98), 26 April 2005

ECtHR, *Dicle for the Democracy Party (DEP) v. Turkey* (no. 25141/94), 10 December 2002

ECtHR, *Doğan and others v. Turkey* (nos. 8803/02–8811/02, 8813/02, 8815/02–8819/02), 29 June 2004

ECtHR, *Emek Partisi and şenol v. Turkey* (no. 39434/98), 31 May 2005

ECtHR, *Fidanten and others v. Turkey* (no. 27501/06 and 104 others), 28 June 2011

ECtHR, *Freedom and Democracy Party (ÖZDEP) v. Turkey* (no. 23885/94), 8 December 1999

ECtHR, *Incal v. Turkey* (no. 22678/93), 9 June 1998

ECtHR, *İçyer v. Turkey* (no. 18888/02), 12 January 2006

ECtHR, *İkincisoy v. Turkey* (no. 26144/95), 27 July 2004

ECtHR, *İpek v. Turkey* (no. 25760/94), 17 February 2004

ECtHR, *Menteş and others v. Turkey* (no. 23186/94), 28 November 1997

ECtHR, *Menteşe and others v. Turkey* (no. 36217/97), 18 January 2005

ECtHR, *Orhan v. Turkey* (no. 25656/94), 18 June 2002

ECtHR, *Öcalan v. Turkey* (no. 46221/99), 12 May 2005

ECtHR, *Sadak and others v. Turkey* (nos. 29900/96–29903/96), 17 July 2001

ECtHR, *Sakık and others v. Turkey* (nos. 23878/94–23883/94), 26 November 1997

ECtHR, *Selçuk and Asker v. Turkey* (nos. 23184/94, 23185/94), 24 April 1998

ECtHR, *Sevgin and İnce v. Turkey* (no. 46262/99), 20 September 2005

ECtHR, *Socialist Party and others v. Turkey* (no. 21237/93), 25 May 1998

ECtHR, *Socialist Party of Turkey (STP) and others v. Turkey* (no. 26482/95), 12 November 2003

ECtHR, *Tanış and others v. Turkey* (no. 65899/01), 2 August 2005

ECtHR, *United Communist Party of Turkey and others v. Turkey* (no. 19392/92), 30 January 1998

ECtHR, *Yazar and others* v. *Turkey* (nos. 22723/93–22725/93), 9 April 2002

ECtHR, *Yumak and Sadak* v. *Turkey* (no. 10226/03), 8 July 2008

ECtHR, *Zana* v. *Turkey* (no.18954/91), 25 November 1997

ECtHR, *Averill* v. *United Kingdom* (no. 36408/97), 6 June 2000

ECtHR, *B.B.* v. *United Kingdom* (no. 53760/00), 10 February 2004

ECtHR, *Beard* v. *United Kingdom* (no. 24882/94), 18 January 2001

ECtHR, *Beck, Copp and Bazeley* v. *United Kingdom* (nos. 48535/99–48537/99), 22 October 2002

ECtHR, *Buckley* v. *United Kingdom* (no. 20348/92), 25 September 1996

ECtHR, *Chahal* v. *United Kingdom* (no. 22414/93), 15 November 1996

ECtHR, *Chapman* v. *United Kingdom* (no. 27238/95), 18 January 2001

ECtHR, *Christine Goodwin* v. *United Kingdom* (no. 28957/95), 11 July 2002

ECtHR, *Connors* v. *United Kingdom* (no. 66746/01), 27 May 2004

ECtHR, *Cossey* v. *United Kingdom* (no. 10843/84), 27 September 1990

ECtHR, *Coster* v. *United Kingdom* (no. 24876/94), 18 January 2001

ECtHR, *Dudgeon* v. *United Kingdom* (no. 7525/76), 22 October 1981

ECtHR, *Finucane* v. *United Kingdom* (no. 29178/95), 1 July 2003

ECtHR, *Grant* v. *United Kingdom* (no. 32570/03), 23 May 2006

ECtHR, *Hugh Jordan* v. *United Kingdom* (no. 24746/94), 4 May 2001

ECtHR, *Jane Smith* v. *United Kingdom* (no. 25154/94), 18 January 2001

ECtHR, *John Murray* v. *United Kingdom* (no. 18731/91), 8 February 1996

ECtHR, *Kelly and others* v. *United Kingdom* (no. 30054/96), 4 May 2001

ECtHR, *Lee* v. *United Kingdom* (no. 25289/94), 18 January 2001

ECtHR, *Lustig-Prean and Beckett* v. *United Kingdom* (nos. 31417/96, 32377/96), 27 September 1999

ECtHR, *McCann and others* v. *United Kingdom* (no. 18984/91), 27 September 1995

ECtHR, *McKerr* v. *United Kingdom* (no. 28883/95), 4 May 2001

ECtHR, *McLaughlin* v. *United Kingdom* (no. 18759/91), 9 May 1994

ECtHR, *McShane* v. *United Kingdom* (no. 43290/98), 28 May 2002

ECtHR, *Magee* v. *United Kingdom* (no. 28135/95), 6 June 2000

ECtHR, *Murray* v. *United Kingdom* (no. 22384/93), 21 October 1996

ECtHR, *Perkins and R.* v. *United Kingdom* (nos. 43208/98, 44875/98), 22 October 2002

ECtHR, *Quinn* v. *United Kingdom* (no. 23496/94), 21 October 1996

ECtHR, *Rees* v. *United Kingdom* (no. 9532/81), 17 October 1986

ECtHR, *Shanaghan* v. *United Kingdom* (no. 37715/97), 4 May 2001

ECtHR, *Smith and Grady* v. *United Kingdom* (nos. 33985/96, 33986/96), 27 September 1999

ECtHR, *X., Y. and Z.* v. *United Kingdom* (no. 21830/93), 22 April 1997

ECOMMHR CASES

ECommHR, *Khristiansko Sdruzhenie 'Svideteli na Iehova'* v. *Bulgaria* (no. 28626/95), 3 July 1997

ECommHR, *Dorigo* v. *Italy* (no. 33286/96), 20 May 1998

Index